Strange Gourmets

Edited by

Michèle Aina Barale,

Jonathan Goldberg,

Michael Moon, and

Eve Kosofsky Sedgwick

Strange Gourmets

Sophistication, Theory, and the Novel

Joseph Litvak

Duke University Press   Durham and London 1997

© 1997 Duke University Press
All rights reserved
Printed in the United States of America on acid-free paper ∞
Typeset in Joanna by Tseng Information Systems, Inc.
Library of Congress Cataloging-in-Publication Data
appear on the last printed page of this book.

For Lee Edelman — *toujours mon amour*

Contents

Acknowledgments

For the reader, a book's acknowledgments are an hors d'oeuvre; for the author, they are a delicious dessert. What a pleasure it is to thank the friends who have nourished me through the years in which I have worked on this book, and for whom I have written it, as a cook lovingly prepares a special dinner for a group of his favorite gourmets. As the reader will discover, this book is crucially informed and enabled by the teaching of four critics, three of whom I am proud to have as friends (about the fourth, see below): John Kucich, whose essay on Trollope, which would figure in his book *The Power of Lies*, provided an early stimulus for my study of sophistication; D. A. Miller, the exhilarating influence of whose reading and writing, not to mention the pleasure of whose company in various restaurants, has helped me get in touch with appetites I had sometimes been too "nice" to own up to; and Eve Kosofsky Sedgwick, who has unfailingly offered moral support while performing numerous acts of practical importance to my work, and who, by her extraordinary example, has affected my style of thinking in ways even more numerous and more decisive.

It was Eve who introduced me to Ken Wissoker of Duke University Press. Ken's interest in this book, as it was taking shape, made it that much more fun and exciting to write. A superb and generous editor, he has also become a wise and valued friend.

I also wish to thank two of the other editors at Series Q, Jonathan Goldberg and Michael Moon, whose praise has meant so much to me.

Among the many reasons why I am delighted to be publishing with Duke is that it puts me in the company of four other wonderful critics and friends who are also recent Duke authors: William Cohen, Jane Gallop, James Kincaid, and Mary Ann O'Farrell. Who could ask for better neighbors than these?

I would also like to recognize the astute and helpful editorial staff at Duke, especially copyeditor Joe Brown. Indeed, everyone I have worked with at Duke has been smart, tactful, and patient.

Other friends whose ideas and whose kindnesses have been inspiring are Joseph Allen Boone, Sheila Emerson, Diana Fuss, William Keach, Paul Morrison, Frank Palmieri, Hilary Schor, Mihoko Suzuki, Yonatan Touval, and Robyn Warhol. Another friend, Bonnie Burns, made my life easier by helping with the index.

At Bowdoin College, I have depended on the support of three exceptional colleagues, who have been there through thick and thin: Susan Bell, David Collings, and Marilyn Reizbaum.

I am grateful to Cynthia Johnson, the coordinator of the Bowdoin English Department, for her help with the manuscript. Christopher Hourigan, the department's research assistant, did an excellent job of compiling the Works Cited. The Bowdoin College Faculty Resources Committee provided financial support that allowed me to complete the book.

I have presented versions of this book as talks at the University of Miami, Harvard University, Tufts University, and to the "Columbus Circle" group at Columbia University, and I thank the audiences at these schools for their many helpful comments and suggestions.

My parents, Joann and Lawrence Litvak, have continued to sustain me with the inestimable gifts of their love, interest, encouragement, and financial support. I also want to mention Dan, Ron, Ed, Trish, Greg, Doug, and Brian Litvak, and Alan, Erica, Leah, Avi, and Sam Edelman. During the writing of this book, I lost my grandparents, Celia and Isadore Litvak, but I could never lose the distinctly Eastern European Jewish appreciation for the pleasures of the table that they taught me long ago, and that, I am happy to think, shows up, not always disguised by a French sauce, in the pages of this book.

How can I begin to enumerate my debts to Lee Edelman? Not only is he the fourth of the convives mentioned above: as this book's dedication suggests, he is my first and last ideal reader. But this book was not just written for him: it was written because of him. Every line of it bespeaks the force of his brilliance, his understanding, and his love. As anyone who has ever eaten in his presence can attest, his own taste is such that he can only regard mine as strange, if not horrifying. Over the years, however, he has succeeded not only in putting up with a strange gourmand (I do not say "gourmet") like me, but even, in his own incomparable way, in nurturing my bizarre otherness. Let this talent of his stand for all his other countless acts of everyday heroism without which neither this book nor my survival in the world would have been possible. He is truly the love of my life.

Versions of parts of this book have been published previously. A version of chapter 1 appeared in *Genders* 24, ed. Ann Kibbey, Thomas Foster, Carol Siegel, and Ellen E. Berry (New York: New York University Press, 1996). A version of chapter 2 appeared in *qui parle* (Fall/Winter 1992). Chapter 3 appeared in *Novel* (Winter 1996). Chapter 4 appeared, in abbreviated form, in a special issue of *Studies in the Novel* (Fall 1996) entitled *Queerer Than Fiction* and edited by Eve Kosofsky Sedgwick. I am grateful to the editors of these journals for granting permission to reprint this material.

Introduction

The Distastefulness of Sophistication

This book seeks, through an analysis of a group of English and European novels and critical texts, to make visible a value (for want of a better term) widely taken for granted both inside and outside academic culture, but apparently regarded either as too frivolously "aesthetic" or as too unproblematically self-evident to merit sustained, sophisticated theoretical or historical attention: the value of sophistication itself.[1] Suffusing our culture, sophistication, I will argue, is by no means simply the unique stylistic disposition of the social groups richest in economic and cultural capital. In its discursive behavior, however, it conforms strikingly to the stereotype of patrician hauteur. Where the question of sophistication is concerned, in fact, the cardinal principle would seem to be some version of the supercilious dictum used to show unwanted customers the door: If you have to ask, you can't afford it. From the novels of Jane Austen to the pages of the New York Times, the pursuit of sophistication has been textually and ideologically generative to the degree that it has remained radically undertheorized.

To begin with the journalistic present: consider this passage from a recent article in the Times entitled "Gucci Reinvents Jet-Set Sophistication":

> Any photo of Mr. Ford's collection would tell the same story: sexy, sleek, and sophisticated.
>
> The term jet set has all but been retired, but Mr. Ford reawakened it at his show: it could only be called "jet set" style, the way fashionable people who travel can look sophisticated in any port.
>
> "That's the way I live and move, and that's why the uniform idea is important," said Mr. Ford, who began playing with a moody mili-

tary theme last spring. "Everybody dresses in uniforms now. It's for people who live an international life. That's our customer." [2]

Temptingly easy though it may be to ridicule this passage as evidence of the loopy self-enclosure of the fashion system, my point here is rather that it exemplifies the way sophistication operates even in more intellectually prestigious contexts, like that of contemporary literary and cultural criticism. For the salient features of the passage—its preference for perform ing sophistication rather than defining it ("The term jet set has all but been retired . . ."); the bland authoritarianism of its prescriptiveness ("Everybody dresses in uniforms now"); its fondness for tautology, whereby *sophistication* acquires meaning only through metonymic resonance with neighboring terms (*sexy, sleek, jet set, fashionable, international*)—these features also characterize *sophistication* as it typically appears in academic prose.

In a review from a recent issue of *Raritan*, for instance, we read: "Having produced an account of homosexuality that is both more theoretically sophisticated and more politically radical than queer theory's reigning interpretations of sexuality . . . Bersani, by concluding with an analysis of how his theory of homosexuality is exemplified in literary texts, manages to make a vital contribution to the politics of AIDS." [3] Whatever you would learn about sophistication from this sentence, you would learn by reading between the lines. You would have to figure out, among other things, that "theoretically sophisticated" and "politically radical" are somehow antithetical—the author does not say "more theoretically sophisticated and *therefore* more politically radical"—and that their reconciliation here (like that of "literary texts" with "the politics of AIDS") constitutes something of a miraculous exception.

Even more classically, while this sentence assumes an opposition between sophistication and radicalism, it also leaves implicit the virtually synonymous, mutually reinforcing relation between sophistication and theory. "Theoretically sophisticated": this phrase, enjoying by now the status of a mantra in academic discourse, reveals the extent to which, in that professional context, sophistication and theory have become almost unthinkable apart from each other: to be sophisticated, these days, just *is* to be theoretical; to be theoretical just *is* to be sophisticated. It is as though there were no other way to be sophisticated except theoretically. As a piece of obviousness, the ritual coupling of *theoretically* with *sophisticated* may in fact exercise an even more imperiously statutory force than the unwritten law requiring the alliterative conjunction of *sexy, sleek,* and *sophisticated* in the mythic universe of haute couture.

In juxtaposing an instance of self-proclaimedly "intellectual" academic writing with the kind of prose that, perhaps like one of Gucci's "moody" models, seems at times to flaunt its vacuity, I have in mind something other than the banal *Schadenfreude* that would delight in reducing literary and cultural criticism to just another fashion system. Or, rather, to say that academic criticism is fashion conscious is to say that academic criticism and the language of high fashion are among the very few places in our culture where, instead of having to undergo various processes of disguise and disavowal, sophistication can be endorsed as a value at all. Yet, if even these discourses demonstrate a reluctance to do much *more* than endorse it, if even they become noticeably inarticulate around it, then one begins to suspect here, not a mandarin disdain for explanation, but, rather, an awkwardly "human" self-consciousness; one begins to sense that, even, or especially, for sophisticates, sophistication, suddenly, weirdly resembling the body odor or the bad breath that it presumably banishes from its kingdom, *causes embarrassment.*

Anecdotal evidence of this embarrassment—an embarrassment typically but not necessarily exclusively middle class—is not hard to come by. Talking about this book, teaching seminars on the topic, I have repeatedly experienced a discomfort best described as a response to a nasty inner voice that won't stop asking the would-be annihilating question, Who do you think you are? Listening to the comments of friends and students, I have repeatedly had occasion to witness a similar discomfort. It is one thing to write reviews and letters of recommendation praising other people's theoretical sophistication, but quite another to take sophistication as the acknowledged object of one's interest—an interest that somehow always betrays itself as a desire: a guilty longing for, or an equally guilty anxiety about, the cultural status that its legitimate possessors or occupants, it would seem, have no need to advertise.

What I am trying to suggest, and what I argue in the following chapters, is that the embarrassment provoked by sophistication has as much to do with sex as with class. More precisely, the class politics of sophistication are inseparable from its sexual politics. While personal testimonies furnish ample proof that sophistication excites and frightens much as, say, a sexual perversion excites and frightens, a glance at the dictionary is all it takes to recall that *sophistication* in fact *means* "perversion." For though *sophistication* might nowadays be defined most readily as "worldliness," as the opposite of "naïveté," its older meaning, as well as its normative meaning, deriving from the rhetorical aberration known as sophistry, is "corruption" or "adulteration," and its opposite would be something like *naturalness*, which, if etymologically related to *naïveté*, enjoys a considerably better press. Indeed, the *Oxford English Dictionary* lists not a single "positive" definition of the term *sophistication*. Rather, it defines sophistication as (1) the use or employment of sophistry; (2) disingenuous alteration or perversion of something; (3) an adulterated article; (4) adulteration. It is not so much that the meaning of the term shifts from negative to positive as that the negative meaning *persists within* the positive, with the result that even the most celebratory invocations of sophistication as worldliness remain haunted by the guilty sense of sophistication as a deviation from, even a crime against, nature.

It is not insignificant, then, that homosexuality figures in both of the examples cited above, implicitly in the text of high fashion, explicitly in the text of high theory. One of this book's guiding assumptions, in fact, is that, while sophistication cannot be reduced simply to homosexuality, gay, lesbian, and queer critics have a particularly vital interest in the analysis of sophistication—which is to say, in the analysis of sophistophobia. That sophistication, again like theory, is its own resistance does not, however, warrant a diagnosis of gay "self-hatred." For the ambivalence attending sophistication—an ambivalence that accounts for my equivocation in calling it a value—means that, while even those most closely associated with it may have trouble owning it, conversely, even those ostensibly hostile to it may have a sizable investment in it, consciously or not. The homophobic, anti-Semitic Republican politician denouncing "cultural elites," for instance, must command enough sophistication to *encode* his attacks— either, in the case of the anti-Semitic ones, so as to evade censorship or, in the case of the homophobic ones, so as to supplement a still-permissible denotative violence with a lavishly ornamental surplus hatred.

Although this last example illustrates how sophistication is not just a gay issue, queer theory and gay and lesbian studies not only inform the readings below but also serve as constant points of reference. We have learned from gay, lesbian, and queer theorists that gay people—especially gay men—have traditionally functioned as objects of such distinguished epistemological and rhetorical aggressions as urbanity and knowingness. But, in the Western *imaginaire*, gay people also function as subjects of sophistication. As the mere name *Oscar Wilde* is perhaps enough to signal, the latter function may render us no less vulnerable than the former. One hundred years after Wilde, his trials get reenacted, albeit in the trivially "comic," putatively innocuous vein of the mass-mediated everyday, every time advertising and journalism, loathing as they do the pretentious and the trendy, derisively dangle before their audience the perennially unpopular figure of the snooty (i.e., gay) salesman in the upscale boutique. It is hard to tell which is worse: having sophistication or wanting it. Not that anyone *can* "have" it, any more than the phallus in Lacanian theory is simply there to be had. Say, rather, that sophistication has us—that it has some of us, seizes some of us, more conspicuously than others. But once we are thus seized, what do we do?

So far, it seems, most of us would rather not even ask the question. In our fear of "our" sophistication, particularly insofar as that fear takes the class-conscious form of a nervousness about "elitism," we continue to deny ourselves full enjoyment of the denaturalizing, destabilizing efficacy that sophistication's self-styled enemies generously accord it—and us. To be not only gay but an academic critic as well, to be part of the reprehensible "cultural elite," is to be doubly identified with the scandal of sophistication. This book aims to help gay, queer, and other would-be adversarial critics make the most of our bad publicity.

In recent years, a lot of these critics have tended to imagine the social and political effects of their critical activity in terms of such ostentatiously performative interventions as "parodic resignification," "acting up," and "troublemaking." Many of my recommendations in the pages ahead participate in this work of opening up the possibilities inherent in strategically taking charge of the spectacular relation to sophistication in which gays and academic critics are already unfavorably, not to say perilously, situated. But the trouble made by a fuller deployment of sophistication would also consist in turning the spotlight on those who, even as they demonize it, surreptitiously and extensively employ it. Showing that sophistication pervades our culture, we would reveal that culture as a *contest of sophistications*, where victory often redounds to those who best disavow their sophistication. This book proceeds from a specifically gay academic perspective, and one of its most urgent motives is to provide analytic resources against homophobia and anti-intellectualism, but its strategy is both to pluralize sophistication and its agents and to demonstrate how some of the most powerful sophistications derive their power precisely from their having adopted the unfashionable garb of antisophistication.

Readers of the work of Pierre Bourdieu will anticipate the extent to which the book's gay-inflected emphasis on the perversity of sophistications—even of those that most cunningly assume the camouflage of the normal—marks a difference from Bourdieu's vast anatomy of distinction. Not that Bourdieu has not exercised an important influence on this project. If I were to identify his most enabling lesson, it would be his almost Proustian impertinence, his flair, as novelistic as it is sociological, for eliciting the dynamics of social game playing latent within activities that represent themselves as "purely" intellectual or aesthetic. "One cannot fully understand cultural practices," Bourdieu writes at the beginning of *Distinction*, "unless 'culture,' in the restricted, normative sense of ordinary usage, is brought back into 'culture' in the anthropological sense, and the elaborate taste for the most refined objects is reconnected with the elementary taste for the flavours of food."[4]

The effect of surprise generated by Bourdieu's procedure, however, depends on an idealizing assumption that distinguished taste has nothing to do with the vulgarity of, say, food and eating. To to put it crudely, the distinction between distinction and sophistication comes down to the fact that while the former can pass itself off as asexually "pure" — at least in France, where the grande bourgeoisie is not required, as in the United States, to masquerade as the petite bourgeoisie — the latter much more quickly arouses the suspicion that it is impure, contaminated from the outset by the desiring, and thus disgusting, body in which, as Mr. Ford would say, it lives and moves.[5] The problem with the concept of distinction is that it is too distinguished, too responsive to the dignity of privilege, and not responsive enough to its risks. To the degree that, as Bourdieu insists, privilege signifies distance from nature, its social elevation simultaneously implies a certain sexual abasement, the indignity embodied, suffered, enjoyed, by those who violate nature's laws. To the degree, in other words, that privilege both estranges and makes strange, *every* gourmet is a strange gourmet, in the Proustian phrase that inspires this book's title.[6] As the composite figure for a set of class attitudes and practices, *distinction* does useful work; its chief drawback is not its illusory character but its narrowness. Even in France, after all, as the examples of Proust and Barthes in this book testify, the experience of the socially exceptional is marked not merely by the honors of distinction but by the vicissitudes of sophistication, its delicious lows as well as its powerful highs.

Yet sophistication's intrinsic vulgarity, its bodily implication, does not exactly guarantee it a compensatory "popular" appeal. Although, as we shall see, sophistication by no means refrains from making use of popular or socially undistinguished practices and artifacts, its impurity more flagrantly betokens its "aristocratic" affiliation, its damaging link with the overrefined "enjoyment of the courtier."[7] Quoting from Kant, master theorist of the pure aesthetic, Bourdieu writes: "The negation of nature leads as much to the perversion of 'unnecessary inclinations' as to the pure morality of aesthetic pleasure: 'Reason has this peculiarity that, aided

by the imagination, it can create artificial desires which are not only un-
supported by natural instinct but actually contrary to it. These desires, in
the beginning called concupiscence, gradually generate a whole host of
unnecessary and indeed unnatural inclinations called luxuriousness.' "[8]
Resembling this unnatural luxuriousness far more than the impossibly
pure or disembodied pleasure of distinguished taste, sophistication offends not only in its artificiality but in its excessiveness: the sophisticate
enjoys (himself or herself) too much, which is to say, at the expense of
others, provoking a populist resentment that almost always parades as an
indignant sexual morality.

In today's academic culture, it is easier to defend sophistication as a
"transgressive" sexual practice than as a manifestation of class privilege.
At certain points in these chapters, indeed, it may seem that a kind of
moral binarism has taken over, opposing a "good," sexually minoritized
sophistication to a "bad," social climbing or socially conservative sophistication. I would emphasize here, however, as I hope to have indicated even
around those apparently moralizing junctures, that we cannot so neatly
dissociate the sophistication whose sexual politics we embrace from the
sophistication whose class politics we abhor. Bourdieu's location of intellectuals and artists within what he calls "the dominated fraction of the
dominant class"—roughly, in U.S. terms, the dissident or left-wing of the
upper middle class—offers a model for resisting the moralistic and self-
exculpatory temptation, for thinking about the structural overdetermination of sophisticated practices.[9] Another difference between this study and
Bourdieu's work, however, has to do with the interpretation of the consequences of that overdetermination. Bourdieu's analysis of the contra-
dictions or contortions defining the dominated-dominant position produces an inexplicit but unmistakable effect of sardonic unmasking, along
with the strong, lingering odor of bad faith that such analytic exercises
inevitably leave in their wake. Where the moment of unmasking usually
represents the triumphant conclusion of Bourdieu's procedure, I attempt
to continue past that moment and to consider the possible affordances,
rather than the disabling ironies, of dominated dominance. Instead of
either piously denying or vindictively laying bare sophistication's politically disconcerting luxuriousness, that is, this book argues for the utopian
exemplarity of "excessive" pleasure—including the pleasure of "excessive" interpretation—in a cultural order intensively involved in the regulation and distribution of sufficient pleasure, in making sure that no one, not
even the rich and famous, takes more pleasure than he or she "deserves."

The Question of the Mouth

This is a book, then, about consumption. Like Bourdieu, I practice a systematic disrespect for the hierarchical difference between aesthetic taste and the "merely" culinary taste that, to the degree that it seems literal, must always, regardless of its mode or object, register as *bad* taste. As I have said, however, the distance between aesthetic and culinary tastes in sophistication is never as great as their distance in distinction. What en ables their proximity in sophistication is a psychosexual dimension of taste missing from Bourdieu's account but prominently featured here. If sophistication raises the question of the mouth, the mouth in question functions centrally not only in the consumption of food but also, thereby, as a sexual organ and a privileged site of sexual fantasy. Or, as Louis Marin has written, "What is edible is always to a certain extent a little bit of all three of the following: a desirable erotic body awaiting consummation, an economically appropriated possession, and a linguistic sign exchanged within a system of communication." [10] In talking about sophistication, one needs to keep all these terms—the culinary, the erotic, the linguistic, the economic—in play; but, since, given a certain tendency toward abstraction in academic commentary, the ones that risk dropping out first are the more "literal" or corporeal ones rather than the more "symbolic" or social ones, I make an effort here not to lose the specificity of the oral, of its pains as well as its pleasures, of the pains it gives as well as the pains it takes.

While, as Bourdieu assumes, aesthetic taste tries to keep its distance from tastes of a less exalted kind, the metaphor of *taste*, as he also argues, at the same time performs the ideological work of naturalizing the biases of the dominant class, legitimating them by grounding them in the supposedly unproblematic, irrefutable truth of the body. [11] As every student of contemporary theory knows, however, the body is not necessarily the best place to look for unproblematic, irrefutable truth. What it permits, instead, is the elaboration of the often surprising, half-submerged logic of the senses implicit in the notion of the aesthetic itself.

It is worth asking, for instance, why the sense of taste in particular, rather than, say, smell, or touch, or sight, emerges as the preferred metaphor for aesthetic judgment. Far from answering this question, the canonical texts of aesthetics go out of their way to beg it. "When a man is possessed of [delicacy of sentiment]," writes Hume, "he is more happy by what pleases his taste, than by what gratifies his appetites." [12] Similarly gesturing toward the dinner table only to rise above it, Kant observes that "to people with a healthy appetite anything is tasty provided it is edible. . . . Only when their need has been satisfied can we tell who in a multitude of people has taste and who does not."[13]

It is to a Frenchman, naturally, that we must turn if we wish to find out why, if the aesthetic seems so eager to disown the oral and the alimentary, it nonetheless articulates itself in analogical relation to them. Seeking to demonstrate how "man's apparatus of the sense of taste has been brought to a state of rare perfection," Jean Anthelme Brillat-Savarin writes:

> As soon as the edible body has been put into the mouth, it is seized upon, gases, moisture, and all, without possibility of retreat.
>
> Lips stop whatever might try to escape; the teeth bite and break it; saliva drenches it; the tongue mashes and churns it; a breathlike sucking pushes it toward the gullet; the tongue lifts up to make it slide and slip; the sense of smell appreciates it as it passes the nasal channel, and it is pulled down into the stomach to be submitted to sundry baser transformations without, in this whole metamorphosis, a single atom or drop or particle having been missed by the powers of appreciation of the taste sense.
>
> It is, then, because of this perfection that the real enjoyment of eating is a special prerogative of man.[14]

Though this evocation of man's rare perfection incongruously congratulates us on our uncanny resemblance to the shark in *Jaws*, the incongruity brings out what Bourdieu theorizes, somewhat cryptically, as the symbolic violence of aesthetic pleasure and what I discuss in this book as the implicit cannibalism of sophistication.[15] For just as the mouth, with its "apparatus" of lips and teeth and saliva and tongue, can be a scary orifice, so the exercise of sophisticated taste rather horrifyingly involves the consumption of the "edible bodies," not just of those lesser animals that ordinarily pass for, or end up as, food, but—symbolically at least—of other consumers. To be sophisticated, that is, is to be more sophisticated than, and to outsophisticate the other is to incorporate the other: to incorporate, at any rate, the other's way of incorporating.

"We like to have victims," writes Proust, "but without putting ourselves clearly in the wrong: we want them to live."[16] To which I would add, we want them to live, but within the interpretive limits to which our greater sophistication has assigned them: we reduce them to a kind of half-life. As the passage from Brillat-Savarin illustrates, the violence of the mouth has two distinct modalities: containing teeth that "bite and break" the object, saliva that "drenches" it, a tongue that "mashes and churns" it, and so forth, the mouth submits the object to a series of more or less brutal transformations that, in the extended orality of speech and language, have their equivalent in a rhetorical operation like sarcasm (literally, the tearing of flesh); in its second modality, the mouth, as an imprisoning cavity, an interior space "without possibility of retreat," where "lips stop whatever might try to escape" and not "a single atom or drop or particle [is] missed," serves as a model for the body itself, indeed, for the sophisticated subject itself, as a mechanism of containment. At once hurting the object and trapping it, the "apparatus of the sense of taste" emblematizes more graphically than any of the other senses the aggressive Darwinian transactions between inside and outside that characterize the object relations of aesthetic judgment.

"Taste," to be sure, can hide its aggression, presenting itself, in the softened light of its most successful public relations, as primarily a faculty of discernment, a sensitive instrument of discrimination, vaguely located in the metaphorized papillae of a tongue that neither mashes nor churns but subtly, fastidiously *appreciates*. Yet this would-be nicest taste can keep up its reputation only by obsessively descending to the crassness of spitting out what displeases it. Promoting such a pacified taste, Hume and Kant elevate it over mere appetite. In maintaining the gustatory metaphor at all, however, they risk entangling the aesthetic *tout court* in that metaphor's nastier implications: they do not so much leave a bad taste in the mouth as leave the bad mouth in taste. The more "perfect," the more sophisticated the taste, the more it will suggest a ravenous maw.

In our account of the mouth as the body's theater of the Grand Guignol, however, we may have elided an essential feature of sophisticated orality. As J. Laplanche and J.-B. Pontalis point out, "Incorporation contains three meanings: it means to obtain pleasure by making an object penetrate oneself; it means to destroy this object; and it means, by keeping it within oneself, to appropriate the object's qualities. It is this last aspect that makes incorporation into the matrix of introjection and identification." [17] If the first aspect—incorporation as a means of obtaining pleasure—evinces most clearly the *erotics* of sophistication, this is an erotics in which identification and destruction are themselves intricately interwoven. The convergence of the libidinal and the aggressive is underscored by Laplanche and Pontalis's arresting formulation: "to obtain pleasure by *making an object penetrate oneself*." The formulation also underscores the convergence, in the danger zone that is the mouth, of active and passive, masculine and feminine, terms that, as we have learned from gay theory, homophobic and heterosexist logics have a particular interest in keeping separate. No wonder that, according to pyschoanalytic orthodoxy, the most important thing to do with the oral stage is outgrow it: the badness of the mouth consists as much in its "innocent" joys as in its voracious cruelties.

For this reason, the very category of taste may be viewed as inherently perverted, not least in its normative manifestations, when it would impose itself as the law of *good* taste. "If B.-S.," as Barthes irreverently refers to Brillat-Savarin, "had written his book today, he would surely have included among the perversions this taste (specifically, of food) which he defended and illustrated."[18] Barthes means that taste, as distinguished from appetite, belongs to the order of desire rather than to the order of need. But the perversity of taste is practical as well as ontological, local as well as global. It is not difficult, especially under today's "health-conscious" dietary and sexual regimes, to imagine various deviant practices of orality and consumption, from fellatio to cigarette smoking to a pathological dependency on ice cream. Even the most "disciplined" taste, however, partakes of the pathology over and against which it establishes itself. As I show in the chapter on Thackeray, for example, "mature" taste, the taste that constitutes itself by the rigor and multiplicity of its refusals, depends on a monstrous feat of ingestion: in order to have identifed itself with the aesthetic law, it must have incorporated that law. As recent queer readings of psychoanalytic theory have taught us, moreover, this identificatory incorporation at once enables and dissimulates a desirous incorporation, so that the move whereby one advertises one's transcendence of infantile orality allows that orality to persist in the very mode of its disavowal.[19]

The name by which this psychic structure has come to be known is *melancholia*, which, further, has been proposed as a general model for (especially male) heterosexuality. Neither letting go of the loved object nor acknowledging the love itself, melancholic incorporation indeed accounts well for much of the apparent boredom, world-weariness, and even depressiveness that mark a certain male-heterosexual style of sophistication. But if I therefore enlist melancholia as a heuristic device for locating and unlocking the denied, "bad" tastes latent within a supposedly homogenized "good" taste, I try to prevent its normative, anaesthetic effects from obscuring its remarkable capacity for keeping, and for keeping secret, tastes that could not otherwise be entertained.

That is, while melancholic, heterosexual disavowal stands, in one opposition, against gay affirmation, it also offers a surreptitious alternative to, and precious leverage against, the normalizing pressure simply to renounce proscribed loves and love objects. The first melancholia is asso-

ciated with the work of Judith Butler, who theorizes it "as a form of for-
getfulness": "In the case of the melancholic heterosexual male, he never
loved another man, he is a man, and he can seek recourse to the empirical
facts that will prove it."[20] The second, more "progressive" melancholia —
really, a different aspect of the first — is implied by certain formulations
of Jacques Derrida, who seems to ascribe to melancholia a savingly re-
calcitrant literality, as opposed to the more dutifully metaphorizing work
of mourning, as it is aptly called: in melancholic incorporation, unlike the
introjection characteristically accomplished by mourning, "the metaphor is
taken literally in order to refuse its introjective effectiveness — an effectiveness that is always a form of idealization."[21]

Attempting, then, to preserve and cultivate the affective and political
ambivalence of melancholia, this book would also resist too easy a division of sophistication itself into heterosexual and homosexual depart-
ments. Not that it erases sexually determined and determining differences
between Thackerayan and Proustian, or between Adornoesque and Barthesian, sophistications; indeed, those differences loom large here. But to
hypostatize or segregate sophistications, sexually or otherwise, deprives
us of the opportunity to understand the larger operations of culture as a
highly elaborated food chain, where, if every act of eating is a speech act
and every speech act an act of eating, we can mean only in relation to
each other's tastes — that is, in relation not just to other people as agents
of taste but to our fantasies of what other people taste like. In the vast
restaurant of culture, there is no room for either naturalness or naïveté.

Sophistication, Theory, and the Novel

This book moves within a relatively restricted historical trajectory, from
late-eighteenth-century England to late-twentieth-century Euro-American culture. Moreover, it has a relatively restricted generic scope — until
the final chapter, its subjects are canonical novels — and its method is that
of close textual analysis. The comprehensive history and anthropology of
sophistication, therefore, remains to be written. Beginning with the Greek
sophists, and ending with postmodernism, that project would have to
cover such topics as Renaissance conduct literature, préciosité, Restoration
comedy, and eighteenth-century libertinism, to say nothing of nonliter-
ary sophistications. It would also have to engage non-Eurocentric cultures, resisting any temptation to regard sophistication as an exclusively,
or even distinctively, white affair. In African-American culture, novels
like Nella Larsen's Passing and Gloria Naylor's Linden Hills and films like Spike

Lee's *Jungle Fever* signal a powerful nonwhite investment in sophistication, an investment to which any would-be thorough study would have to attend.

My decision to limit the purview of this book to the past two hundred years, or rather, even more exclusively, to a handful of English and European authors and texts from this period, has to do, like any such "decision," with the contingent circumstances of my training, inclinations, and—why mince words?—tastes. Yet the book's shape and procedures have a less arbitrary logic as well. Recent criticism of the nineteenth-century novel has taught us that it constitutes at once a matrix and an anatomy of life in the contemporary middle-class West. Let me suggest here how this book uses the concept of sophistication to expand our sense both of the nineteenth-century novel's modernity and of what is characteristically nineteenth century about not just our culture but, more specifically, our criticism.

Austen, Thackeray, Proust, Adorno, Barthes: What story does this sequence of names tell? None of these authors seems an unlikely or unorthodox choice for the canon of sophistication; each, in his or her own way, virtually epitomizes sophistication in one of its more familiar, even stereotypical, modes. The only peculiarity of this list is that it ends by veering away from the novel into literary and cultural theory and criticism. But this inconsistency is only superficial. For each of the book's first four chapters—two on Austen, one each on Thackeray and Proust—reads the novels in question as, in part, allegories of modern and contemporary critical and theoretical practice, the practice exemplified by the texts discussed in the book's last chapter. *Pride and Prejudice* is taken as a commentary on the politics of oppositional criticism. *Northanger Abbey* emerges as a lesson in the new-historicist management of the relations between "history" and "literature." *Vanity Fair* addresses the tension between the queerly utopian and the bitchily misanthropic, between hedonism and depressiveness, in current critical performance. *The Guermantes Way* illustrates the strategic "immaturity" of gay theory. And, while this allegorical perspective brings out a "theoretical" dimension of the novels, little effort is required to reveal "novelistic" tendencies in the writing of Barthes and Adorno, both of whom quite consciously and programmatically mix autobiographical and fictional with more conventionally scholarly styles. But what do *theoretical* and *novelistic* mean here? What makes these allegorical juxtapositions possible?

In *The Power of Lies*, his recent study of dishonesty and transgression in Victorian culture, John Kucich proposes that Victorian "fiction could be seen as a kind of conduct literature defining exactly how one might achieve an aura of shared sophistication through deceit. Imitating privileged groups that could negotiate the gray areas between clear-cut truth and falsehood, sometimes even inverting them, was fundamental to the pursuit of cultural power."[22] Demonstrating the centrality of sophistication to the project of middle-class self-definition, Kucich effectively invalidates the received wisdom according to which the cultural work of the Victorian novel (except where it unwittingly subverts itself) consists of promoting an ideology of sincerity, simplicity, and moral transparency. An ambitious and intricate pedagogy of sophistication, Victorian fiction teaches its readers how to act by dramatizing the considerable power and prestige to be gained through a sophisticated manipulation of cultural codes. The importance of imitation in this pedagogy attests, after all, its novelistic mediation. Yet this pedagogy is theoretical as well, not just in the usual, tautological sense (whereby sophisticated equals theoretical), but insofar as what it teaches is how to produce a metalanguage: what does it mean to "negotiate the gray areas between clear-cut truth and falsehood, sometimes even inverting them," if not to elaborate, out of existing languages in binary opposition, a new, more comprehensive, more flexible language with the capacity to comment on both?

To say that the novel thus teaches theory, then, is also to explain the prevalence of novelistic devices in the preeminently sophisticated theoretical texts of Barthes and Adorno. An enabling premise of this book is that, for many late-twentieth-century middle-class readers, the pedagogical function of the Victorian novel has been taken over by literary and cultural criticism—that, where our forebears turned to fiction to learn the sophisticated art of operating, and of operating on, other people's languages, we find our conduct literature in Adorno and Barthes and the cultural studies industry of which they are themselves forebears.

Although inspired by Kucich's work, the present study interprets sophistication as a process of creative interposition not so much at the level of linguistic morals, of truth versus untruth, as at the level of manners, of propriety versus impropriety. Since this interpretation implicitly understands the Victorian novel in general to be more "Austenian" than traditional literary history allows, Austen plays a major, paradigmatic role in this book.[23] If the history of modern sophistication in some sense begins with the Victorian novel, then Jane Austen is the first "Victorian" novelist. The inaugural figure in the sophisticated pedagogy undertaken by later nineteenth-century fiction, Austen, of course, has recently been acclaimed as our contemporary as well. Although a certain common sense would ascribe Austen's current mass-cultural allure to conservative nostalgia—"We gaze upon Austen's world with a form of manners envy,"[24] opines one journalist—her appeal has to do, not with some collective longing for a lost gentility, but rather with a persistent, perhaps inexhaustible, middle-class desire for instruction in the hermeneutics of social performance.

"Manners envy," however, has the merit of exemplifying, if not of comprehending, the negotiations that sophisticated writing must learn to conduct. Substituting *manners* for *penis*, the author might appear to enact the corrective decorum that he thinks "manners" represent. And yet, the very substitution bizarrely suggests, at the same time, not an antithetical, but rather an almost synonymous relation between *manners* and *penis*, an interchangeability predicated on the canny recognition of just how titillatingly taboo a subject like manners can seem, especially when *manners* no longer means just officially certified good manners but the whole repertoire of sociality's unwritten rules. In its naughty oscillation, that is, between propriety and impropriety, between the prudent and the prurient, "manners envy" reveals its author as a diligent pupil in Jane Austen's school for sophistication—an academy that, despite constant changes in both faculty and curriculum, has never gone out of business.

To study in this school, moreover, is to learn how little incompatibility exists between the subject matter of sophistication and the terroristic techniques used to teach it—to learn how much a school for sophistication can resemble a school of hard knocks. Reading an Austen novel means undergoing an education through intimidation, one of whose most striking (if not, for all that, most memorable) lessons is that sophistication *hurts*, that smartness *smarts*. In the book's first chapter, I make a point of staging my own uneasy education at the delicate, and yet oddly rough, hands of *Pride and Prejudice*, a novel I may not be the only reader to approach somewhat resentfully, but a novel, as well, in which one might find a happier sophistication than it first seems to permit. Austen's "lightest" novel, I argue, participates in a certain construction of sophistication itself as a regime of lightness, under which heavy bodies constitute both an affront to the imperative of "self-discipline" and an obstacle in the way of the smooth course of the marriage plot. But, while the novel's heroine, Elizabeth Bennet, seems to triumph because of her exemplarily sophisticated levity, the chapter shows that she in fact practices a richer and more expansive sophistication, in which the "disgusting" or vulgar body is not repudiated but *stylized*. Negotiating the space between aristocratic refinement and middle-class coarseness, Elizabeth defines a new, hybrid class style—the style, indeed, of a new, hybrid class, to which today's academic critics, even or especially self-styled oppositional critics, belong. If one consequence of this reading is to underline the connections between privilege and perversity in oppositional criticism, that consequence leads in turn, not to an immobilizing irony à la Bourdieu, but to a call for the mobilization of the oppositional possibilities of sophistication *as* perverse privilege.

While the first chapter—the book's shortest and most manifesto-like— might have as an alternative title "Jane Austen: Politics," the second might be called "Jane Austen: History." But it is the politics of history, or of the discourse about history that has established itself as the new historicism, with which the chapter more precisely concerns itself. The chapter shows how Austen's *Northanger Abbey* narrates the heroine's social ascent via marriage as simultaneously an education in the politics of genre. Catherine Morland, I argue, gets ahead by learning to transform the paranoia she has cultivated as a reader of Gothic novels into the more prestigious, proto-Foucauldian paranoia she might derive from reading books of history. The charm of this transformation, like that of the new historicism itself, consists in the possibility of combining the pleasure of literature with the authority of history. Yet this same literarily historical charm becomes problematic, it turns out, insofar as it is embodied in the figure of an attractively sophisticated young man. Anticipating the fate of male charm in the Victorian novel, *Northanger Abbey* already takes steps to reduce and contain its too-eligible husband material, the proliferation of which, compounded by novel-induced habits of readerly overidentification, poses the twin threats of feminization and *mass* sophistication.

Increasingly plausible in the context of Victorian subject making, the horror of universal sophistication furnishes the stimulus for Thackeray's *Vanity Fair*, the subject of the third chapter. Reading Thackeray's novel in conjunction with his *Book of Snobs*, the chapter interprets his attack on snobbery as an attempt, if not to restore an ostensible, and an ostensibly salutary, middle-class unsophistication, then to impose a stable hierarchy of sophistications. What imperils such a hierarchy, however, is precisely its condition of possibility: sophistication's intrinsically, paradoxically unstable status as not a single, monolithic entity but a process, a relational activity based on parasitism, projection, second-guessing, and one-upmanship. Presenting sophistication as an unending, invidious, high-stakes game of middle-class self-positioning and self-promotion, Thackeray illustrates, with what would appropriately be called a vengeance, the rivalrous transitivity of *sophisticate* as a verb. In this ruthless

game, to sophisticate oneself, to upgrade one's own language or performance, is to desophisticate others, to recast their knowingly managed
public appearances as so many stupid or pathetic exercises in "vanity."
The more Thackeray himself wins the game—the more, that is, he approximates totalitarian mastery as ironic metacommentator or put-down
artist—the more sophistication itself approximates the stereotype of cosmopolitan jadedness. But this totalitarian, melancholically heterosexual
sophistication has an unsuspected underside; its bottom, as it were, is
not so much the snob as the snob's brother pervert, the bon vivant—in
Vanity Fair, the fat, effeminate dandy Jos Sedley, who embodies an almost
obscenely naive fantasy of sophistication, a fantasy whereby sophistication af-
firms its link with pleasure and posits, in place of a dog-eat-dog world,
an erotic and gastronomic utopia.

The fourth chapter moves not only from the nineteenth century to
the twentieth but from the Francophobic sophistication of the Victorian
novel to French sophistication itself, which is to say, to what most Anglo-
phone readers would regard, whether contemptuously or admiringly or
both, as an absolute, a quintessential sophistication. That this supersophis-
tication in turn finds its monumental expression in the work of a gay
writer—namely, Proust—only reinforces the sense of a profound and
intimate solidarity between the homosexual and the sophisticated. All the
more surprising, then, that the Proustian apotheosis of homosexuality as
smartness should resemble the merely naive sophistication of Thackeray's
protogay scapegoat. But this chapter shows how closely Proust's sophisticated intelligence is bound up with an insistent, incorrigible immaturity.
Whether associated with childhood or with adolescence, Proust's regressive practice in fact enables his most powerfully sophisticated effects.
Focusing on The Guermantes Way, the third volume of Remembrance of Things
Past, I demonstrate the extent to which Proustian sophistication, conjoining both ends of the digestive tract, bespeaks a highly cultivated taste
for waste—temps perdu meaning "time wasted" as well as "time lost"—an
acute fascination with the excremental subtext of everyday life. I suggest,
however, that, just as Jos Sedley loosens the inevitable-seeming connection between sophistication and melancholia, so Proust's gastronomie de la
merde provides (oddly enough, some might say) a recipe for happiness. As
though building on Jos Sedley's example, Proust elaborates a gay science
in which what begins to take shape, against his novel's more famous pessimistic prescriptions, is the life-giving, almost miraculous possibility of
a sophisticated optimism.

Adorno exerts a major influence over the readings in the Thackeray and Proust chapters. In the final chapter, he emerges, with Barthes, as a conduit between Proust's sophisticated naïveté and that of contemporary cultural studies, in which theoretical finesse converges with interest in, even enthusiasm for, "middle-" or "low-brow" artifacts and practices. At first, Adorno's and Barthes's sophisticated naïveté seems to boil down to nothing more than an arrogant obtuseness about the complexity and contestatory affordances of a mass culture for which they conspicuously lack affection. It is because of this apparent obtuseness, I point out, that, although acknowledged as precursors of cultural studies, Adorno and Barthes have to be kept at a distance from current work in the field. The chapter argues, however, that Adorno's and Barthes's embarrassing, "dated" disdain for mass culture nevertheless offers us far more effective strategies for dealing with the violence of that culture—a violence systematically inflicted by means of the most affable homophobia and anti-intellectualism—than do hipper, more "populist" postmodern protocols.

Yet this argument does not necessarily render Barthes and Adorno any less embarrassing. If we wish to come to terms with them, we must come to terms with an irreducible compound of luxury and sadism in their critical stances and procedures. But not just their stances and procedures: we late-twentieth-century practitioners of literary theory and cultural studies may not be as far from Adorno and Barthes as we like to think. Our distaste for them, in other words, is also a distaste for the less politically and erotically defensible aspects of the sophistication we have inherited from them. Luxury means taking too much pleasure; sadism means taking it at the expense of others. But, before we renounce luxury and sadism, perhaps we should ask what makes "enough" pleasure enough and what makes "good" pleasure good. Before we give up luxury and sadism, that is, we should know what, and whom, we are giving them up for. We might in fact set a better example, and be better critics, by retaining our expensive tastes than by repudiating them.

So much does this book attend to the costs of those tastes—both for the eater and for the eaten—that it could hardly undertake simply to celebrate sophistication as an unproblematic pursuit or experience of pleasure. Yet an important motive of the book is to speak not only about sophistication but for it. It by no means lacks detractors, who are quick to point out its various offenses. But, since one of those "offenses" is its association with intellectuality and homosexuality, both of which are resented as by definition excessive, as self-indulgent and unproductive, it has seemed to me worthwhile to affirm it precisely on the basis of this association.

I have suggested above, as I will suggest below, that, in addition to revealing existing economies of taste and pleasure, sophistication-affirmative criticism can help us imagine alternative ones. In writing this book, I have tried to practice such a criticism performatively as well as constatively—hence an interpretive method that understands and presents itself as text based and style conscious rather than as obviously historicist or materialist. *Obviously, of course,* hints that historicist or materialist concerns nonetheless have a place here. It is fair to say, however, that what these chapters mostly do is close readings of canonical literary (and literary-critical) texts. This does not mean that more overtly historical approaches cannot be sophisticated. The point, rather, is that the kind of rhetorically oriented analysis that I practice here has seemed best suited to promote the particular sophistication—to be precise, the composite of sophistication and naïveté—that I admire in writers and critics like Proust, Adorno, and Barthes and for whose continuing pertinence I hope to make a convincing case.

If sophisticated naïveté arrives at some of its most trenchant insights by regressing or by staying behind, then the adherence to a frankly literary method and frankly literary objects will indeed strike a number of readers as positively perverse. More than just an instance of the conservatism of the libido, however, this "childish" fixation on old texts and old ways seeks to prove the interpretive advantages of dilatory, anachronistic attachment over a restless determination, like that of Proust's Duchesse de Guermantes, always to stay ahead of the game. Abiding, like Proust's narrator, with what others have left behind, one sees things that they cannot. By persisting in my "naive" cathexis, what I see, and what I try to show, is the uniquely literary character of sophistication's politics, by which I mean, not just the stereotypical sense in which sophistication and literariness (like sophistication and theory, or like sophistication and homosexuality) seem to invoke each other, but, more broadly, the way sophistication works through and as an interminable, obsessive process of revision, of restyling and reframing, both of one's own words and of the words of others. The pedagogy of sophistication does its most compellingly formative work at the level of the sentence; it is at sophistication as a kind of syntax, accordingly, that the present study looks most carefully. If, as I began by noting, high theory and high fashion may offer the only two relatively uncloseted discourses of sophistication in our culture, this is only fitting, for sophistication, literary or sartorial, is nothing if not style or fashion conscious—in more familiarly critical terms, nothing if not keenly aware of how cultural meanings are differentially inscribed. And if there is an old-fashioned quality to this consciousness of the fashion consciousness that *all* sophistications share, I don't mind it: nowadays, being old-fashioned may be the best way of producing something novel, not to say something strange.

I

Delicacy and Disgust, Mourning and Melancholia,

Privilege and Perversity: *Pride and Prejudice*

Let it be understood in all senses that what the word *disgusting* de-nominates is what one cannot resign oneself to mourn. —Jacques Derrida

In a well-known passage from one of her letters to her sister Cassandra, Jane Austen records her own response to *Pride and Prejudice* (1813):

> I had some fits of disgust. . . . The work is rather too light, and bright, and sparkling; it wants shade; it wants to be stretched out here and there with a long chapter of sense, if it could be had; if not, of solemn specious nonsense, about something unconnected with the story; an essay on writing, a critique on Walter Scott, or the history of Buonaparté [*sic*], or anything that would form a contrast, and bring the reader with increased delight to the playfulness and epigrammatism of the general style.[1]

That Austen can be driven to disgust, not just by her own writing, but by its very *refinement*, by what is most "light, and bright, and sparkling" in it, comes as no surprise: the hyperfastidiousness she evinces here conforms perfectly with the venerable stereotype of gentle Jane, where the gentleness or gentility in question easily assumes a pathological or ideologically suspect character. Of course, what disgusts Austen is not so much her novel's "general style" itself as the lack of a "contrast" that would "bring the reader with increased delight to [its] playfulness and epigrammatism." In its belated wish to interpolate a certain differential heaviness, however, Austen's acute calculation of rhetorical effects bespeaks the characteristic work of an aesthetic of *distinction*.[2] Gagging on the stylistic consistency — the *overconsistency* — of *Pride and Prejudice*, getting sick from what amounts to too much of a good thing, Austen thus presents herself as her novel's ideal reader. For reading *Pride and Prejudice* — reading any Austen novel — means submitting, consciously or not, to a rigorous aesthetic discipline, undergoing subtle but incessant schooling in the ever-finer classifications, discriminations, and aversions that maintain Austen's exacting (because never quite explicit) norms of good manners and good taste, of "rectitude and delicacy," according to which anyone, even a distinguished hero or a delightful heroine,[3] or anything, even an unrelieved "playfulness and epigrammatism," can fall under the dreaded rubric of the disgusting.

But what if, instead of merely providing evidence of how well Austen has learned her own lessons, her "fits of disgust" signified a protest against that discipline? There is more than one way, after all, of being disgusted by *Pride and Prejudice* — indeed, by the very aesthetic properties that would seem to make it irresistibly appetizing. For if the novel functions discreetly and thus all the more efficaciously as a kind of conduct book, the good manners and good taste it works to implant operate in the service of a eugenic teleology of *good breeding*: that is, of the marriage plot, whereby the traditional novel idealizes heterosexuality and its reproduction. Much of the most adventurous recent Austen criticism has concentrated on uncovering just this ideological labor in her fiction. As a result, it has become possible not only to see how her novels serve up what D. A. Miller calls "social prescriptions that readers are palatably, even deliciously made to swallow," but also to begin to resist such dubious nourishment, spitting out — even spitting up — what no longer tastes quite so delicious.[4] In expressing her disgust on reading *Pride and Prejudice*, Austen may be doing something other than just voicing her fear of dulling (or offending) our palates with too much brilliance: she may in fact be seen as at once authorizing and enacting an *ill-mannered reading* of her own text.

If *Pride and Prejudice* is disgusting because it is "too light, and bright, and sparkling," its seductive surface does not so much conceal a disciplinary core as constitute and convey a new and improved discipline of its own. The lightness of the style, I would argue, functions much like that of today's lighter, leaner cuisine, which, as we are constantly reminded not just by doctors and dietitians but, even more dishearteningly, by restaurant critics and cookbook authors as well, is both what we want and what's good for us. *Pride and Prejudice*, whose low-fat, low-cholesterol language positively makes our mouths water, begins to seem uncannily "modern," a prescient fictional precursor of our own food and drug administration.[5]

But the stylish askesis the novel purveys is not merely a question of style. In thematizing its *écriture minceur*, it articulates the strict moral regimen enforced by and on what it would project as a whole interpretive community of weight watchers. The "easy playfulness" (p. 70) of Elizabeth Bennet's manners is matched, not surprisingly, by her "light and pleasing" (p. 70) figure, and she therefore serves as a fitting embodiment of the verbal ethos of the novel in which she stars. Thus streamlined, moreover, she can figure over and against characters like Mr. Collins, whose "heavy looking" (p. 109) body almost automatically convicts him of the "stupidity" (p. 163) with which he is soon charged and that accounts for most of the rare morsels of "solemn specious nonsense" to be found in the text; or like the "indolent" (p. 81) Mr. Hurst, whose vice is confirmed, and whose character irreversibly discredited, in the summary observation that, "when he found [Elizabeth to] prefer a plain dish to a ragout, [he] had nothing to say to her" (p. 81). If we haven't yet internalized the precept that less is more, those of us unfortunate enough to share Mr. Hurst's taste are reminded that the only appropriate response to a ragout is *dégoût*.

Even more telling, of course, is Elizabeth's moral superiority to the novel's various comically aberrant female characters, all of whom, in different ways, betray both an excessive appetite and an inability or an unwillingness to control it: Mrs. Bennet, who has never learned how to "hold her tongue" (p. 305); Lydia Bennet, who has inherited not only her mother's shameless garrulity but also her none-too-discriminating taste for soldiers; Miss Bingley, who, with her invidious sarcasm, repeatedly and haplessly bites off more than she can chew; Lady Catherine de Bourgh, whose similarly self-subverting freedom in "delivering her opinion" (p. 198) more efficiently delivers proof of her "ill breeding" (p. 207). Reduced — or, rather, expanded — to comic types, these characters, paradoxically, can never really "grow": they can only repeat themselves. Even the notoriously "fast" Lydia is stuck in a one-joke role. Along with Collins, these "literary fat ladies," as Patricia Parker would call them, indeed provide whatever precious textual padding remains amid the general svelteness.[6] Modeled against the static backdrop that they compose, the self-disciplined Elizabeth should seem to move even more sleekly through the novel's marriage plot, which, although it places obstacles in her path, does so, apparently, in order that we may marvel at the "liveliness" and general lightheartedness with which she negotiates them.

As Austen anticipated, however, the novel may not be sufficiently "stretched out" or larded to make us consume it with such "increased delight." Not every reader, at any rate, will choose to join the "admiring multitude" whom the marriage of Elizabeth and Darcy is destined to "teach . . . what connubial felicity really was" (p. 325). What one hears as a certain sarcasm in this very phrasing may even bespeak *Austen's* distaste for the ideological project in which she finds herself enlisted. In carrying out this project, she is hardly unique among eighteenth- or nineteenth-century English novelists, and *Pride and Prejudice* is hardly the only one of her novels in which the exigencies of the marriage plot ultimately take precedence over every other claim for narrative interest. What makes *Pride and Prejudice* unusually hard to swallow, I have been suggesting, is not so much the marriage plot per se as the particular ideologico-aesthetic ruse that is supposed to make it go down so easily. For no matter how the novel's distinctive lightness (liteness?) gets glamorized, it remains a fetish in a symbolic economy of *privation*: indeed, it has to be turned into an object of *desire* precisely insofar as it represents—and requires—the systematic denial of *pleasure*.

For all its "Mozartean perfection," in short, *Pride and Prejudice* seems to me the least enjoyable of all of Austen's novels. Where the other novels offer us various juicy tidbits to sink our teeth into on the way to the wedding, *Pride and Prejudice*, although not *entirely* fat free, generally exercises an almost stingy restraint in dispensing preclosural gratifications, withholding any that might tempt us to stray too far or too unproductively from its foreordained linear trajectory, catering only to those tastes whose indulgence will leave us, like the heroine, lithe and trim enough to be put through our paces.

Novels such as *Sense and Sensibility* and *Emma* obviously have to conduct their heroines (and their readers) toward the triumphant genital heterosexuality enshrined in the institution of marriage, but, as critics have shown, the very plotting of that development through a progression of proto-Freudian "phases" at least affords their heroines (and their readers) various perversely "pregenital" and/or nonprocreative excitations.[7] Faced with *Pride and Prejudice*, however, the reader who is not especially tantalized by the prospect of a wedding feast is going to be left feeling more than a little hungry.

In this situation, is there anything to do with one's mouth besides complain? As I have suggested, one way of resisting the heterosexist teleology of Austen's master plot is to cultivate—indeed, to *savor*—whatever perverse reader relations that plot may permit, if only so as, precisely, to master them. To tease out the kinkiness of the interaction between Emma and Knightley, for example, or to play up the seductive theatricality of Mary and Henry Crawford, is fantasmatically to perpetuate a relation with a lost or occluded object: in the first example, a perversity *between* characters, which the normalizing narrative has to cover up; in the second, an energy more visibly located within characters themselves, who must therefore be dealt with more punitively, expelled from the text in a climactic paroxysm of moral revulsion. Instead of reenacting that expulsion, instead of casting the Crawfords out, as one is expected to do, an ill-mannered reader of Mansfield Park may try to keep them in, guarding them, perversely, in what French Freudian theory has helped us picture as a crypt within — or on — one's own reading body.

In other words, if the disgusting "is what one cannot resign oneself to mourn," purgation is not the only response to it; what has been theorized as the fantasy of incorporation suggests an alternative form of nonmourning. The fantasy of incorporation promotes what Freud calls the work of melancholia, where the refusal to mourn signals a refusal of loss. Neither a mere throwing up and casting out nor, as in mourning, an idealizing, metaphoric introjection of the lost object, incorporation, as Derrida has suggested in his commentary on the work of Nicolas Abraham and Maria Torok, "involves eating the object . . . in order not to introject it, in order to vomit it, in a way, into the inside, into the pocket of a cyst." [8] Insisting on a certain literalization of the object, at once killing it and keeping it alive, incorporation is a fantasy not only of eating one's cake and having it but also of becoming one's cake, of identifying oneself with it and thus of denying its absence, which the metaphoric substitutions characteristic of mourning would implicitly acknowledge. [9]

In view of what I've said about the slim pickings presented by Pride and Prejudice, however, the question would seem to be, How can one perpetuate a fantasmatic relation with something one never had in the first place? One possible answer might begin by recalling that, under the novel's terroristic regime of good taste, no one, not even Elizabeth Bennet, is immune from the charge of vulgarity. For example, Elizabeth's very athleticism — the clearest demonstration that hers is a disciplined body — provokes Miss Bingley's disgusted censure when, in a burst of unladylike impetuosity, Elizabeth undertakes the walk to Netherfield to visit her sister Jane and shows up in a dirty petticoat. If Miss Bingley's sneering assertion that this behavior displays "a most country town indifference to decorum" (p. 82) testifies more damningly to her own bad moral taste, there might nonetheless be some advantages to not sanitizing Elizabeth too quickly, to keeping her dirtiness in view, allowing it to reveal a weight and density comparable to those enjoyed by the incorporated object in the work of melancholia.

Although, Lydia's worthy efforts notwithstanding, the novel as a whole may not satisfy one's appetite for certain perverse pleasures, Miss Bingley's ill-advised mudslinging, like Lady Catherine's later judgment that Elizabeth's marriage to Darcy constitutes a "pollution" (p. 396) of the woods of Pemberley, has the oddly appealing effect of stigmatizing the heroine as not only a transgressor of class distinctions but also a sexual threat. However transparent a betrayal of her own jealousy, snobbishness, and sheer mean-spiritedness—however disgusting in its own right—Miss Bingley's disgust suggests one way of cathecting what we might otherwise pass up as an excessively wholesome text: by recognizing that, through the very plotting of its heroine's upward mobility, of her inevitable ascent toward marriage, it affords us a way of articulating sex with class—specifically, of eliciting from it a certain *social* perversity, in which the older sense of *vulgarity* as social offense already anticipates or implies the newer one of *vulgarity* as sexual offense.

In fact, far from being adventitious or merely occasional, Elizabeth Bennet's implication in the disgusting to a great extent defines her. It is this very stance, moreover, that she takes (rather self-congratulatorily) to define herself. What she shares with her father, and what qualifies the two of them to figure as the novel's most conspicuous author surrogates, is a sophisticated "delight . . . in any thing ridiculous" (p. 59). Self-styled connoisseurs of the stupid and the vulgar, bemused practitioners of the art of treating the disgusting as a delicacy, these two characters demonstrate the classic middle-class technique, recently delineated by John Kucich, of making oneself look classier than the rest of the middle class.[10] But this raises a potentially unsettling question: To what extent are they therefore not only author surrogates but critic surrogates as well?

One reason for retaining a certain psychoanalytic frame of reference is that, inflected by an awareness of the politics of sophistication, it can help us not only resituate the "easy" ironic "playfulness" that informs this lightest and liveliest of Austen's novels but also rethink our own way of consuming it. If the interesting characters in Austen's novels usually fall into two asymmetrical categories—the category inhabited primarily by the heroines, who can (or must) do the essentially interiorizing work of mourning, and the category of those who, endowed (or afflicted) with no such interiority, live exclusively in the nauseating vicariousness that, for Austen, virtually *is* the social—if, in short, the characters can be classified as either elegiac or emetic, what makes the jaunty Elizabeth Bennet differently interesting is that, oddly like the melancholic, she marks out a liminal zone between the interior and the exterior. While she dwells exclusively neither among the disgusting nor among the mournfully refined, she effects a certain commerce between these two realms. As a refined con-

sumer of the disgusting, she may have tastes more like those of an oppositional critic than we might imagine and more to teach us about our own
refractory middle-class fantasies of incorporation than we already know.

That is, if *Pride and Prejudice*, more saliently than any of Austen's other
novels, mobilizes the marriage plot in such a way as to legitimate the
nascent social conjunction that has been called a "middle-class aristocracy," [11] the concomitant middle-class sophistication embodied by Elizabeth Bennet has the capacity to signify more than just a binding of
potentially unruly social energies: its overdetermination can provide an
instructive context for the contestatory projects of recent bourgeois academic criticism. It is an irony worth remarking, in other words, that the
discursive strategy impelling Elizabeth's success story—in which what
really succeeds, more balefully, seems to be ideological containment itself
—looks a lot like the discursive strategy whereby latter-day middle-class
sophisticates would disrupt the very ideology in whose interest Elizabeth
fares so well.

Much of the appeal of *Pride and Prejudice*, in any case, consists in its fulfillment of the wish that middle-class readers *can* be sophisticated. While the
middle-class heroine of *Northanger Abbey* can only aspire to the sophistication epitomized by her socially superior husband, Elizabeth Bennet not
only possesses sophistication before the novel has even begun but proves
herself more charming than Prince Charming himself—more charming,
more clever, more witty than all the aristocratic Darcys and Bingleys and
Hursts and de Bourghs put together. But what exactly is this middle-class
sophistication that makes Elizabeth, according to her author, "as delightful
a creature as ever appeared in print"? Just what is it in Elizabeth's "general
style" that enables her not only to win Darcy but, in so doing, to out-
class and infuriate snobs like Miss Bingley and bullies like Lady Catherine,
making her the prototype of all those wisecracking comic heroines of
literature and film, those avengers of their class against its supercilious
would-be oppressors?

Consider the following exchange, in which Elizabeth attempts to re-
cuperate her mother's embarrassing monologue about a suitor of Jane's
who once wrote verses for her:

> "And so ended his affection," said Elizabeth impatiently. "There
> has been many a one, I fancy, overcome in the same way. I wonder
> who first discovered the efficacy of poetry in driving away love!"
> "I have been used to consider poetry as the *food* of love," said Darcy.
> "Of a fine, stout, healthy love it may. Every thing nourishes what

is strong already. But if it be only a slight, thin sort of inclination, I
am convinced that one good sonnet will starve it entirely away."

Darcy only smiled; and the general pause which ensued made
Elizabeth tremble lest her mother should be exposing herself again.
(p. 90)

Clearly framed as a diversionary tactic, Elizabeth's rather panicky "playfulness and epigrammatism" here work, not just to take the spotlight away
from her vulgar mother, but to establish Elizabeth's distinction over and
against that vulgarity, with which she might otherwise seem too closely
affiliated. But, although Elizabeth may come off looking distinguished,
the playful epigrammatism thanks to which she does so is not entirely
distinct from the abjected discourse of the mother.[12]

For Elizabeth's wit obeys a chiastic logic, whereby Darcy's apparently
refined, metaphoric defense of poetry as the "food of love" gets set up
as a mere received idea, against which her own ironic, deidealizing reading must, if it is to emerge as superior in analytic sophistication, invoke
a certain irreducible antimetaphoric insistence: that of the body and its
appetites in their ineloquent, almost stupid, but strangely heroic materi-
ality. While the "fine, stout, healthy" body in love can take poetry or
leave it, such merely metaphoric food will hardly nourish what Elizabeth
rather surprisingly disparages as a "slight, thin sort of inclination." (Even
if *stout*, in Austen's day, may have meant "vigorous" rather than "thickset,"
we can indeed imagine here a happy prolepsis, not unlike that of *vulgarity*,
whereby the body for which this health-conscious novel secretly longs
is neither slight, nor even light, but perhaps best described by the distinctly un-Austenian adjective, *zaftig*.)[13] Indeed, so paradoxically offensive
is the idealized metaphoricity of poetry as the food of love that it can
have the literally disgusting effect of "starv[ing]" that weak inclination
"entirely away." The savvy, down-to-earth Elizabeth advertises a robust
middle-class materialism that—at once appealing to the debunking force
of what a nicer aesthetic would find repulsive and thereby evincing its
own disgust vis-à-vis the latter—chokes on the spiritualizing clichés that
the aristocratic Darcy, for one, has not been too proud to swallow.

This is not to say that Elizabeth has no saving interiority: her grief
and humiliation in the wake of the disgrace caused by Lydia and Wickham, her anguished recognition that "never had she so honestly loved
[Darcy], as now, when all love must be vain" (p. 295), testify to her appetite for the work of mourning. But Elizabeth owes her success to more
than just her refined and refining inwardness. If, on the one hand, what

makes middle-class sophistication middle class, as Norbert Elias suggests, is its displacement of merely exterior, superficial aristocratic civility into a psychologized cultivation, it just as constitutively distinguishes itself, on the other hand, by activating the resulting self-consciousness through an endless putting into quotation marks of its own lower stratum, of the vulgarity that thereby figures within it as an indelible prehistorical trace.[14] Through her witty remarks on poetry and love, Elizabeth distinguishes herself from Darcy and her mother alike, playing the high metaphorizing taste of the one off against the low literal mindedness of the other — the terms in which she champions the body and literality, for instance, are themselves figurative — and thus exhibiting a rhetorical virtuosity that neither of them can claim.

Playing both sides against the middle — against itself — middle-class sophistication vulgarizes mere (i.e., aristocratic) sophistication and sophisticates mere (i.e., lower-class) vulgarity. Elizabeth invites Darcy to acknowledge the charm of the latter tactic when, at the end of the novel, she asks him "to account for his ever having fallen in love with her":

> "My beauty you had early withstood, and as for my manners — my behaviour to *you* was at least always bordering on the uncivil, and I never spoke to you without rather wishing to give you pain than not. Now be sincere; did you admire me for my impertinence?"
>
> "For the liveliness of your mind, I did."
>
> "You may as well call it impertinence at once. It was very little less. The fact is, that you were sick of civility, of deference, of officious attention. You were disgusted with the women who were always speaking and looking, and thinking for *your* approbation alone. I roused, and interested you, because I was so unlike *them*." (p. 388)

Resorting again to chiasmus, Elizabeth identifies her manner, as well as her "manners," in terms of an alluring "impertinence" as opposed to a disgusting "civility." Yet, if she has "interested" Darcy where other women could not, this is not simply because of her difference from their "deference" — not simply because he finds refreshing what would otherwise seem disgusting — but because she has had the wit to *stylize* the vulgarity that keeps threatening to reclaim the rest of her family. "*Bordering* on the uncivil," Elizabeth's stylistic practice is a strategically displaced, ironically mannered version of what she has avowed in herself as a certain "coarseness of . . . *sentiment*," itself bordering on the incorrigible Lydia's "coarseness of *expression*" (p. 247). And, while Elizabeth by no means celebrates such contaminating contiguity with Lydia—or, for that matter, with any of the more disgusting members of her family, which is to say, just about everyone but Jane, the Gardiners, and perhaps her father—her remarks to Darcy above make disarmingly clear that she has grasped the rhetorical and social advantages of vomiting vulgarity into the inside, of incorporating it into a new, more capacious, and more versatile class style.[15]

The evident upward mobility of this style might represent something of an embarrassment for those of us who recognize in it an uncanny precursor of our own would-be "impertinent" deployment of the "disgusting": if not unabashedly downward, the movement of oppositional criticism is supposed to be audaciously and unpredictably lateral, transgressing disciplinary divisions, cultural boundaries, and so forth. The point is not to unmask oppositional criticism as merely another mode of bourgeois careerism but to mark the different, almost opposite, ethical and political valences with which strikingly similar strategies can be charged. For the fantasy of *incorporation*, which I have associated with an admirably perverse resistance to the normalizing (i.e., heterosexualizing) pressures of the marriage plot, bears a strong resemblance to the far less attractive operation of *containment*—more specifically, to "the endless 'rediscovery' of the carnivalesque within modern literature" (and criticism), which Peter Stallybrass and Allon White have demystified as "a counter-sublimation, a delirious expenditure of the symbolic capital accrued (through the regulation of the body and the decathexis of habitus) in the successful struggle of bourgeois hegemony."[16]

Perversely cultivating a taste for what the regime of "family values" demonizes as the disgusting, much recent gay, lesbian, and antiheterosexist criticism could probably be historicized as a "countersublimation" of the kind Stallybrass and White describe. But less than the question of whether that criticism is "really" oppositional or "really" complicit in the success of bourgeois hegemony, what interests me is why the problematic of class and the problematic of sexuality so rarely engage each other in contemporary academic discourse. Not that our culture as a whole abounds in places where they can be found in dialogue; in this respect, the academy indeed mirrors the world from which it might be imagined to differ. While every television talk show nowadays strikes another blow against the poor old repressive hypothesis, what remains largely unspoken, in as well as out of the academy, is not sexuality but the class relations *around* sexuality. Yet, if this issue seldom gets addressed, it nevertheless—or for that very reason—gets acted out, generating powerful or even violent effects, as demonstrated currently by a whole range of attacks on "cultural elites," attacks launched most notoriously and most risibly in and through the mass media by Republican politicians, but also increasingly in evidence within the field of lesbian and gay studies itself, where a resentful activism sets itself up in opposition as much to a supposedly triumphant ivory-tower mandarinate as to the aforementioned guardians of the family.[17]

If the example of the impertinent Elizabeth Bennet confronts "perverse" criticism with a hypothetical narrative of its own class origins, it should go without saying that, far from constituting one more discrediting assault, this genealogy is designed to promote the cause of perversity. Instead of neutralizing "perverse" criticism by exposing its position of class privilege, it would suggest that privilege—or what gets stereotyped under that rubric—can itself have the dangerous force of the perverse. In a culture that tolerates the sophisticated even less than the disgusting—indeed, for which the sophisticated paradoxically represents the disgusting at its most egregious—and that constructs its middle class as the sacred repository of normality itself, the sophisticated middle-class connoisseur of the disgusting commits an offense that includes but is not limited to the sexual. Or, rather, her sexual offense counts as a social offense, and vice versa. Not only has she developed unorthodox appetites, but she has the effrontery to flaunt them, as though looking down her nose at those members of her class who, less knowingly fluent than she in their command of the operative codes of good and bad taste and therefore less adept at scrambling them, have to content themselves with merely upholding them. And, since pride must always be met by prejudice, the bold infractions of elite criticism have to get recoded as pathological, as symptoms of sexual abnormality in its most repellent form, so that what might seem an enviable cosmopolitanism can take on instead the horrifying, abject alterity of what one avoids like the plague.

That this repellent form, especially in the age of "AIDS," is almost always male homosexuality reveals what we might call the other face of countersublimation: if the continuing success of bourgeois hegemony is best allegorized by the rising heroine of the marriage plot, her recasting in the homophobic image of the gay man reminds us how easily the privileged middle-class subject can turn into a scapegoat.[18] Rather than designate one figure or the other as the "true" embodiment of elite middle-class culture, we might try to imagine them as a telling composite, as an emblem of the dynamic interdependence of perversity and privilege in oppositional criticism. For if the former obviously inflames our culture's numerous arbiters of taste, the outrage that it signifies is scarcely separable from that of the latter. Privilege may not seem the most likely

feature in the repertoire of an oppositional politics, but, while its provocative potential may be hard to admit in theory, its provocative effects
are everywhere legible in contemporary social practice.

Only if we presume to know that *privilege* can mean only one politically
suspect thing does its intimate relation with the perverse appear necessarily to give away the game of oppositional criticism—give it away, that
is, as "nothing more than" a game, in which, for example, what is at
stake is merely the familiar (or quasi-familial) antagonism between fractions of the dominant class, between, say, the Elizabeth Bennets and the
Lady Catherine de Bourghs of the late twentieth century.[19] The pleasures
of such sociological reduction are not to be denied; but privilege has its
pleasures, too, and, if oppositional critics have not exactly denied them,
neither have we been particularly eager to affirm them, whatever certain
"activists" and "populists" would say to the contrary. By exhibiting our
shameful "elitism" as tastelessly as our engrossed detractors like to accuse
us of doing—as saucily, in other words, as we flaunt the sexual transgressiveness with which that "elitism" is symbolically interfused—we revolting critics might do more than just play into the hands of the enemy. By
living up to our bad press, with the full insolence we are already thought
to enjoy, we might find ourselves in an even more privileged position to
repel sexual and aesthetic regimes that, as many people (not all of them
middle-class academic critics) might say, are strictly from hunger.

2

Bon Chic, Bon Genre: Sophistication and
History in *Northanger Abbey*

Recounting the history of the relations between "history" and the novel
as those genres are deployed in eighteenth-century conduct books, Nancy
Armstrong has identified a significant realignment at the end of the century. Until then, history—more precisely, an insistently psychologizing
reading of history—is prescribed by conduct-book authors as a kind of
prophylaxis against the dangerously seductive effects of fiction on the
female mind. Armstrong cites a typical exhortation to "Use no Monstrous, Unnatural, or Preposterous Fictions to divert her with, but either
ingenious fables, or real histories."[1] If the protectors (and producers) of
the new feminized middle-class subject thus seem to cast the novel in the
role of a ruinous aristocratic rake, they do not hesitate to censure it at
the same time as an alarmingly effective conduit for the vulgarity of lowlife. In the intertwined eighteenth-century projects of class and gender
construction, novels and romances figure as historiography's doubly demonic other: so much is at stake ideologically, and so great is the anxiety
aroused by fiction, that it must be phobically overdetermined as at once
too high and too low, as both emblem and agent of the promiscuous era-
sure of social boundaries. In the last decade of the century, however—the
decade in which Jane Austen began and wrote most of *Northanger Abbey*—
"a sudden shift of categories can be observed. . . . One finds abundant
evidence to suggest that the classification of fiction had suddenly become
more sophisticated."[2] Although anticipated, as Armstrong shows, by de-
velopments earlier in the century, this shift of categories—whereby, not
just in conduct books but in novels themselves, novels and histories start
to look more alike than different—is an index of the large-scale cultural
reorganization delineated in Armstrong's revisionist version of the rise
of the novel, her story of how it became respectable, its contradictory

stigmatization in the eighteenth century giving way dramatically to its refashioning and mobilization as a privileged instrument of middle-class hegemony in the nineteenth century.

Located (although somewhat problematically) at Armstrong's turning point, *Northanger Abbey* recapitulates the process up to and including that point: if history and the novel appear as antitheses in chapter 5, by chapter 14 their relation has somehow become one of mutual supplementarity.[3] And, while "history" is never again referred to explicitly, I will argue that it persists covertly throughout the rest of the narrative, at once as what can be taken urbanely to go without saying and as a mildly nagging unanswered question, thereby rendering even more "sophisticated" its sustained interplay with its novelistic counterpart. In the process, moreover, I want to consider the unanswered—indeed, mostly unasked—question of "sophistication" itself: that is, of its role in the formation of what, in our gender-minded histories of the novel, we are often too quick to homogenize as "middle-class identity."

Tellingly, Armstrong herself has to qualify Austen's enterprise as the construction of a "middle-class *aristocracy*" (emphasis added).[4] It would be easy enough, of course, to dismiss Austen as the polished product of the transition from a less firmly *embourgeoisé* eighteenth century (and Regency) to nineteenth-century culture "proper." Indeed, despite the energetic de-idealizing efforts of generations of anti-Janeite critics, Austen's works continue to signify an embarrassingly anachronistic gentility—anachronistic, that is, even in relation to nineteenth-century fiction. But I would suggest that, insofar as the sophisticated classification of fiction and history in a novel like *Northanger Abbey* works to classify—to class—both its heroine and its reader in terms of sophistication, Austen in fact foreshadows the determinative indeterminacy that, well into the Victorian regime of domesticity and interiority, keeps marking the nineteenth-century novelistic subject, whose "bourgeois" constitution cannot quite seem to take place without leaving certain telltale "aristocratic" residues.[5] Articulating "history" with "sophistication"—an issue whose class politics, as we shall see, cannot be extricated from a complex gender politics—this chapter will pose a question about more recent history as well, asking what we are doing when we do sophisticated historical readings of literary texts, readings that allow us to satisfy both our refined professorial taste for difficulty and difference and our newer, lustier appetite for the beefy world outside the academy.[6]

"From" Paranoia "to" Sophistication

Readers of *Northanger Abbey*—and of the body of criticism around it—know that the high-profile metacommentary in the book is not about the novel and history but about the novel and Gothic romances. It is generally understood that Austen offers not a debunking, rationalistic parody of works like Radcliffe's *Mysteries of Udolpho* but rather a streamlined, modernized—in short, sophisticated—Gothicism that follows in their footsteps. In different ways, numerous critics have made the case that Catherine Morland's progress toward "a more sophisticated use of cultural forms" constitutes an education in dialectics, whereby realism evolves as a refinement on rather than a denial of Gothic.[7] In the novel's paradigmatic phrase, "The anxieties of common life beg[in] soon to succeed to the alarms of romance" (p. 203). Even the long passage in which Catherine displays her new sophistication by condescending to the author she had once naively adored can be read, as one critic puts it, as representing "a complex admission rather than rejection of the Gothic":[8]

> Charming as were all Mrs. Radcliffe's works, and charming even as were the works of all her imitators, it was not in them perhaps that human nature, at least in the midland counties of England, was to be looked for. Of the Alps and Pyrenees, with their pine forests and their vices, they might give a faithful delineation; and Italy, Switzerland, and the South of France, might be as fruitful in horrors as they were represented. Catherine dared not doubt beyond her own country, and even of that, if hard pressed, would have yielded the northern and western extremities. But in the central part of England there was surely some security for the existence even of a wife not beloved, in the laws of the land, and the manners of the age. Murder was not tolerated, servants were not slaves, and neither poison nor sleeping potions to be procured, like rhubarb, from every druggist. (p. 202)

Although this xenophobia might seem to have domestic reassurance as its intended effect, the apparent non sequitur, "Catherine dared not doubt beyond her own country," gives one pause. After all, if the passage opposes English law and order to Continental viciousness, the line should read: "Catherine dared not doubt within her own country." But, as the passage continues, we discover that, far from marginalizing the motives for the Gothic, its tendentious narrowing from geocultural "extremities" to a figural linkage of middles and centers with the putative virtues of English moderation actually enables a tightening of the Gothic screw. Exemplifying the perversity of paranoia, the passage moves from a presumably calming invocation of the median and the middling to the disconcertingly paradoxical conclusion that this stable middle ground in fact supplies a basis for nothing so much as intensified suspicion:

> Among the Alps and Pyrenees, perhaps, there were no mixed characters. There, such as were not as spotless as an angel, might have the dispositions of a fiend. But in England it was not so; among the English, she believed, in their hearts and habits, there was a general though unequal mixture of good and bad. Upon this conviction, she would not be surprised if even in Henry and Eleanor Tilney, some slight imperfection might hereafter appear; and upon this conviction she need not fear to acknowledge some actual specks in the character of their father, who, though cleared from the grossly injurious suspicions which she must ever blush to have entertained, she did believe, upon serious consideration, to be not perfectly amiable. (p. 202)

Having gone from geographic middleness to cultural moderation, the passage proceeds from cultural moderation to psychological mixture. Thus rehearsing its own representational logic, "realism" makes the (bad) dream of female Gothic paranoia come true: where Catherine was just paranoid before, now she recognizes that she really has something to be paranoid about.[9] As though to provide her—and us—with further reassurance of the need for anxiety, the narrative goes on to confirm with a vengeance her belief that General Tilney is "not perfectly amiable": a few chapters later, after all, he kicks her out of his house because he discovers that she isn't as rich as he had thought and because he's afraid that she's after his fortune. But, even before this climactic reinscription of the Gothic, the narrative has managed to cast the permanent shadow of a doubt. Catherine "would not be surprised if even in Henry and Eleanor Tilney, some slight imperfection might hereafter appear," if only for the reason that Henry at least, as many critics have observed, has been exhibiting such "imperfections" from the outset, revealing himself, to the suspicious gaze, not as Gothic hero to his father's Gothic villain, but as the practitioner of a more systematically euphemized, more suavely generalized, and thus more conveniently misrecognizable male sadism than that directed against Catherine by his rather too anxiously and ineptly malevolent parent.

That Catherine does misrecognize Henry's sadism—that she takes his elaborate sarcasms and insults, for instance, as manifestations of a charm even more seductive than that of "Mrs. Radcliffe's works"—accounts for why the novel's paranoid or Gothic realism seems much less paradoxical than my framing of it. In other words, because Catherine's education necessarily assumes the diachronic form of a linear narrative, of a female bildungsroman that is also a heterosexualizing "love story," she seems not to descend from a relatively abstract and innocuous paranoia to a more concrete and insidious one but rather to ascend from paranoia *tout court* toward something more epistemologically legitimate and more socially desirable, something that, in promoting (and in promoting Catherine to) "a more sophisticated use of cultural forms," the novel signally invests in the "lover-mentor" Henry himself—that something, of course, is sophistication *as* a cultural form, as a class-specific, and thus, as we shall see, gender-marked, style or disposition.[10]

Catherine's refined paranoia depends heavily on a thematics and an imagery of middleness, and, although this middleness gets mapped along national and regional axes, the resulting symbolic cartography also inscribes an allegory of *class*. Since the socially middling can be defined only in relation to the extremes it is always having to avoid, Catherine's realistic paranoia could be traced to the disciplinary system that, as critics have shown, keeps the normative, implicitly feminized middle-class subject of the nineteenth-century novel in line by keeping that subject fluctuating between, but never quite reaching, opposite "extremities," uncertain about *where* the lines that would define its normative status have been drawn.[11] In the liberal police state that is realism's utopia, nothing succeeds like anxiety in maintaining not just the suspense but also the suspension of both novel reader and novel character, especially when the latter is a novel reader, as in *Northanger Abbey*. But if middle-classing them means keeping them up in the air, hovering uneasily between lowlife and high society, they must also, given the strong teleologies that impel nineteenth-century narratives, seem to be on the move, going places, up and coming, even if only on the intellectual and ethical scale that a novel like *Great Expectations* would have us substitute for a social and economic one. (Pip may end up having to lower his expectations, but, in renouncing the "bad" sophistication of snobbery, he accedes to the "good" sophistication of quasi-authorial narrative privilege.) As a result, what *Northanger Abbey* and its successors disclose is an odd asymmetry in the formation of their middle-class protagonists, those essentially labile desiring subjects whose middleness, as John Kucich has suggested with regard to Trollope, is always slightly off center, tilted sometimes toward the lower end of the social order but gravitating (or levitating) more often than not toward the upper echelons.[12] At least in nineteenth-century fiction, it would seem, it is the "middle-class aristocracy," that hybrid, centrifugal, exogamous, overachieving, self-displacing social trope, that you have always with you.

The (self-)decentering or asymmetry of Catherine Morland, for example, can be discerned in the mechanics of the novel's final explanations and resolutions: while John Thorpe's socially anxious misrepresentations of her family's economic position precipitate both her hyperbolic rise and her equally hypobolic fall in General Tilney's estimation, thereby enabling her "true" status to be fixed at some presumptive midpoint between the false extremities of wealth and need, of *having* more land and *wanting* more land, that determination is what in the end compels the general to consent to her *marrying* more land—namely, his son's—than her middle-class father owns. Figuring the "more" of middle-class culture, which keeps pushing it, as though by some indomitable inner law, some Cinderella instinct, toward alliances and identifications with its "aristocratic" other, the "more" built into this middle-class heroine consists in the way she exceeds herself merely by *becoming* herself—that is, by getting ranked accurately in the social hierarchy (thanks to the intervention, not coincidentally, of a viscount and a viscountess), so that she can advance, via marriage with Henry Tilney, from the lower to the upper gentry.

What I am trying to describe here is a process in the novel whereby refinement as particularization, as in the "realistic" psychology of mixed character and the "bourgeois" ethos of moderation, seems inevitably to upgrade itself by tending toward refinement as "aristocratic" style.[13] Or, in terms put into productive analytic play by Pierre Bourdieu in his sociology of aesthetics, the act of *making* distinctions comes to *confer* distinction on the one who is making them; the classifier classifies herself, showing by means of her classifications that, in vulgar parlance, she has class, proving in her own person that, as is "only natural," class will out.[14] Teaching her how to make distinctions, Catherine's course in refined Gothicism prepares her to become distinguished, to attain a condition in which, someday, in her life after the novel's close, she might seem to have left Gothicism—even refined Gothicism—behind. At the beginning of the novel, she is "in training for a [Gothic] heroine" (p. 39); at the end, she is in training, with her husband as tutor, for assimilation into the elite culture that he embodies. Were we to project that training beyond the limit of the novel, we would have to imagine that her refined Gothic paranoia will ultimately refine itself to the point where, although it may retain the form of Gothic paranoia, it will no longer look Gothic or paranoid, so successful will its sublimation have been.

The trouble with Gothic, the reason why it has to produce its own

Aufhebung, derives from its very centrality to Catherine's aesthetic education. It centers her — middle-classes her — but as a result of its own too-conspicuous fluctuation between extremities. And, in thus centering her, it proves itself lacking in that extra quantum of energy that will simultaneously decenter her: it is too antithetical and therefore too symmetrical to give Catherine the precisely calculated boost, the hydraulic lift, that she needs to reach the *off-center* center of the *upper-middle* social register. However realistically middling and mixed a perspective her Gothic curriculum may ultimately secure, it leaves too many traces, in the process, of its own spectacular, promiscuous shuttle between the poles of its aristocratic subject matter and highly artifical conventions, on the one hand, and its irrecuperably vulgar social reputation and distinctive (but undistinguished) corporeal effects, on the other. Notwithstanding Austen's famous spirited defense of her sister novelists, including her Gothic forerunners, in chapter 5, her heavily ironic emphasis on Gothic fiction's absent referential ground (Catherine's Gothic future is in doubt because "There was not one lord in the neighbourhood; no — not even a baronet" [p. 40]), as well as the metonymic taint that no amount of palimpsestic revision can ever quite obliterate once the gold-digging, social-climbing Isabella Thorpe has gotten her hands on *The Mysteries of Udolpho*, indicate the need for some other, less visibly contradictory, more discreetly upscale literary paradigm through which to chart her heroine's progress.

In other words, despite the legitimating shift of categories noted by Armstrong, *Northanger Abbey*, at any rate, still evinces the necessity of living down the bad press that the novel as genre had received in the preceding century and that the social and aesthetic extremism of the Gothic novel in particular seems destined to reactivate. This, of course, is history's cue to reenter the discussion. For if the classification of fiction becomes more sophisticated in Austen's time, and if the novel's cultural stock rises concomitantly, those changes have a great deal to do with the move whereby novels take historiography as their model. It is well known, of course, that fictional narratives had modeled themselves on and even called themselves histories before the end of the eighteenth century; what is significant about the shift in question, however, is precisely the sophistication with which that generic self-definition was negotiated.[15] In this historical framework, Scott would be the obvious canonical name to invoke. But, while Austen could hardly be classified as a "historical novelist," a work like *Northanger Abbey*, I would suggest, improves its class standing considerably by enlisting history as its secret partner, enacting a sophisticated reclassification of itself.

I want to signal the distinctively understated presence of this "history," or of this "historicism," alongside or within the novel's more aggressive thematization of the Gothic—as, for instance, in Henry's speech to Catherine, where he reproaches her for indulging in the sort of Gothicizing fantasy for which he has in fact set her up:

> Dear Miss Morland, consider the dreadful nature of the suspicions you have entertained. What have you been judging from? Remember the country and the age in which we live. Remember that we are English, that we are Christians. Consult your own understanding, your own sense of the probable, your own observation of what is passing around you—Does our education prepare us for such atrocities? Do our laws connive at them? Could they be perpetrated without being known, in a country like this, where social and literary intercourse is on such a footing; where every man is surrounded by a neighbourhood of voluntary spies, and where roads and newspapers lay every thing open? Dearest Miss Morland, what ideas have you been admitting? (pp. 199–200)

Sounding for all the world like a Foucauldian new historicist *avant la lettre*—not only does the ubiquitous existence of informal networks of "voluntary spies" evoke the generalized panopticism of modern culture, but "social *and* literary intercourse" constitutes that panopticism's disciplinary lining—Henry provides Catherine with the perverse model for her transformation of the supposedly reassuring discourse of enlightened reason into grounds for redoubled paranoia. Yet, when he speaks the language of paranoia, it seems not so much like a discreditably *female* (if justified) paranoia ("Dearest Miss Morland, what ideas have you been admitting?") as like a seductively urbane, indeed, imperturbably *male*, rhetoric of authority.

The point is not to reduce Foucauldian self-consciousness to mere psychopathology. Where the term *paranoia* is ordinarily applied diagnostically and/or disparagingly, I am using it here—inspired by feminist revisions and revaluations of female paranoia—in such a way as to problematize the familiar distinction between legitimate, male knowledges and illegitimate, female ones, to demonstrate the surprising continuity between a relatively privileged discourse of historicist "truth telling" and a relatively unprivileged one of novelistic, or novelistically induced, "delusion." [16] To demonstrate this continuity is to uncover one of the most ingenious mechanisms of this novel's marriage plot, which is to say, its narrative of upward mobility. In marrying Henry, that is, Catherine marries his "sophistication"; but, since his "sophistication" is structurally similar to her "naïveté," the marriage happily combines something old with something new. Nothing less than a social coup on the part of the heroine, it somehow seems "natural" as well. And this impression of naturalness is helped, as we shall see, by the fact that, while sophistication is initially represented by a man, it unfolds as a class style characterized by a less rigorous policing of gendered tastes than Catherine has known in her polarized milieu: the world into which she ascends includes sophisticated women as well as sophisticated men. Though "Dearest Miss Morland" puts up for now with Henry's male condescension, its resemblance to that to which it condescends already offers her the hope (however illusory) that to join him in matrimony would be to join him in his urbane superiority.

Having mastered his paranoia in the sense of having perfected it, at any rate, Henry may seem instead to have mastered it in the sense of having triumphed over it. Far from supplanting Gothic paranoia, historicist sophistication merely renders even more systematic what is already an obsessively and defensively systematizing activity in the first place.[17] But, in showing Catherine an underlying connection between paranoia and sophistication, Henry also shows her how to progress from the former to the latter; he shows her how one can seem to rise above Gothicism by means of Gothicism. His lesson, in short, promotes history as Gothicism disciplined.

"From" the Novel "to" History

If *Northanger Abbey* takes pains to stage its relation with Gothic fiction, its inscription of history, I have been suggesting, is no less consequential for being less ostentatious—which is to say, more Austenian. Indeed, the strategic importance of that inscription resides precisely in its subtlety, in the quiet good taste with which it is performed—with which, indeed, the name of the author is virtually synonymous. I have pointed out the implicit functioning of "history" in more noticeably Gothic-centered passages; but, even where its name does comes up, it behaves, one might say, like a gentleman, never parading its attractions or pushing its own claims at the obvious expense of other literary or artistic forms.

Admittedly, the novel's first reference to history, which occurs in the context of Austen's defense of the novel in chapter 5, is not particularly honorific. If she allows history writing to preserve a certain air of tedious gentility amid the Grub Street jumble to which she consigns it, her apparent revenge on the literary class structure nevertheless has the general effect of subjecting history not just to a declassification but to a not-so-subtle *déclassement*. By chapter 14, however—in what is almost but not quite the middle of the book, in what constitutes its slightly lopsided centerpiece—Austen appears to have felt a certain compunction about what she might fear has looked like an unseemly display of resentment, for in this later chapter she intimates a reclassification of history that re-affirms its upper-middle status. It is as though, rehearsing in miniature the development of the novel as a genre, the author had herself reenacted the progress from its terrible childhood through its rebellious adolescence to its reasonable maturity, where, finally on an equal footing with its literary progenitors, it can come to terms both with its own history and with history itself. Thus, when Catherine, Henry, and his sister, Eleanor, discuss *The Mysteries of Udolpho*, Eleanor asks Catherine:

> "You are fond of that kind of reading?"
> "To say the truth, I do not much like any other."
> "Indeed!"
> "That is, I can read poetry and plays, and things of that sort, and do not dislike travels. But history, real solemn history, I cannot be interested in. Can you?
> "Yes, I am fond of history."
> "I wish I were too. I read it a little as a duty, but it tells me nothing that does not either vex or weary me. The quarrels of popes and kings, with wars or pestilences, in every page; the men all so good for nothing, and hardly any women at all—it is very tiresome: and yet I often think it odd that it should be so dull, for a great deal of it must be invention. The speeches that are put into the heroes' mouths, their thoughts and designs—the chief of all this must be invention, and invention is what delights me in other books. (p. 123)

This passage makes clear that, while Catherine may be anti-intellectual, she is hardly unintelligent. Her lower-middle-brow naïveté, in fact, furnishes her with an alibi for the rather sophisticated feminist critique of traditional history that she broaches here and that Austen seems obliquely to endorse a couple of pages later in her ironic aside about the social and political advantages of female "ignorance." While this passage thus provokes a sympathetic recognition in many contemporary readers, it also calls up—just as grippingly—the sense of panic familiar to some academic critics in the face of the current imperative always to historicize.[18] A feminist critique of patriarchal history, of course, need not signify antihistoricism; many feminisms are also sophisticated historicisms, and many antihistoricisms are also antifeminisms, or at least nonfeminisms. What I would emphasize as valuably feminist in Catherine's skepticism toward history is her recognition of, and resistance to, the compulsory character of the historicism with which she is faced, a historicism that itself *means* sophistication. Especially in the current critical context, where the virtue of historicizing has almost acquired the status of an orthodoxy and where the failure to historicize (or to honor the most familiar historical paradigms) can still be alleged humiliatingly against certain feminist as well as, for instance, many gay, lesbian, and queer (including Foucault-inspired) critical practices, Catherine's resistance, however anxious, however easily overcome, usefully suggests a sophisticatedly naive reading of sophistication itself—that is, of the "sophistication" that, bearing down on its objects with all the coercive pressure of such values as maturity, responsibility, and discipline, necessarily asserts itself over a literariness associated with immaturity, irresponsibility, and (mere) pleasure, so that to be a (merely) literary literary critic, one who fails to locate the literary work in its proper historical setting, is simply, or simplemindedly, to refuse to join the ranks of the grown-ups.[19] This is why Catherine's resistance is hard for her (and for some of us) to sustain, why, to the well-read, well-bred Eleanor's cool acknowledgment that she is "fond of history," we may find ourselves responding, with Catherine, "I wish I were too."

Yet there is another kind of sophistication implicit in Catherine's complaint about "history, real solemn history," and, in the next paragraph, the novel unpacks it in such a way as to offer the lure of a more *literary* history than the one we wish we were fond of. Picking up on Catherine's insight into history's "invention" or fictionality, Eleanor comments:

> Historians, you think . . . are not happy in their flights of fancy. They display imagination without raising interest. I am fond of history— and am very well contented to take the false with the true. In the principal facts they have sources of intelligence in former histories and records, which may be as much depended on, I conclude, as any thing that does not actually pass under one's own observation; and as for the little embellishments you speak of, they are embellishments, and I like them as such. (p. 123–24)

Just as Henry shows Catherine how to refine Gothic paranoia as historical discipline, so Eleanor opens up for her a passage from fiction to history, *by way of* fiction. For as Henry also illustrates, history is not the opposite of fiction but fiction in a particularly displaced form: in place of the "dull" history of which Catherine complained, the Tilneys offer her a *new* historicism, one that, claiming all the authority and distinction of a discipline, also affords the compensatory "embellishments" of the un-discipline known as the literary.[20] Eleanor's worldliness vis-à-vis the referential status of historiography in no way disrupts her confidence in her access to the world, the world with which historiography presents her: she professes herself "very well contented to take the false with the true," untroubled by her recognition that the difference between them may be undecidable. To be sophisticated about history, Eleanor's example shows, is not just to know that history is a kind of fiction: it is to know that and *not make a big deal out of it.* Liking what she gets, if not exactly getting what she likes, the sophisticated reader of history knows how to convert her boredom into a virtue.

That the normative interpretation of history is mediated here by Eleanor, moreover, is not lost on Catherine: "You are fond of history!—and so are Mr. Allen and my father; and I have two brothers who do not dislike it. So many instances within my small circle of friends is remarkable" (p. 124). Although the fondness for history on the part of the Morland men might seem to diminish its cultural cachet, what is most "remarkable" is that Eleanor's fondness for it helps make a difference between the upper middle class and the merely middle middle class. In the class fraction represented by the Morlands, that is, history is what fathers and brothers "do not dislike"; in the class fraction represented by the Tilneys, a taste for history is found in women as well as in men (Henry wastes no time in praising the historians' "method and style" [p. 124]). Once this difference has been established, history can define the novel's desired class style itself, another finely regulated mixture, this time at the level of gender stereotypes. Unlike the rigid sexual division of taste in families like the Morlands, this style signifies a pseudoequality of the sexes, whereby women consume and talk about the patriarchal texts of history with the same ease with which their brothers consume and talk about the supposedly feminine and feminizing texts of Gothic fiction. By imitating Eleanor, Catherine can get closer to Henry; she can get, that is, from a middle-class and female Gothic paranoia to an upper-middle-class historical sophistication whose definitive maleness consists precisely in the subsumptive "androgyny" of its total *comprehension.*[21]

No sooner does history get raised as a question, however, than it gets dropped as a subject. After this discussion, the Tilneys move on to such other topics as the picturesque and, not surprisingly, the insistent Gothic novel. Yet it is this very eclecticism that accounts for Eleanor and Henry's allure as embodiments of a certain privileged cultural style. Not for them the gauche pedantry of the pushing autodidact: what emanates from their conversation is not so much knowledge as the sexier mystique of know-ingness.[22] Enfolded in their spaciously cosmopolitan discourse, the subject of history acquires much of the discreet charm with which they treat it. And, while it may thus look like merely one status symbol among others in the catalog of topics for cultivated name-dropping, we should not take its self-effacement at face value. For one thing, as I have shown, history returns implicitly in Henry's speech about the policing of England and in Catherine's subsequent reflections on the English character. For another, once it has been put into subtextual circulation as the prescribed refine-ment of Gothic, it keeps suggesting itself all the more fantasmatically as the half-concealed paradigm for the novel's own discursive procedures.

This odd effect becomes most evident at the end of the novel when Austen, blithely exposing the arbitrariness and fictionality of her narra-tive, does not so much undermine it as frame it in much the same way that Eleanor frames history—as a mixture of, for instance, "the false with the true." That we will be "very well contented to take" it as such, just as Eleanor takes the works of Hume and Robertson, seems indeed the au-thor's confident expectation, so little does her ironic parabasis interfere with her concurrent rhetoric of reference. If history in general is dis-placed fiction that still tells the truth, then this fiction in particular may be displaced history that still has its tropes: the two forms appear finally to supplement and to frame each other, but without any of the melodrama one might associate with a certain style of deconstructive criticism. In-deed, what we have here is a case of the un-uncanny: what the conclusion performs most emphatically is *exemption* from anxiety. When, for instance, Austen writes, "The anxiety, which in this state of their attachment must be the portion of Henry and Catherine, and of all who loved either, as to its final event, can hardly extend, I fear, to the bosom of my readers, who will see in the tell-tale compression of the pages before them, that we are all hastening together to perfect felicity" (p. 246), who can get anxious about this alienation effect? Who's afraid of Austen's "I fear"? And, if we suspect that "perfect felicity" is not *exactly* what is in store for us, we can remain "very well contented" with the suspicion itself, since our ability to entertain it, to consider it *fearlessly*, demonstrates our own sophisti-cation, our inclusion in the charmed and charming circle that Austen's novel describes. Reading *Northanger Abbey*, we have learned not only how to be suspicious without seeming anxious but also how to have our world without giving up our worldliness. In short, even though Austen may be too well mannered to specify the extent to which history figures in her text, it is as though we had learned how to read that text "historically."

The Most Charming Young Man in the World

Like all good pedagogues, Austen knows that the best way to make a boring subject like history interesting is to make the students develop a crush on the teacher. Catherine Morland of course has not one but two seductive teachers in the brother-and-sister team of Henry and Eleanor Tilney, whose intricate relation to Catherine mirrors Austen's intricate courtship of the reader. In other words, if Catherine's graduation neatly coincides with the inevitable tying of the knot that cinches the marriage plot, the entanglement of desire and identification leading up to that telos can never be straightened out along exclusively heterosexual lines. The admirable Eleanor obviously functions as a role model for Catherine, but it would take a willfully obtuse "common sense" to pretend that wanting to be like Eleanor has nothing to do with wanting Eleanor, period. Even in the 1950s, Austen criticism could bring itself to acknowledge lesbian energies in her novels, if only in the disapproving terms of a more or less popular Freudianism.

But, while some Austenians have at least recognized the possibility in her novels of desire between women—on the condition, of course, that it appear under the pathological, moralistic rubric of, say, narcissism—both male and female critics, both sexists and feminists, have been notably reluctant to look at the various charming young men whose desirability drives Austen's heterosexualizing master plot as surely as Henry Tilney, in pointed contrast to the bumptious John Thorpe, with his dubious boasts about how "[w]ell hung" (p. 67) his gig is, drives the carriage that takes Catherine from Bath to Northanger Abbey:

> Henry drove so well,—so quietly—without making any distur-
> bance, without parading to her, or swearing at [the horses]; so differ-
> ent from the only gentleman-coachman whom it was in her power
> to compare him with!—And then his hat sat so well, and the in-
> numerable capes of his great coat looked so becomingly important!
> To be driven by him, next to being dancing with him, was certainly
> the greatest happiness in the world. (p. 163)

Perhaps critics worry that repeating Catherine's gaze would land them in the passenger's seat, in the unglamorous subject position of an impres-

sionable femininity. Regarding Henry—rather, refusing to regard Henry
—they have chosen between two apparently antithetical but mutually reinforcing tactics: the patriarchal one of imitating his condescending wit
and irony while pretending not to notice its sexual performativity and
the antipatriarchal one of registering that sexual performativity, but only
as the manifestation of a somewhat abstract male chauvinism.

This scopophobia might adduce its moral justification in Austen's other
novels. Judith Wilt has observed that, after *Northanger Abbey*, charm in
Austen's young men (Wickham, Willoughby, Frank Churchill) begins to
signify duplicity or villainy, with the result that, "by the time of *Mansfield
Park*, Henry Tilney has metamorphosed into the charming villain, Henry
Crawford."[23] Where the charming Ann Radcliffe merely gets assimilated
into a higher, more refined Gothicism, it is not long before the charming
young man who replaces her meets with the less genteel violence of re-
pudiation. Within Austen's fiction itself, that is, male sex appeal begins its
long nineteenth-century slide toward the demonized figure of the pretty
boy with an ugly problem, whose apotheosis hangs ignobly at century's
end in the picture of Dorian Gray. Indeed, the story of the nineteenth-
century English novel might be told as the story of how social intercourse
itself stops getting embodied by the charming man and starts getting embodied either by the disgusting man (Uriah Heep in *David Copperfield*, Slope
in *Barchester Towers*, Casaubon in *Middlemarch*) or by the equally disgusting,
because theatrically bewitching, woman (Becky Sharp in *Vanity Fair*, Alcha-
risi in *Daniel Deronda*) and of how, faced with this hideous progeny, all we
can do is follow the lead of the rebarbatively "plain" heroes and heroines
of Charlotte Brontë, as they retreat from social existence in general into
an intensively psychologized, protosuburban paradise.[24]

Limiting our scope to the Austen canon itself, we might ask, How do we
get from attractive Henry Tilney to repulsive Mr. Collins, from an image
of the social as an object of desire to an image of the social as an object of
disgust, as the site of what I referred to in the previous chapter as a "nauseating vicariousness"? Is male charm in *Northanger Abbey* already somehow
contaminated, already inhabited, à la Dorian Gray, by its phobogenic
opposite? Just what *makes* a man charming, according to this novel, and
just what would make his charm vulnerable to self-subversion? Henry's
charm, at any rate, is announced from the moment of his introduction
to Catherine in the pump room at Bath:

> The master of ceremonies introduced to her a very gentlemanlike
> young man as a partner;—his name was Tilney. He seemed to be

about four or five and twenty, was rather tall, had a pleasing counte-
nance, a very intelligent and lively eye, and, if not quite handsome,
was very near it. His address was good and Catherine felt herself in
high luck. . . . He talked with fluency and spirit—and there was an
archness and pleasantry in his manner which interested, though it
was hardly understood by her. (p. 47)

What does it mean to be "not quite handsome" but "very near it"? What
exactly separates "handsome" from "very near handsome"? That Austen
withholds this crucial information—as though it were not crucial information, as though everyone knew the difference but no one cared—and
that she seems to qualify and evade Henry's attractiveness even as she asserts it might suggest that she already has reservations about male charm.
And, if we were to seek a plausible reason for these reservations, we
would not have to look much further than the "archness and pleasantry,"
which even Catherine, "fear[ing] . . . that [Henry] indulged himself a little
too much with the foibles of others" (p. 50), isn't too bedazzled to recognize as precursors of the Schadenfreude with which he will soon treat her.

But is it the aggressivity of archness that gives Austen pause? As its ety-
mology reminds us, archness is the rhetorical prerogative of those at the
top of the social hierarchy, those who command the authority to articulate that hierarchy in the first place. If charm, as Bourdieu has argued,
"designate[s] the power, which certain people have, to impose their own
self-image as the objective and collective image of their body and being;
to persuade others, as in love or faith, to abdicate their generic power
of objectification and delegate it to the person who should be its object,
who thereby becomes an absolute subject, without an exterior (being
his own Other), fully justified in existing, legitimated," then, precisely to
the extent that it foreshadows his more elaborated sadism, Henry's archness not only constitutes his charm but constitutes it as the novel's proudest
achievement: the historicist sophistication that objectifies the would-be
objectifying surveillance of a whole "neighbourhood of voluntary spies"
and that thus transforms paranoia into panopticism.[25]

Yet there remain in the novel other traces of an anticharismatic tendency that cannot be explained away quite so easily. Henry's inability to
do more than approximate handsomeness resonates strikingly, for example,
with Austen's arch refusal, in the novel's final chapter, to let us see "the
most charming young man in the world" (p. 247), as she tantalizingly
refers to the wealthy peer who shows up like a deus ex machina to marry
Eleanor and thus enable General Tilney to consent to the marriage of
Henry and Catherine as well. Although Austen's excuse that "the rules of

composition forbid the introduction of a character not connected with my fable" (p. 247) and her mocking assurance that, despite this interdiction, "the most charming young man in the world is instantly before the imagination of us all" (p. 247) are in themselves charming instances of self-conscious fictiveness, they may not be quite charming enough to satisfy readers who, still wondering about "not quite handsome," want to see, not just imagine, the character she is keeping from us and who want to know why she is doing so. Why can the novel tolerate only one charming young man, and why does even he have to fall slightly short of the charms we desire for him?

Unpersuaded that "too much" charm can get to be as boring as, say, history before it became literary, we might hypothesize that the problem with two charming young men is rather one of excessive excitement: this doubling raises the specter of social intercourse as uncontrolled and uncontrollable imitation. "The problem, perceived by many commentators on eighteenth-century mores," Jerome Christensen has written, "was usually associated with the 'present rage of imitating the manners of high life [that] hath spread itself so far among the gentlefolks of lower life, that in a few years we shall probably have no common folk at all.'" [26]

Although it maintains a strict quota system in order to regulate mimetic desire between men, Northanger Abbey does represent one rather disturbing case of cross-gender desire and identification between "the gentlefolks of lower life" and the "high life" for which they yearn. The example of Isabella Thorpe shows that, much as the novel needs Henry's charm to stimulate the desire of the middle class for the "aristocracy," it also needs to guard against the danger of stimulating too much desire—that is to say, of producing an overidentification that would end up blurring the line between middle-class women and "aristocratic" men. When Henry is described as "forming his features into a set smile, . . . affectedly softening his voice" and speaking "with a simpering air," the narrative has little trouble absorbing these potentially discrediting mannerisms into the general "fluency and spirit" (p. 47) required of the "very gentlemanlike young man." When a similar theatricality shows up in a character like Isabella Thorpe, however, the narrative is not so tolerant. In Isabella, affectation bespeaks not social distinction but a fatal vulgarity and inauthenticity. The contrast between her and Eleanor is decisive:

> Miss Tilney had a good figure, a pretty face, and a very agreeable countenance; and her air, though it had not all the decided pretension, the resolute stilishness of Miss Thorpe's, had more real elegance. Her manners shewed good sense and good breeding; they

were neither shy, nor affectedly open; and she seemed capable of being young, attractive, and at a ball, without wanting to fix the attention of every man near her, and without exaggerated feelings of extatic delight or inconceivable vexation on every little trifling occurrence. (p. 76)

But, where Eleanor's defense of history serves indirectly to recommend her brother's "historical" practice, underscoring the superiority of the class style he thereby embodies, here her mediation has the rather embarrassing effect of bringing out—by disavowing—the *resemblance* between Henry's style and Isabella's mere "stilishness." Although Eleanor is interposed as a screen or a buffer against any awareness of such slippage across class lines, it is clear not only what Isabella's "pretension" is pretending to but also that this "pretension" comes a bit too close to the more accomplished "affectation"—the more artfully opaque "archness and pleasantry"—that is its model. (Isabella's confession to Catherine that she "had long suspected the [Tilneys] to be very high" [p. 139]—that is, haughty— bespeaks more poignantly her envious aspiration to that height.) And, when the same chapter that contains a warning that "Dress is a frivolous distinction, and excessive solicitude about it often destroys its own aim" (p. 92), also features an extended discussion of dancing as a metaphor for marriage, in which Henry's rhetorical conceits are all too visibly dressed to kill, we can see how his example might make it difficult to distinguish between good distinction and its "frivolous" perversion.

Undeniably, the force of the passage in which Catherine contrasts Eleanor with Isabella and, indeed, much of the appeal of the first half of the novel itself derive from a powerful fantasy of legibility at the heart of Austen's fiction as a whole: the fantasy that, at least in reading one's acquaintances, one *does not* have "to take the false with the true" since one can learn to distinguish reliably between those with genuine class and those who are merely vulgar poseurs—between the Tilneys and the Thorpes of the world. Culminating almost ritually in the heroine's embrace by the former and in the equally gratifying exposure and expulsion of the latter, the fantasy's power consists in large part in its implicit flattery of the reader, whom it congratulates for *having* the distinction necessary to *make* distinctions, for setting herself apart from the upstarts by whose pretentious impostures she might otherwise have been taken in—or, worse, in whose pretentious fantasies she might otherwise have had to recognize her own.[27] If the novel makes its heroine a reader, it even more delightfully makes its reader a heroine.

Fully committed to the punitive, projective logic that accounts for so much of the pleasure of the "realistic" text, *Northanger Abbey* indeed sees to it, for example, that Isabella gets what's coming to her, finding herself abandoned by the "fashionable" (p. 141) Captain Tilney just as she had abandoned Catherine's brother. If the target audience for this revenge plot consists of the multitude of the socially insecure (that is to say, of the middle class), the annoying Isabella obviously makes an irresistible target herself, but where *target* means "scapegoat." The social insecurity— the destabilizing of the class structure—that her "pretension" threatens to effect, however, can ultimately be traced, not to her undisciplined desire, but rather to the advertising campaign whose function it is to incite that desire in the first place. Though her transgression obviously consists in not knowing her place, what induces that libidinal errancy, that grotesque imitative identification, is the spectacle of the charming young man, the sex symbol who, what Isabella wants to be even more than to have, figures as the object of her affectations. Isabella may pursue the irresponsible Frederick Tilney, but the eroticized class style that she is after finds its fullest embodiment in the novel in his supposedly good younger brother.

Showcasing Henry as the object of a desire that is not limited to Catherine, the novel risks setting in motion a general imitativeness whose effect would be to erase the distinctions it has so painstakingly drawn— and to implicate itself in the social promiscuity for which fiction in general had been denounced throughout the previous century. One of Isabella's most obnoxious traits is her arch way of attributing archness to others; eventually, she even has the rhetorically unadventurous Catherine pretending to the "arch penetration" (p. 132) with which Isabella charges her. As though fancying herself (to pun badly on the name of James's noble heroine) a sort of Isabella Archer, she brazenly lays claim to a supercilious rhetoric that not only links her obscenely with Henry but also calls Henry's identity into question; in imitating him, she makes him seem to imitate her. Here, as throughout Austen's fiction, the arriviste's aping of "the manners of high life" furnishes her with one of her favorite and most egregious examples of social interaction as nauseating vicariousness. What could be more disgusting than the vulgarian's pretentious emulation of the sophisticate? Only the resulting undifferentiation, which announces itself under the sign of a second, perhaps even more disturbing vicariousness: the vicariousness, strategically thematized by Jacques Derrida in a reading of the disgusting in Kant's aesthetics, in which imitation takes place not just between people but between parts of the same body.[28]

As when, in the following passage, Henry Tilney's hair "imitates" his penis: "The Mysteries of Udolpho, when I had once begun it, I could not lay down again; —I remember finishing it in two days—my hair standing on end the whole time" (p. 121). Catherine expects all men to be like the boorish John Thorpe, who is as vulgarly contemptuous of novels as she is vulgarly enamored of them, but Henry's interest in Gothic fiction looks forward to the appropriative hipness of a certain opportunistic style of "male feminism." Impressing his interlocutors with the arresting (if proverbial) image of his "hair standing on end the whole time," he stages his petrification (or castration) in the paradoxical, apotropaic mode of erection.[29] Indeed, Henry disarmingly, that is, aggressively, installs himself in the space of novelized "femininity," all the better to engage in a menacing display of cultural capital as phallic privilege. Affirming his superior command of Gothic fiction, he warns Catherine:

> Do not imagine that you can cope with me in a knowledge of Julias and Louisas. If we proceed to particulars, and engage in the never-ceasing inquiry of "Have you read this?" and "Have you read that?" I shall soon leave you as far behind me as—what shall I say—I want an appropriate simile;—as far as your friend Emily herself left poor Valancourt when she went with her aunt into Italy. Consider how many years I have had the start of you. I had entered on my studies at Oxford, while you were a good little girl working your sampler at home! (p. 122)

But Henry's "feminism" may not be entirely distinguishable from his "feminization": it may not be reducible, that is, to the sort of power play that characterizes patriarchy with a baby face. Though his cute receptivity to Gothic novels rectifies itself as a defensively offensive stiffness, his reference to his "studies at Oxford," in addition to casting him in the subordinate role of the student, evokes the whole constricting network of family ties in which he must play the other, less escapable subordinate role of the younger son. And, as he lets slip in a startlingly fratricidal fantasy a few pages later, that is a role that he has every reason to resent. For while Catherine was "a good little girl working [her] sampler at home," Henry was, and must remain, a good little boy—perhaps, since he'll have to cede the title of most charming young man, the best little boy in the world. But he is charming enough and could easily be added to the company of the charming young men in Austen's novels of whom Sandra M. Gilbert and Susan Gubar observe: "Willoughby, Wickham, Frank Churchill, and Mr. Elliott are eminently agreeable because they are self-changers, self-shapers. In many respects they are attractive to the heroines because somehow they act as doubles: younger men who must learn to please, narcissists, they experience traditionally 'feminine' powerlessness and they are therefore especially interested in becoming the creators of themselves." [30]

Where Bourdieu describes charm's characteristic *effects*, Gilbert and Gubar provide it with a *genealogy*, and the traditionally "masculine" power of the charming (or absolute) subject, which masquerades as pure cause, therefore gets demystified as itself an effect: an effect of "traditionally 'feminine' powerlessness," a peculiar afterglow of the anxious rhetorical performance perhaps best exemplified, in our time and idiom, by the abused child struggling to survive the dysfunctional family. That many abused or "merely" dominated children grow up to be "self-changers," "self-shapers," and even self-creators (less honorifically, "narcissists") may thus signify not so much triumph over the familial reign of terror as continuing subjection to it. Where Henry's charming "archness and pleasantry" initially seemed to define charm in general as a *supersocial* disposition—not just the social disposition par excellence but the social disposition that panoptically rules over and thereby *transcends* the social—now, while pleasantry emerges as an almost Pavlovian reflex forcibly instilled in those "who must learn to please," archness begins to resemble a professional deformation, a curvature of the tongue imposed on those who cannot enjoy the rewards, or who cannot afford the risks, of straight talk.

Henry is not exactly an abused child, but, if Catherine begins to sense that General Tilney "seemed always a check upon his children's spirits" (p. 163), she soon learns, through painful firsthand experience, that his "parental tyranny" extends beyond mere oppressiveness (p. 248). Henry of course finally rebels against this tyranny; yet his rebellion and his consequent proposal of marriage to Catherine seem to entail a curious stylistic change. Expressing his "embarrassment on his father's account" (p. 239) through a gratifying profusion of "blushes" and other "pitiable" somatic signs, Henry seems almost to have been assigned a new class body: the charming, easy body of the "aristocrat" seems to have been replaced by the awkward, self-conscious body of the petit bourgeois.[31] For a moment, it appears not that Cinderella is ascending to the level of Prince Charming but that he is descending to hers and that their union heralds not a bold reentry into the symbolic order but a panicky exit from it.

If this humbling of Henry does not entirely divest him of his "aristocratic" charm, it furnishes one more piece of evidence that, even in *Northanger Abbey*, the homophobic aversion therapy of nineteenth-century fiction is already being prepared. Even here, where so much effort goes into making the (presumptively female) reader mad about the boy, we can see intimations of the dreary cultural project thanks to which the charming young man will cease to be engrossing and become merely gross. *Northanger Abbey,* moreover, intimates the logic of this revulsion, showing how charm itself implies not only the archcommentator's arch penetration of the social text but also his inscription in that text, and thus the possibility of his penetration by others. Just as the most charming young man in the world gets linked, through his servant, with the "washing-bills" Catherine misidentifies in her Gothic wishfulness, and hence with dirty linen, so Henry threatens to reveal the nauseating versatility of the body in charm.

What disconcerts Austen, and a whole novelistic tradition after her, is a sense that upper-middle-class sophistication, the very stock in trade of nineteenth-century fiction in general, might turn every upper-middle-class male body into that nauseating body. Indeed, as the style of the middle-class aristocracy becomes increasingly associated with the style of what John Kucich has called the antibourgeois intellectual elite—or with the style of what Bourdieu calls the dominated fraction of the dominant class—men like Henry Tilney become increasingly troubling for their "perverse" combination of cockiness with complaisance, of cosmopolitanism as mastery with cosmopolitanism as marginality. In order to save upper-middle-class men for the upper-middle-class and would-be upper-middle-class women whose fate it is to love them, Austen begins remodeling the former along the virile, although rather charmless, lines of, say, Darcy—making them more like lawyers or businessmen than like literature professors—and annexes the remaining sophistication as the legitimate function only of a relatively disembodied female authorship, not of a relatively embodied male characterhood. As the charming young man sinks into villainy, and as his dirty linen expands itself as the general sleaze that ultimately defines him, the archness and pleasantry that he also leaves behind become the property of Jane Austen herself. If her gender permits her to let down the hair that previously stood on end and to develop Henry's archness and pleasantry into the "irony" and "wit" for which she is famous, it is because *irony* and *wit* are the names we must give to resentment and sarcasm to find them charming—that is, to misrecognize the violence of a social order that, barring women from the exercise of power, grants them the authority of a "style" that can only keep biting the hand that doesn't feed it.[32]

3

Kiss Me, Stupid: Sophistication and
Snobbery in *Vanity Fair*

In boredom there is the lure of a possible object of desire, and the lure of the escape from desire, of its meaninglessness. —Adam Phillips, "On Being Bored"

39. Manuscript Silver diary, 8 January 1862. A further detail from the same source may be relegated to the decent obscurity of a note: "Thackeray says one of the first orders he received [at Charterhouse] was 'Come & frig me'" (21 October 1858). —Gordon N. Ray, *Thackeray: The Uses of Adversity*

At the end of *Vanity Fair* (1847–48), Becky Sharp hires solicitors to challenge the insurance company that, suspecting her of having killed Jos Sedley for his life insurance policy, refuses payment of it. Since the challenge succeeds, we are led to conclude that Becky not only gets away with murder but profits from it. The fact, however, that her solicitors are "Messrs Burke, Thurtell, & Hayes" (p. 796)—the names of three notorious murderers [1]—does not just make Becky look even guiltier: it signals the murderousness of the law itself, its implication in the violence it seeks, if not to punish, then to excuse or deny.

But, if the law's violence thus gets figured as a killing literality, the end of the novel merely thematizes the subtler brutality of a law that pervades, even constitutes, *Vanity Fair* as a whole: the brutality that, while seeming to assume the mitigating disguise of sophistication, more fundamentally is sophistication, the fatal sophistication of the novel's narrator, the man about town whose famous irony extends an iron fist all the more powerful for being inseparable from the velvet glove that covers it.

That sartorial image suggests the mode in which Thackeray's narrative violence most tellingly operates: the mode, in fact, of *la mode*. Enforcing the law of sophistication with a vengeance, the Thackerayan narrator reminds us that the most sadistic of the police, if not the most abusive, are the fashion police, those arbiters of taste whose profit, that is, whose cultural authority, does not come without a certain risk of its own: the risk of a distinctly problematic relation to the norms of middle-class heterosexual masculinity.

Is there something "inherently gay" about the role of arbiter of taste? Without unpacking the question's numerous historical and theoretical implications, and without addressing the more local issue of Thackeray's sexuality, I would simply point out that he was obviously not "gay identified" and—as my second epigraph might signal—that the meaning of his not being gay identified is anything but obvious. The execution of Jos Sedley bespeaks Thackeray's own anxious awareness of sophistication's homosexualizing potential. Becky may kill Jos to cash in on his insurance policy, but she thus fronts for the real culprit, the narrator himself, whose credibility apparently requires the abjection—indeed, the extermination—of his effeminate double, the fat dandy who represents not just naïveté but, far worse, a naive travesty of sophistication itself. As though to justify the death sentence he finally pronounces on Jos, Thackeray enthusiastically plays up the scandal of that oxymoronic figure, the obtuse style queen.

If it seems anachronistic to intimate Thackeray's homophobia, this is only because, not unlike, say, modern homophobia, it masks itself as (and models itself on) a set of anxieties not about sexuality but about class: as the downright normal, thoroughly respectable condition we might call snobophobia. Just before publishing Vanity Fair, Thackeray in fact produced a series of articles collected under the rubric of The Book of Snobs, which, although disarmingly subtitled By One of Themselves, works overtime to diminish the impression that it takes one to know one, and which affords an especially acute perspective on the violence at work in the novel that was to make Thackeray a star.

Thanks to Eve Kosofsky Sedgwick, we recognize "it takes one to know one" as the very mantra of the epistemology of the closet.[2] That epistemology builds explicitly on René Girard's epistemology of snobbery: "One must be a snob oneself," Girard observes, "in order to suffer from the snobbism of Others."[3] Thackeray's snob already doubles, I hope to show, as a protohomosexual. As John Sutherland points out in his editor's introduction to The Book of Snobs, Thackeray's own "class identity in 1846 was ambiguous," not only as a result of his family's financial vicissitudes, but also because of his own awkward professional position between the world of the salons and the gutter journalism of Punch.[4] Sutherland cites G. M.

Young's image of Thackeray "among a great Victorian railway crowd: "I see a passenger whose joy is darkened by one anxiety—he is not quite sure if his ticket entitles him to travel first class" (p. 13). But can one "see" that passenger—arriviste and départiste at once—can one conjure up this tableau, thus scoring points for urbane wit and knowingness, without having, precisely, known that anxiety oneself? And is it possible, in the densely populated scene resurrected here, for *ambiguity* and *anxiety* not to take on a certain sexual coloring? Insofar as the anxiety is also a desire—a desire for the particular companionship of other strangers on a train—the ambiguity in turn becomes as much a matter of sexual as of class identity.[5]

The anxiety and ambiguity informing Thackeray's sophisticated practice characterize his use of the word *sophistication* itself. Not only does Thackerayan *sophistication* hover between an older construction of the term, as meaning "corruption," and a newer one, as meaning something like "worldly refinement": the mode of its circulation in his text anticipates what I would call the double discourse of sophistication, an ideological incoherence (or ruse) everywhere discernible in, for instance, late-twentieth-century mass culture. In *Vanity Fair*, for example, while describing the vulgarly opportunistic interest of the Osborne sisters in the rich mulatta, Miss Swartz, Thackeray snidely refers to the former as "dear unsophisticated girls" (p. 245). On the one hand, "sophistication" is thematically disowned (the Osborne sisters are ironically ridiculed for *being* sophisticated, i.e., materialistic, socially ambitious, insincere); on the other hand, it is rhetorically performed (the irony with which the sisters are ridiculed is itself a sophisticated device).

Thus, if snobbery, for Thackeray, amounts to a kind of pseudosophistication, he seems at first to define it, not against some *authentic* sophistication, but against the unsophistication of such middle-class virtues as honesty, sincerity, simplicity, and, above all, naturalness—values that the middle class nonetheless deplorably fails to uphold. Here is a representative passage from a chapter on "dinner-giving snobs," in which Thackeray rails against the middle-class practice of throwing pretentiously lavish dinner parties:

> Why should JONES and I, who are in the middle rank, alter the modes of our being to assume an *éclat* which does not belong to us—to entertain our friends, who (if we are worth anything, and honest fellows at bottom) are men of the middle rank too, who are not in the least deceived by our temporary splendour; and who play off exactly the same absurd trick upon us when they ask us to dine?

Thackeray quickly reminds us, however, how hard it can be to kick the habit of trying to keep up with the Joneses:

> This rule I have made, and found the benefit of. Whenever I ask a couple of Dukes and a Marquis or so to dine with me, I set them down to a piece of beef, or a leg of mutton and trimmings. The grandees thank you for this simplicity, and appreciate the same. My dear JONES, ask any of those whom you have the honour of knowing, if such be not the case. (p. 103)

Although the shared middle-class identity of Thackeray and his friends would all but confirm them as "honest fellows at bottom," it turns out that some of his friends (or are they just acquaintances?) are in fact aristocrats — whom, to be sure, he entertains with refreshing and exemplary "simplicity." One might take this contradiction as a slyly self-mocking illustration of how, as Thackeray suggests, "it is impossible for any Briton, perhaps, not to be a snob in some degree" (p. 22). Perhaps. But, then, how to account for the unusual vehemence of denunciation, if anything heightened by a continued lurching between universalizing and minoritizing paradigms,[6] in the paragraphs that follow?

> And being perfectly contented, (indeed humbly thankful — for look around, O JONES, and see the myriads who are not so fortunate), to wear honest linen, while magnificos of the world are adorned with cambric and point-lace: surely we ought to hold as miserable, envious fools, those wretched Beaux TIBBS's of society, who sport a lace dickey, and nothing besides. The poor silly jays, who trail a peacock's feather behind them, and think to simulate the gorgeous bird whose nature it is to strut on palace-terraces, and to flaunt his magnificent fan-tail in the sunshine.
>
> The jays with peacocks' feathers are the SNOBS of this world: and never since the days of AESOP were they more numerous in any land, than they are at present in this free country.
>
> How does this most ancient apologue apply to the subject in hand — the dinner-giving Snob? The imitation of the great is universal in this city, from the palaces of Kensingtonia and Belgravia, even to the remotest corner of Brunswick Square. Peacocks' feathers are stuck in the tails of most families. Scarce one of us domestic birds but imitates the lanky, pavonine strut, and shrill, genteel scream. O you misguided dinner-giving SNOBS, think how much pleasure you lose, and how much mischief you do with your absurd gran-

deurs and hypocrisies! You stuff each other with unnatural forced-meats, and entertain each other to the ruin of friendship (let alone health) and the destruction of hospitality and good-fellowship— you, who but for the peacock's tail might chatter away so much at your ease, and be so jovial and happy! (pp. 103–4)

In asking how the Aesopian fable "appl[ies] to the subject in hand— the dinner-giving Snob?" Thackeray betrays an awareness of a potentially embarrassing disjunction—or conjunction—in his discourse, digressing as it has from its focus on dinner-giving snobs to a diatribe against imitation dandies, or against "jays with peacocks' feathers," digressing from the culinary to the sartorial *and back*, as though in a daffy relay between dandies and *dindes*. What is potentially embarrassing is not just the hint of a fundamental confusion (exacerbated by the mention of "those wretched Beaux TIBBS's of society, who sport a lace dickey, and nothing besides") between those who are "honest fellows at bottom" and those caricatured as "poor silly jays" with peacocks' feathers "stuck in the[ir] tails" ("Scarce one of us domestic birds but imitates the lanky, pavonine strut, and shrill, genteel scream"); it must also give Thackeray pause that his excursion into birdland has a weirdly literalizing effect on "the subject in hand," *changing* the subject by treating it too visibly as an object, making it too easy to imagine the dinner-giving snob as himself dinner—if not exactly a bird in the hand, then a morsel at the end of one of those silver forks eponymously memorialized by the school of novelists Thackeray both parodied and participated in. (Indeed, one of the illustrations earlier in the text [p. 5] shows one man—presumably Thackeray himself—chasing another—presumably a representative Snob—and about to pierce him with a gigantic fork.)[7]

The blurring of the line between eaters and eaten (not to mention the line between satire, on the one hand, and pornography and horror fiction, on the other) is reinforced first by the image of dinner-giving snobs "stuff[ing] each other with unnatural forced-meats" and then by the rather startling genocidal fantasy with which the chapter reaches its climax:

And to think that all these people might be so happy, and easy, and friendly, were they brought together in a natural unpretentious way, and but for an unhappy passion for peacocks' feathers in England. Gentle shades of MARAT and ROBESPIERRE! when I see how all the honesty of society is corrupted among us by the miserable fashion-worship, I feel as angry as Mrs. Fox just mentioned, and ready to order a general *battue* of peacocks. (p. 105)

In view of Thackeray's ostensible devotion to the "natural," especially insofar as it grounds the social hierarchy itself, it seems a little odd that his hostility here should be directed, not at the poor silly middle-class jays engaged in "misguided" and "absurd" imitation of their aristocratic betters, but at the latter, at the "gorgeous bird[s] whose nature it is to strut on palace-terraces," and whose "general *battue*" or slaughter he now blithely pronounces himself "ready to order." The bloody-mindedness of this revolutionary fantasy might be attenuated by the evident irony with which Thackeray invokes the "gentle shades" of Marat and Robespierre, were it not that this irony, so typical of what Sedgwick calls "Thackeray's bitchy art," with its "feline gratuitousness of aggression," functions rather clearly as a form of violence in its own right.[8] Much as the author invites us to misread *bitch* as *butch*, to misrecognize his Austenian instinct for the jugular as a manly taste for the jocular, as the very essence of beefy, beef-eating middle-class English masculinity, his projection of a scene of carnage that might be titled *The Silence of the Peacocks* has the effect, especially given the Grand Guignol overtones of the tableau of mutual force-feeding, of casting Thackeray himself as the hungriest cannibal in the whole corrupted *société de consommation*, whose unnatural eating habits he has been condemning with such disgusted gusto.

Representing snobbery as a male-homosocial orgy of oral and anal perversion, Thackeray, then, does not exactly manage to keep his own nose clean: he may be more deeply implicated in middle-class pseudo-sophistication than his disarming subtitle lets on.[9] The apparent distance or distinction that he nevertheless keeps derives, not from his saving remnant of naturalness, but from his success in practicing (if not preaching) cannibalism as sophistication itself, as the true, or naturalized, sophistication that eats both screaming aristocratic peacocks and silly middle-class jays for breakfast. However difficult, the ruse of rendering sophistication and cannibalism virtually synonymous is hardly implausible, as my allusion to Hannibal Lecter suggests. Like that cinematic icon—who, feline not just in the gratuitousness of his aggression but also in the creepiness of his high-cultural hyperliteracy, embodies, through his very oral-sadistic pathology, what counts as "sophistication" in the popular imaginary, Thackeray's writing, for all its purported antisophistication, all its noisy promotion of naturalness and jollity, all its bullying championship of the ideology of the middle, epitomizes a certain connection between the "high" style of sophistication and the "low" practice (or, at least, the bad habit) of eating other people.

His writing allows us, that is, to think about sophistication as not only a particular discipline or disposition of taste but also a particular internalizing relation to the tastes (in both senses of the word) of others, as a question not only of *what* and *how* you eat but also of *whom* you eat.[10] "In matters of taste, more than anywhere else," Pierre Bourdieu has suggested, "all determination is negation; and tastes are perhaps first and foremost distastes, disgust provoked by horror or visceral intolerance ('sick-making') of the tastes of others."[11] Far from being simply the excluded outside of taste, distaste is what inheres in it most intimately; the most advanced or refined taste—the taste to which is accorded the name of *sophistication*—would therefore be, not the "pure" taste that most fastidiously *casts out* the tastes of others, but the omnivorous taste that most aggressively *incorporates* them, taking them in fantasmatically so as to constitute itself as their *Aufhebung*, as the simultaneous experience and transcendence of them implied by the term *consumption*.

There seem to be two kinds of incorporation at work in the chapter we have been discussing, a "good" and a "bad": the kind that Thackeray reprehends as the middle-class "imitation of the great" and that, in its "absurd" attempt to *take in* aristocratic manners and so to reproduce them in and on the bourgeois body, virtually constitutes dinner-giving snobbery—perhaps the paradigm of snobbery *tout court*—as a homophobically projected scene of oral and anal relations between men; and the kind that (looking like the cat that swallowed not the canary but, even more disgustingly, both the jay and the peacock) Thackeray himself performs as his famous irony, as the comic appropriation and reframing of both the snobs and the objects and causes of their desires.

Yet, as the phrase *homophobically projected* signals, these two kinds of incorporation may not be all that different from each other. That is, in projecting or expelling a "bad," snobbish incorporation, Thackeray may be trying to *minimize* its resemblance to the "good" incorporation whereby he imitates the objects of his satirical scorn. Just as Thackeray's ironic *mocking*, as the term suggests, involves both derision and mimicry, or involves derision *in* mimicry, so the "miserable, envious" snob "imitat[ing] the lanky, pavonine strut, and shrill, genteel scream" of the aristocrat may be acting out, not just a starry-eyed infatuation *with* him, but, precisely by way of misery and envy, a mordant aggression *against* him.

If Thackeray's incorporation is no less imitative than the snob's, the snob's incorporation is no less ironic than Thackeray's—where irony, seeming to place mitigating or pacifying quotation marks around an act of violence, functions more effectively, as was suggested above, *as* an act of violence. Nor is irony's violence merely rhetorical: impelled by such powerful energies as misery and envy, driven by a murderous desire to take the place of its object, irony necessarily inflicts a political and an erotic violence as well. While Thackeray's displacement of the aristocrats from their preeminent position in the cultural pecking order may be an act of symbolic violence, the symbolic character of that violence, in other words, does not signify its abstractness: Thackeray's relation to the bodies of the peacocks whose slaughter he fantasizes, and whose screams he parodically rehearses, is no less rapt and ravenous, no less avid in its attentiveness to and reproduction of how aristocrats walk and talk, than the mimetic desire of the snob in his "fashion-worship" and his "passion for peacocks' feathers."

If the distinction between snobbery and "naturalness" breaks down, it is less surprising that the distinction between snobbery and distinction itself proves equally precarious: naturalized or not, sophistication—which means adulteration or denaturing before it means refinement—is by definition pseudo, and therefore the difference between the real thing and its perversion can only amount to more of the same. It is customary to see Thackeray as an emblematic figure in the process whereby the Victorian gentleman displaces the Regency dandy as arbiter of taste.[12] But, once the ambitious, endemically imitative middle class buys into sophistication as a cultural value, as both a means and an index of social success, the arbiter of taste risks becoming as redundant as "false sophistication" itself.[13] Or, as Time magazine lamented in the title of the 8 August 1994 cover story, "Everybody's Hip (and That's Not Cool)." What's not cool, as far as both Time and Thackeray are concerned—although both adduce less selfish, more intellectually prestigious reasons—is that a generalized hipness, a mass sophistication, threatens to put them out of business.

If, as we saw in the previous chapter, Jane Austen confronts us with the unthinkable, horrifying paradox of a universal sophistication, she quickly reassures us by restoring the image of a world in which, as is only logical, some people can be distinguished to the precise extent that others cannot. More cruelly driven by the journalistic dread of appearing insufficiently au courant, Thackeray, for his part, has a much harder time dismissing the unnerving prospect of a culture in which, as Oscar Wilde might have said, "it isn't easy to be sophisticated nowadays. There's such a lot of beastly competition about." Notwithstanding Thackeray's effort to cast the competition as a lot of beasts—as bêtes in both nominal and adjectival senses—notwithstanding all his angry-sorrowful clucking about what "fools" the fashion worshipers are, about their "absurd grandeurs and hypocrisies," the real Thackerayan nightmare, never far from the surface either of *The Book of Snobs* or of *Vanity Fair*, is one in which the universal imitation of the great signifies not that there are too many stupid people but that there are too many smart people.

In other words, one suspects that the fashion of fashion worship makes Thackeray mad—and sad—less because it symptomatizes the folly of refusing to accept one's proper station than because the general diffusion of smartness as *stylishness* implies the general diffusion of smartness as *intelligence*, an "unnaturally" (or maybe just inconveniently) wide distribution of the cultural capital needed in order to recognize, interpret, and exchange the various signs that constitute a thoroughly commodified world. Claiming to be "as angry as Mrs. Fox," Thackeray not only enmeshes himself further in a food chain notable for its reversibility, for the phantasmagoric suddenness with which the hunters can turn into the hunted, but also acknowledges that, in a culture already centered on the semiotics of consumption, even the ordinary consumer is necessarily foxy:[14] *every* shopper is a smart shopper, for every shopper has to be sly, knowing, and wary if she is to move safely within the dense forest of status symbols from which there is never any question of exiting. What is suggested by the image of dinner-giving snobs "stuff[ing] each other with unnatural forced-meats" (as if fattening each other up for the kill) is that, although conspicuous consumption is a compulsory feature of middle-class life, it is not enough: in a marketplace mobbed with cool customers, the successful consumer must be able conspicuously to consume not just commodities but other consumers; or—to put it more tastefully—she must consume the *consumption* of other consumers, distinguishing herself from it by assuming toward it the same relation of ironic comprehension—of simultaneous possession and distance—that Thackeray exhibits through his mocking incorporation, what might be called his in(di)gestion, of both aristocratic and bourgeois tastes.

If it is possible thus to shift from a generically female consumer to a uniquely male metaconsumer (whose slaughter of the too-desirable peacocks would, however vainly, mark an all-consuming end of consumption itself), this possibility has everything to do with the trick whereby Thackeray stages his consumption so that its feminizing—in a context of male rivalry, effectively homosexualizing—voracity gets transmuted into the distinguished distance, or the killing melancholic disavowal, constitutive, as Judith Butler has argued, of male heterosexuality itself.[15] Inflecting this ideal as much in terms of class as in terms of gender and sexuality, moreover, Thackeray is at pains to promote his distinguished melancholia as at the same time distinctively bourgeois, as at once exceptional and normative.

We have glimpsed the outlines of this trick in the dream of meta-consumption at work in *The Book of Snobs*. It is to *Vanity Fair*, however, that we should turn if we wish to consider the fullest elaboration of both trick and dream. Even before the novel begins, in the preface titled "Before the Curtain," the "Manager of the Performance," as Thackeray's narrator styles himself, demonstrates his ideological virtuosity:

> As the Manager of the Performance sits before the curtain on the boards, and looks into the Fair, a feeling of profound melancholy comes over him in his survey of the bustling place. There is a great quantity of eating and drinking, making love and jilting, laughing and the contrary, smoking, cheating, fighting, dancing, and fiddling: there are bullies pushing about, bucks ogling the women, knaves picking pockets, policemen on the look-out, quacks (*other* quacks, plague take them!) bawling in front of their booths, and yokels looking up at the tinselled dancers and poor old rouged tumblers, while the light-fingered folk are operating upon their pockets behind. Yes, this is VANITY FAIR: not a moral place certainly; nor a merry one, though very noisy. Look at the faces of the actors and buffoons when they come off from their business; and Tom Fool washing the paint off his cheeks before he sits down to dinner with his wife and the little Jack Puddings behind the canvas. The curtain will be up presently, and he will be turning over head and heels, and crying, "How are you?" (p. 33)

The "feeling of profound melancholy" that "comes over" the Manager of the Performance prefigures his transformation from avowed "quack" into the novel's ideal reader, or consumer, whose subsequent trajectory is anticipated in the move from the "great quantity of eating and drinking" on display at the fair to Tom Fool sitting down to dinner with his wife and children:

> A man with a reflective turn of mind, walking through an exhibition of this sort, will not be oppressed, I take it, by his own or other people's hilarity. An episode of humor or kindness touches and amuses him here and there; — a pretty child looking at a gingerbread stall; a pretty girl blushing whilst her lover talks to her and chooses her fairing; poor Tom Fool, yonder behind the wagon, mumbling

his bone with the honest family which lives by his tumbling; but the general impression is one more melancholy than mirthful. When you come home you sit down, in a sober, contemplative, not uncharitable frame of mind, and apply yourself to your books or your business. (p. 33)

Since Vanity Fair is both a marketplace and a spectacle, the melancholic, bourgeois-gentlemanly reader interpellated here can be cast as both a consumer and a spectator, with the result that his relation to this Rabelaisian microcosm is defined at once by the most intimate consubstantiality and by the privilege of immunity or extraterritoriality: if to read this fat novel is to eat it, that potentially sick-making ingestion gets recuperated as a salutary separation. The "books" and "business" to which "you" "apply yourself" "when you come home" somehow both are and are not continuous with the book—the one in your hand—that you will have been busy consuming *before* your homecoming. Just as the profundity of the narrator's melancholy derives from the vulgarity and immorality of the scene he "survey[s]," so the reader's redemptive retreat into domestic and interior space depends on the very unwholesomeness of his diet up to that point. Yet the books and business to which he turns, or "sit[s] down, in a sober, contemplative, not uncharitable frame of mind," seem to signal a turn *away from* the book(s) and business that produced that frame of mind (or, precisely, "turn of mind") in the first place. Unlike "poor Tom Fool," whose name (especially in contiguity with that of "the little Jack Puddings") suggests that, even when "he sits down to dinner," he is never far removed from the danger of being eaten himself, the normative middle-class male reader learns from the narrator (who, never very temptingly duck-like in the first place, seems to rise from his quackery even as he "sits before the curtain on the boards") how to manage his performance so that it appears to transcend performance: he learns how to find in Vanity Fair, and in *Vanity Fair*, an escape from the theater of consumption *through* the theater of consumption.

When Tom Fool—"mumbling his bone with the honest family which lives by his tumbling"—sits down to dinner, he does so in the narrowest margin of the flimsiest pseudoprivacy: his domestic existence seems as unhidden, as undifferentiated, and as unpsychologized as that of an animal in a cage. Less demonstrably heterosexualized, the reader-*flâneur*, whose relative leisure may well connote bachelorhood, nonetheless enjoys the heterosexual man's ability both to move freely and panoptically through public space and to withdraw from it into a private realm of which he is equally the master. When the reader sits down to his book, his consumption of it, far from implicating him in a risky public sphere, takes place within—indeed, seems to have earned him the right to enjoy—an inviolable refuge from that sphere.

The difference between a "reflective" or "contemplative" degustation and a merely bestial "mumbling" works to project a hierarchical relation between a framing authorial-readerly sensibility marked as bourgeois and a framed novelistic world marked as popular.[16] What is striking, however, is how little of the novel itself actually concerns itself with life below the ranks of the middle class and the aristocracy. A few sentences later, Thackeray writes: "There are scenes of all sorts: some dreadful combats, some grand and lofty horse-riding, some scenes of high life, and some of very middling indeed" (p. 34). This is a bit disingenuous, for it is not just "some" but virtually all of the scenes in the novel that unfold in high or middle society. The superciliousness of "very middling indeed," with its not-so-subtle hint that middle equals mediocre, links the general déclassement to which the preface subjects the novel's dramatis personae with Thackeray's misrepresentational strategy in The Book of Snobs, where the spread of snobbery was reassuringly characterized as a problem of excessive stupidity rather than of excessive intelligence. Advertising itself as a carnivalesque grande bouffe, Vanity Fair can ignore the extent to which it is about how to survive in a world composed neither of Tom Fools, nor, higher up on the social ladder, of the "miserable, envious fools" lampooned in The Book of Snobs, nor of "other quacks," but of other melancholics—which is to say, of other middle-class sophisticates.

To remark, after all, as numerous critics have done, Thackeray's ambivalence toward Becky Sharp—the mixture of admiration and condescension with which he treats her—is to observe the novelist in the process of distinguishing himself from a character too "gay, brisk, arch, distinguée" (p. 291) for his own good. The sharper Becky seems, the more Thackeray needs to shove her back into the frame of his moralistic puppet show, reducing her to a laughably girlish naïveté, as when Lady Steyne and her daughter leave their cards at Becky's house:

> Lord! lord! how poor Mrs. Washington White's card and Lady Crack-enbury's card, which our little friend had been glad enough to get a few months back, and of which the silly little creature was rather proud once—Lord! lord! I say, how soon at the appearance of these grand court cards, did those poor little neglected deuces sink down to the bottom of the pack. (p. 561)

That the next figure to appear on the scene of this reading will be silly little Thackeray follows with all the assurance of "it takes one to know one." The inevitable deconstructive collapse of the sophisticate into the snob announces itself in the form of what might look like so much rhetorical padding. The narrator's "Lord! lord!" redoubled by his "Lord! lord! I say" functions not just as a formulaic interjection but, it soons turns out, as an invocation, perhaps even a slightly frantic one, of a decidedly secular deity: the lord—namely, Lord Steyne—whose relation to Becky is at least that of benefactor and sponsor in aristocratic society and whose relation to Thackeray, no less scandalously, becomes legible as that of authorial mouthpiece, in the full prurient sense that a knowing reader would tease out.[17] For Lord Steyne ("my Lord Steyne," to be precise) promptly answers Thackeray's call, making his descent in fact in the very next paragraph: "My Lord Steyne coming to call a couple of hours afterwards, and looking about him, and observing everything as was his wont, found his ladies' cards already ranged as the trumps of Becky's hand, and grinned, as this old cynic always did at any naïve display of human weakness" (pp. 561–62). A few paragraphs later, this all-observant old cynic treats Becky to the following authoritative piece of demystification:

> "You've got no money, and you want to compete with those who have. You poor little earthenware pipkin, you want to swim down the stream along with the great copper kettles. All women are alike. Everybody is striving for what is not worth the having! Gad! I dined with the King yesterday, and we had neck of mutton and turnips. A dinner of herbs is better than a stalled ox very often. You will go to Gaunt House. You give an old fellow no rest until you get there. It's not half so nice as here. You'll be bored there. I am. My wife is as gay as Lady Macbeth, and my daughters as cheerful as Regan and Goneril. I daren't sleep in what they call my bedroom. The bed is like the baldaquin of St. Peter's, and the pictures frighten me. I have a little brass bed in a dressing-room: and a little hair mattress like an anchorite. I am an anchorite. Ho! ho! You'll be asked to dinner next week. And *gare aux femmes*, look out and hold your own! How the women will bully you." This was a very long speech for a man of few words like my Lord Steyne; nor was it the first which he uttered for Becky's benefit on that day. (pp. 562–63)

Nor, as the reader of The Book of Snobs will recall, is this speech so different from the one in which Thackeray, equally keen in his detection and derision of "any naïve display of human weakness," lays down the laws of middle-class dinner-giving etiquette, prescribing—in the slogan of the beef industry—real food for real people. The echoing of the middle-class satirist who brags, "Whenever I ask a couple of Dukes and a Marquis or so to dine with me, I set them down to a piece of beef, or a leg of mutton and trimmings," by the aristocratic character who can toss off the line, "I dined with the King yesterday, and we had a neck of mutton and turnips," indicates more than just a Victorian precedent for the counterchic of comfort food. It points to a broader imaginary relation between the aristocratic man of few words and the middle-class man of many words, a fantasy of cross-class identification whereby, in legitimating middle-class simplicity, the aristocrat betrays its *need* for such legitimation, for the royal cachet that is perhaps in fact its raison d'être. For though Thackeray would seem to claim melancholia as a middle-class privilege, his incorporation of Lord Steyne suggests, more globally, that the demystified and demystifying, in short, the depressive, position from which the narrator speaks throughout *Vanity Fair* bears the lordly stain of a prior, itself disavowed identification with a stereotypically "aristocratic" boredom and disillusionment.

To note that the word *blasé* may derive from the Dutch *blasen*, meaning "to blow," is not only to blazon a certain "bad taste" but also to evoke the excitement latent in boredom itself, to recall that, in the words of D. A. Miller, "boredom, as the example of pornography perhaps best illustrates, overtakes not what is intrinsically dull, but what is 'interesting' to excess." [18] If *The Book of Snobs* expends considerable energy ridiculing the conspicuous consumption, the ostentatiously perverse, quasi-cannibalistic desire, of other middle-class men ("You stuff each other with unnatural forced-meats"), *Vanity Fair* would offer itself as massive testimony that the author has reached an even more advanced stage in the process of decathecting the whole orally fixated social order, of extricating himself from the parasitic chain of brownnoses, suck-ups, and ass kissers that just about is the world according to Thackeray. The yawn that would seem to recommend itself as the novel's logo cannot necessarily be distinguished, however, from the gaping orifice that would incorporate, along with the totality of the social, the figure who apotheosizes incorporation itself, the man of preeminently jaded appetite who has already eaten his way through the entire menu of Vanity Fair and can therefore make such magisterially totalizing pronouncements as "All women are alike" and "Everybody is striving for what is not worth the having!"

What is most saliently on display in *Vanity Fair* may well be Thackeray's "escape from desire," in the phrase from this chapter's first epigraph. "Been there, done that" could serve as the motto of an author who makes a show of jovial hospitality all the better to kill whatever appetite we may have for the food that—as in the chapter misleadingly entitled "In which we enjoy three Courses and a Dessert"—he typically promises with one hand only to take away with the other:[19]

> It is all vanity to be sure: but who will not own to liking a little of it? I should like to know what well-constituted mind, merely because it is transitory, dislikes roast beef? That is a vanity; but may every man who reads this have a wholesome portion of it through life, I beg: aye, though my readers were five hundred thousand. Sit down, gentlemen, and fall to, with a good hearty appetite; the fat, the lean, the gravy, the horse-radish as you like it—don't spare it. Another glass of wine, Jones, my boy—a little bit of the Sunday side. Yes, let us eat our fill of the vain thing, and be thankful therefor. And let us make the best of Becky's aristocratic pleasures likewise—for these too, like all other mortal delights, were but transitory. (p. 584)

Maybe we'll just have the salad. Or maybe, instead of assuming the depressive position into which Thackeray would bully us, we should read him as unironically as Becky reads the peerage (p. 561) and think about what it would mean to "make the best of [her] aristocratic pleasures." To begin with, it might mean recognizing Thackeray's apparently ironic, aversive relation to those pleasures as the product of his wholesale internalization of them. If, to be sure, that internalization has to be followed by an equally extensive anaesthetization, we should keep in mind that, much as this anaesthesia looks like an escape from desire, it is also an object of desire, the end of a desiring operation. For, as we have seen, Thackeray's desire not to desire is at the same time a desire to be, as well as a desire for, the kind of man whose apparent libidolessness only signifies the more decisively, and the more seductively, that he has had and done it all. The point is not simply to bring Thackeray out as a snob—nothing, indeed, could be simpler—but, from a perspective other than that of disavowal or of homophobic projection, to consider the possibility that, pace Lord Steyne, what a snob wants is "worth the having."

In a remarkable passage on the European tradition's other great snob novelist, Theodor Adorno writes:

> If the pimp, the antithesis of the snob, acknowledges the intertwining of sex and gain through his profession, an intertwining that

bourgeois society covers up, then conversely the snob demonstrates something equally universal, the deflection of love from the immediacy of the person to social relationships. The pimp socializes sex; the snob sexualizes society. Precisely because society does not actually tolerate love but rather subordinates it to the realm of its ends, it keeps a fanatical eye out to make sure that love has nothing to do with it, that it is nature, pure immediacy. The snob disdains the socially accepted love match that has an ulterior purpose but falls in love with the hierarchical order itself, which drives love out of him and which simply cannot tolerate being loved. The snob lets the cat out of the bag, the cat the Proustian oeuvre then bells. . . . Like every love, snobbery wants to escape from the entanglement of bourgeois relationships into a world that no longer uses the greatest good of the greatest number to gloss over the fact that it satisfies human needs only by accident.[20]

Might not the feline Thackeray be the cat that lets itself out of the bag? If so, however, his aggression would no longer seem so gratuitous: his cattiness might emerge as a reaction formation against the desire that it simultaneously inscribes, as a strategy for displacing the kiss of a love that bourgeois society cannot tolerate into the bite of a sarcasm that, for all its bestial implications, often finds itself not just tolerated but even celebrated, provided that it issues from one of the culture's official (heterosexually identified male) hepcats.[21] To turn Thackeray's bite back into a kiss would be not to defang him, as though a kiss were just a kiss (or as though a bite, for that matter, were just a bite), but to specify both the love and the loved object that his particular kind of heterosexually melancholic sophistication works at once to deaden and to preserve.

In Proust, as Adorno suggests, snobbery and homosexuality virtually imply each other as modes of forbidden desire. A little later in the paragraph quoted above, the theorist who can write, "Totalitarianism and homosexuality belong together,"[22] remarks, more perceptively: "The impossibility of love that Proust depicts in his socialites, and especially in the Baron de Charlus, who is actually the central figure of the novel, and who ultimately retains the friendship only of a pimp, has since then spread like a deadly chill over all of society, where a functionalized totality stifles love wherever it stirs."[23]

At least as a reader of Proust, Adorno proves smarter, and less homophobic, than his theory, and it is on this Adorno, needless to say, that I attempt to build here (as well as in the next two chapters). Vanity Fair serves up no such delectable fat cat as the Baron de Charlus—we will see why Jos Sedley can only be a Charlus manqué—but, in its fantasmatic identification with the worldliness of a Lord Steyne, it entertains an "unnatural" desire whose almost canonical association with the unpardonable sin of snobbery furnishes a convenient alibi for the ongoing cultural assault on a less visibly thematized homosexuality: Thackeray's identification with worldliness is a desire precisely for a world, not so much "the hierarchical order itself" as what Adorno, elsewhere in the paragraph from which I have quoted, calls a "fairytale image" of that order.[24]

If calling this desire the love that must keep biting its own lips further evokes its affinity with the love that dare not speak its name, that formula would also describe the sarcastic or mordant discipline that Thackeray feels compelled to impose on a certain naive fantasy of sophistication at work in the novel itself, a fantasy of escape not from desire but into a metropolitan utopia, somewhere over the rainbow, where desire is not obliged to unmask itself as so much vanity (i.e., as "mere" mask), or, better yet, where vanity might even stand a chance of transvaluation, of refiguring itself as something other than the grimacing harlequin's face of a universal shame.

Here, finally, is where Jos Sedley comes in, for it is he who most spectacularly (and most poignantly) embodies this fantasy, as in the following passage, as bulky as Jos himself:

> He did not live with his family while in London, but had lodgings of his own, like a gay young bachelor. Before he went to India he was too young to partake of the delightful pleasures of a man about town, and plunged into them on his return with considerable assiduity. . . .
>
> . . . But he was as lonely here as in his jungle at Bogley Wollah. He scarcely knew a single soul in the metropolis; and were it not for his doctor, and the society of his blue-pill, and his liver complaint, he must have died of loneliness. He was lazy, peevish, and a bon-vivant; the appearance of a lady frightened him beyond measure; hence it was but seldom that he joined the paternal circle in Russell Square, where there was plenty of gaiety, and where the jokes of his good-natured old father frightened his amour-propre. His bulk caused Joseph much anxious thought and alarm; now and then he would make a desperate attempt to get rid of his superabundant fat; but his indolence and love of good living speedily got the better of these endeavours at reform, and he found himself again at his three meals a day. He never was well dressed; but he took the hugest pains to

adorn his big person, and passed many hours daily in that occupa-
tion. His valet made a fortune out of his wardrobe; his toilet-table
was covered with as many pomatums and essences as ever were
employed by an old beauty; he had tried, in order to give himself
a waist, every girth, stay, and waistband then invented. Like most
fat men, he would have his clothes made too tight, and took care
they should be of the most brilliant colours and youthful cut. When
dressed at length, in the afternoon, he would issue forth to take a
drive with nobody in the Park; and then would come back in order
to dress again and dine with nobody at the Piazza Coffee-House. He
was as vain as a girl; and perhaps his extreme shyness was one of
the results of his extreme vanity. If Miss Rebecca can get the better
of him, and at her first entrance into life, she is a young person of no
ordinary cleverness. (pp. 59–60)

As I began by observing, Miss Rebecca does ultimately get the better
of Jos, although not by marrying him. As I also observed, however, she
apparently gets away with murder because, just a puppet after all, she
merely acts out the violence dictated by the author—an author, one of
whose prior comic personae had been "the Fat Contributor" and who
in fact "weighed very heavy,"[25] busy vomiting up a figure who would
otherwise inscribe, more grossly and more damagingly than Becky does,
a mise en abyme of his own abysmal, all-consuming worldly appetite. For
while Becky's femaleness allows Thackeray to reinforce the hierarchy of
sophisticated author over desophisticated character by mapping it onto
the hierarchy of "man" over "girl," the girlish Jos threatens to expose
sophistication itself as already sissified. Unlike such paragons of urbanity
as the depressive Lord Steyne or the melancholic stage manager and ideal
reader, moreover, the "lonely" Jos is merely pathetic, a sad case because
he fails to be sad in the proper jaded way, to live his worldliness as world-
weariness. On second thought: not "merely pathetic" but also pathogenic,
sick making, disgusting in his lack of disgust for "the delightful pleasures
of a man about town," pleasures that real men, if they partake of them
just as voraciously, know how to make look like unpleasures.[26]

"Historical context" may prevent this portrait of the would-be "gay
young bachelor" from making things perfectly queer, but only a historicism itself invested in keeping them straight will pretend not to see that
the role of the Regency dandy here has begun to expand in the direction
of more modern sexual identities and anxieties. Lest we fail to pick up on
the passage's protohomophobia, somehow missing the point of Jos's fear

of "the jokes of his good-natured old father," or of his fear of women, the evidence on his toilet table goes to show us that, as Proust might have said, Jos practically *is* a "woman." "As vain as a girl," as grotesque as an "old beauty" struggling, of course in vain, to turn back the clock, Jos, like the demented Tennessee Williams heroine whom the knowing reader has no trouble decoding as an aging queen, wears a heterosexual mask as transparent as the cosmetic stratagems he so desperately employs. Let him go through the motions of making love to Miss Rebecca: buffoon-ishly dependent on such artifical stimuli as chili peppers and rack punch, undermined by everything from his "extreme shyness" to his butch little nephew's contempt for him to his (Lecterish?) habit of "br[inging] home men to dine" (p. 697), his charade doesn't fool us for a minute.

But, if the function of vanity is thus to betray itself, if vanity as nar-cissism cannot help turning into vanity as futility, Jos offends in part be-cause he does *not* submit entirely to this program of self-subversion. Bad enough, when the bourgeoisie has so much at stake in reorienting society around the values of naturalness and unpretentiousness, to display inordi-nate interest in display, conflating the sin of caring too much about oneself with that of caring too much about what others think of one; to aban-don, even temporarily, one's "anxious thought and alarm" about one's image is to force that same bourgeoisie, always eager to misrecognize its loathing of fat people as a humane concern for their health, to confront the thoroughly coercive, which is to say the thoroughly social, character of its religion of doing what comes naturally. "Precisely," as Adorno says, "because society does not actually tolerate love but rather subordinates it to the realm of its ends," it is enraged, like Caliban both seeing and not seeing his own face in a glass, not only by the eroticization of itself but also by an equally perverted "love of good living," not only by the snob but also by his *semblable*, the sensualist bent on pursuing happiness outside the "paternal circle" (and the marriage plot that merely reproduces it), and rendered even more disreputably alien if frenched as a bon vivant.

Jos is not a snob, but, as a bon vivant, he shares the snob's insufferable utopianism. For, like the snob, the bon vivant projects a "fairytale image" of society, sexualizing it by inhabiting it as though it were a site of plea-sure not melancholically fated to reveal its own emptiness. If the snob, moreover, uncovers the sociality of the generalized love that bourgeois ideology locates in what it pretends to consider a "good" nature, the bon vivant uncovers that sociality's imaginative impoverishment: threatening to look like the worldly or social love par excellence, the love of good living must get expelled into the chaos of a "bad" nature, of an abjectly asocial outer darkness reserved for those who ought not show their faces, or their bodies, until they have learned that, just as *eating well* does not mean eating good food but eating food that's "good" for you, so *good living* does not mean realizing your desires in and for the world but doing what a naturalized social regime would have you know without being told. Instead of having the decency to stay at home, as his shyness should have taught him to do, Jos Sedley tastelessly, unforgivably obtrudes his "big person" on the world, as though it could make room for one who, not despite but because of his prodigious appetite, has not made adequate room in himself for it—who, not despite but because of his fashion-conscious hyperconsumption, has not fully internalized the principle, no pain (less catchily, no disavowal), no gain.

Not that, for all his hedonism, Jos is incapable of *taking* pains, indeed "the hugest pains to adorn his big person"; but these are obviously the wrong kind of pains, and they even more obviously accentuate the wrong kind of gain. ("Like most fat men, he *would* have his clothes made too tight.") Having failed to mortify his flesh, poor silly Jos undergoes a mortification vengefully imposed from outside. The homicidal imperative registered by the remark "he must have died of loneliness" finds its fulfillment in the death by a thousand cuts—the social death—that the narrator starts administering from the moment that Jos, who persists in showing up where he isn't wanted, starts compromising the distinction, not just between *amour-propre* as healthy self-discipline and *amour-propre* as reprehensibly masturbatory self-indulgence, but between a normative self- or fashion consciousness and excesses of the most repulsive cultural illiteracy.

In his very will to smartness, Jos dooms himself to appear tragically unhip, irremediably witless. But his fate as a fashion victim does not simply constitute another example of Thackeray's knack for putting down the competition. In seeing to it that, far from getting good life, the good liver gets mortified, Thackeray punishes—by refusing to gratify—Jos's desire not just for sophistication but for what sophistication itself desires: namely, a *public*, in the sense both of an audience and, more broadly, of a pleasure-giving social sphere (call it the town) beyond the rigorous confines of the family plot. When Jos "take[s] a drive with nobody in the Park" and goes to "dine with nobody at the Piazza Coffee-House," what kills him is not so much that, desperate to make the scene, he finds himself ignored as that, even worse, he finds that there is no scene to make, no town for the would-be man about town to be about. All dressed up with no place to go, the well-stuffed peacock dreams of a no-place in which, instead of shriveling into an invidious economy of scarcity or war of appetites, social intercourse might actually open up into a fairytale image of *good company*, where that eminently social pleasure would make a space for, and prove as erotic as, the more private-seeming pleasures, say, of good food, good clothes, and good sex.

What could be more naive than this fantasy of sophistication, more discrediting than the credulity of its investment, haplessly unhistoricized, unproblematized, untheorized, in the "goodness" of the various goods it promotes? Unlike the bon vivant, the snob at least has the merit of not wanting to belong to any club that would have him as a member.[27] In other words, although the academic critic might feel compelled to privilege Jos and his abject flamboyance, it is hard to resist (if not to acknowledge) the pull of an identification with his self-hating confrere: with the snob in his distaste for the pleasures, desires, and talents of the people around him and thus for his own. Even if we were programmatically to align our critical troublemaking with the queer spectacle enacted by Thackeray's Fat Boy, we might soon find ourselves engaged in the competitive project of—to borrow a resonant phrase from the novel— "out-Josephing Joseph" (p. 67). Every drag queen, as we know, is a prima donna: to the extent that gay reading is "reading" (in the *Paris Is Burning* sense of the term), its utopianism becomes complicated.

Complicated, but not negated: the similarities between the snob and the bon vivant are more interesting than their differences. Against Thackeray's official view of the world as divided between a joylessly carnivalesque public sphere and a bourgeois privacy consecrated to (and by) the distinguished enjoyment of the joylessness that being in public induces, the dinner-giving snob and the dinner-taking bon vivant propose complementary perversions: by means of what is aptly termed *entertaining*, the snob, as we have seen, perpetrates the obscenity of "a privateness oriented to an audience";[28] and, if the snob illicitly introduces the public into the private, the bon vivant just as illicitly inserts the private into the public.

Either way, society gets sexualized—and the ways in which it is *already* sexualized become annoyingly obvious. What makes the snob and the bon vivant both so unlovable, and what links them with a certain homophobic stereotype of the gay man, is that, by taking the hugest pains to make a good impression, they remind everyone else what a huge pain it is to be social at all. But when Thackeray cries, "O you misguided dinner-giving SNOBS, think how much pleasure you lose . . . !" his crocodile tears don't quite wash away the traces of his own longing for the pleasures that snobs (and other party animals) would gain—the pleasures of a "social life" not unlike the one enviously attributed to the same stereotypical gay man. Leaving those traces, *Vanity Fair* leaves us to contemplate a social life in which *social* would indeed mean "sexual"—not in the merely euphemistic sense with which we are familiar, but in a sense sophisticated enough, and large enough, to be naive.

4

Taste, Waste, Proust

Sa haine des snobs découlait de son snobisme, mais faisait croire
aux naïfs, c'est-à-dire à tout le monde, qu'il en était exempt.
—Proust, *Le Côté de Guermantes*

Dining with Proust

Vanity Fair, as we have seen, contains a naive fantasy of sophistication, but,
if Thackeray succeeds in projecting an aura of sophistication *tout court*,
he does so precisely by containing (or seeming to contain) the oxymoronic scandal of his naive (self-)parody, unloading it onto the sad figure
of Jos Sedley. Yet, while this procedure may help allay the straight man's
anxiety — about, for instance, what it means for him to *be* sophisticated —
it does not necessarily make everybody happy. The dumb gay man, like the
dumb Jew, is an embarrassment, even a source of shame, for members of
an oppressed minority who have traditionally consoled themselves with
the thought that they are at least *smarter than their oppressors*.

   Of all the gay male writers in the Western literary canon, perhaps the
one who least threatens to embarrass us, the one whose primary canonical function may even be to epitomize gayness *as* intelligence, is Marcel
Proust. Other names (Wilde, James) may come to mind, but one could
argue that they signify specialized variants of intelligence (wit in the
case of Wilde, subtlety in the case of James) rather than intelligence in
the more general, more powerful, arguably more basic form of what
Theodor Adorno calls an "organ for untruth and thus for truth."[1] And,
if the almost perfect fit in Proust between smartness-as-intelligence and
smartness-as-stylishness provides a happy instance of what Lee Edelman
has taught us to think of as homographesis, we feel all the more entitled

to read *Proust*, both the name and the work, as the definitive gay inscription of sophistication in the sense that our culture accords to it.[2]

Yet, for all that Proust represents "sophistication," the closest thing to an equivalent term in his text, *la mondanité*, or worldliness (in French, unlike English, *sophistication* retains the negative meaning of "adulteration"), acquires an almost equally negative charge. And, for all that he represents "intelligence," he spends as much time criticizing it as celebrating it. It is hardly the case that we are back to the "nature" that Thackeray pretends to like, but what I will persist in calling Proust's intelligence and sophistication turns out, insofar as it depends on a "naïveté" of its own, to have more in common with the "nature" that Thackeray hates than we might imagine. (Why is it, by the way, that, if you can't really say *sophistication* in French, you can't really say *naïveté* in English? *Problème à résoudre.*) Again, Adorno proves helpful:

> The compulsion to adapt prohibits one from listening to reality with [Proust's] precision, from taking its soundings. One need only make the effort to refrain from dealing directly with subject matter or pursuing one's aims in a conversation and instead follow the overtones, the falseness, the artificiality, the urge to dominate, the flattery, or whatever it may be that accompanies one's own or one's partner's voice. If one were aware of their implications at every moment one would fall into such fundamental despair about the world and what has become of oneself in it that one would lose the desire, and probably the strength as well, to continue to play along.
>
> Proust, however, did not go along with the renunciation of responsiveness, nor with the false maturity of resignation. He kept faith with the childhood potential for unimpaired experience and, with all the reflectiveness and awareness of an adult, perceived the world in as undeformed a manner as the day it was created, in fact developed a technique to resist the automatization and mechanization of his own thought. He strives indefatigably for immediacy, for a second naïveté, and the position of the pampered amateur from which he approached his literary task works to the advantage of these efforts.[3]

Idealizations of "the childhood potential for unimpaired experience" may not be to everyone's taste, but what Adorno—to be sure, not exactly one of the guiding lights of gay studies—calls Proust's "second naïveté" bears significant implications for any account of what is distinctively gay about Proustian sophistication. To the extent, for example, that this naï-

veté resists "the compulsion to adapt," or to the extent that it offers an
alternative to "the false maturity of resignation," it becomes readable as
a gay strategy for surviving—or (since it is itself a recovered naïveté) for
recovering from—the ruthless cultural project of universal heterosexual-
ization, whereby "growing up" in fact means shutting down, tuning out,
closing off various receptivities that make it possible to find the world
interesting.

As Adorno points out, of course, this self-occlusion functions as a
strategy for survival in its own right: if the well adapted were any less
obtuse, they might indeed—to invoke another Victorian novelist, one
with whom Proust had much closer affinities than with Thackeray—die
of that roar which lies not so much on the other side of silence as on
this side of it, in the endless chitchat of everyday life. An even better listener than George Eliot, whom he so much admired, Proust, cultivating
the dangerous ability to hear the grass grow and the squirrel's heart beat,
sets a paradoxically saving example for those of us for whom, at some
point in our lives, "fundamental despair" starts to seems less frighten-
ing a prospect than being bored to death in exchange for the social and
psychological advantages derived from "playing along."

Not only saving, Proust's example of a second or—better yet—a sophisticated naïveté seems infinitely more attractive, needless to say, than the
naive and therefore failed sophistication of a Jos Sedley, especially now
that, exacerbating his affront to gay sensibilities, the stupidity with which
the latter is well wadded begins to look almost normal. Before we put Jos
behind us, however, let us note that the self-indulgent Fat Boy of whom
we are ashamed shares this much with the "pampered amateur" of whom
we are proud: their different naïvetés are both, in effect, perversions. The one
through amour-propre and "love of good living," the other through a "love"
that it is one of the aims of this chapter to delineate, both "childishly"
persist in amatory investments guaranteed to fill their more "mature" age-
mates, if not with fundamental despair, then with a no less "fundamental"
disgust. Fixated not just aurally, as Adorno's metaphors suggest, but, like
Jos, orally as well, and in a way that extends far beyond the initiatory act of
ingestion for which he is famous—the eating, of course, of a tea-soaked
cake that bears a woman's name—Proust, in search of temps perdu—time
wasted in addition to time lost—manifests thereby an equally perverse and
almost insatiable appetite for waste, for what it is only the vulgar beginning of a description to call the very bullshit (the "untruth") with which
Adorno pseudomisanthropically identifies social discourse as such.[4]

If it helps to define the intelligence of Proust's naïveté (as opposed to the stupidity of Jos's) as a "subversive" art of cutting through crap, the vulgarity may be forgiven. But not, I hope, too quickly: far from promoting the impossibly redundant project of eliminating waste, the obsessive insistence of Proust's truth telling underwrites, as it were, an even more obsessive fascination with the very substance apparently in need of being wiped away.[5] To do justice to the full perversity of Proust's "naive" gastronomy, we may in fact require more vulgarity, not less. Let us note, for example, that, as a *second*, "sentimental" naïvete, as indeed the perversely cultivated product of a pampered amateur, it can give off a far more nauseous stench (coprophagia assuming the bad odor of its object) than anything emitted by Jos Sedley, an already sufficiently repulsive *spoiled boy*. In other words—Freud's, more or less—while Jos has simply *remained* a pervert, Proust has deliberately and defiantly *become one again*. If the naïveté of the former can thus be dismissed as a pitiable failure or inability to "develop normally," as the quasi-biological defect of one who "can't help being that way," the naïveté of the latter may suggest the cheeky, not to say smart-ass, attitude of an overgrown rich kid intent on rubbing less privileged noses in the fact that he doesn't *have* to "act his age" and that his only "work" consists in the leisurely, even luxurious *recherche*—more academically speaking, the research—of forbidden pleasures, childish things he delights in *not* putting aside.

I am alluding, of course, to my earlier account, in the chapter on *Pride and Prejudice*, of the "disgust"—that is to say, the envy and resentment—provoked by the oppositional critic, especially when his or her reprehensible "cultural elitism" gets flaunted under the explicit heading of gay and lesbian studies or queer theory. But, if that chapter ended with a complaint that oppositional critics are not oppositional *enough*, are not as obnoxious or as revolting as they are reputed to be, I want here to mark at least the possibility of a certain bathos in the slippery ease with which I have just glossed Proust's *recherche* as academic "research." For though it is all too demonstrably the case that, as far as many champions of traditional academic values (or even of less traditional academic values, such as getting one's money's worth) are concerned, academic research just *is* the narcissistic self-indulgence of a bunch of pampered amateurs, it is also the case that this alleged ludic imposture, this insolent playing-at-work and working-at-play (as opposed to the *appropriate* activity of simply "playing along"), acquires much of its power to enrage from its location within an institutional and professional system whose rules, while relatively relaxed, remain those of capitalist production and of bourgeois reproduction.

The point is not only the obvious one that, unlike Proust's writing, even the most privileged or prestigious academic work operates under a specific set of political and economic—that is, ideological—constraints, such that, if one knows what's good for one, one tries (to borrow a phrase of Barbara Johnson's) not to bite off more of the hand that feeds one than one can chew:[6] even more obviously, those constraints are temporal as well. If time, simply put, is money, money is time; just as simply, it takes time to go in search of time. Undeniably a massive labor in its own right, Proust's indefatigable striving for a second naïveté presupposes the luxury of a permanent sabbatical, a vast temporal expanse, deliciously free of paper grading, committee meetings, letters of recommendation, and so on, in which it is possible to cultivate not only that naïveté but also cultivation—indeed, sophistication—itself.

Indeed, the privilege of perversity means the privilege, not just to regress, but to do so in an ostentatiously distinguished way, a way that displays privilege. This is why, far from mitigating the odium of Proust's perversion retrouvée, the "reflectiveness and awareness of an adult" with which he conducts the operation of retrieval will register, in the nostrils of the resentful, as a second offense. Although sophistication, that is, often gets legitimated as the sign of an adroitly grown-up relation to the world, it can easily get stigmatized, à la française, as the symptom of an unhealthy overgrowth, a noxious overrefinement, a putrefacient hypertrophy of sensibility, a vile corruption of taste as waste—in short, as "decadence." For the phobically normal, "sophisticated naïveté" would constitute not a paradox but rather the obscene tautology of a double perversion, the insult of the unnatural added to the injury of the all-too-natural.

Who, however, even in the most "pampered" of academic circles, can afford to smell this bad? The question is clearly rhetorical, yet it implicitly poses another, more genuine (if not stupidly, Jos Sedleyishly naive) one: Please tell me, how can I be like Proust? "Noblesse oblige: the privileged status of the multi-millionaire, which permitted him his boundless refinement, obligated him," Adorno writes, "to be the way everyone ought one day to be able to be."[7] As I will argue later, it takes more than money to be able to be that way. One of the major obstacles, however, may be identified simply as everyday life itself, which, if it makes sure that none of us runs the risk of fundamental despair, similarly guarantees that none of us, either, risks becoming as disgustingly smart as Proust. Perhaps there is a kind of comfort in this normalizing, desensitizing distraction: it saves us from the considerable embarrassment, not to mention the unpopularity, attendant on the cultivation of a coolness that, even on Proust, looks, as I have been trying to suggest, queerer than it's safe to assume. And yet, the appeal of the fantasy that might be called *devenir Proust* resides, as the earlier passage from Adorno indicates, in its promise of a certain way of *inhabiting* the everyday, not of withdrawing from it. This appeal is equally well conveyed by Jean-François Revel, an equally unlikely theorist of gay sophistication, for whom Proust exemplifies "the capacity to have an everyday life as exempt from depression as from exaltation, or rather, in which exaltation and depression would not be the only means of avoiding boredom."[8]

Boundless refinement *as* everyday life, not in spite of it: "real life," as Proust himself asserts at the end of *Remembrance of Things Past*, "is literature."[9] Mythically associated with an ascetic-aesthetic retreat from the world ("Literature is the only real life"), Proust exercises a seductive power over *some* readers, at any rate, by virtue of the indomitable relish with which he dines out on—that is, serves up—the world, a world that, to be sure, his sophistication exposes as another Vanity Fair but that, more generously if not more openly than Thackeray's sophistication, which, like a certain stereotype of sophistication in general, seems not to avoid but, on the contrary, to *embrace* boredom, it thereby allows us to *savor*, as though for the first time.

Much closer to home than Adorno or Revel, Eve Kosofsky Sedgwick has acknowledged her own investment in something like a fantasy of becoming Proust, whose "interminable meditation on the vanity of human wishes was a galvanizing failure for at least one reader: it was, if anything, the very sense of the transparency and predictability of worldly ambitions that gave me the nerve and skill to have worldly ambitions of my own."[10] In this canny articulation of the magical effect of Proustian "disenchantment," the word *worldly*, like the *ambitions* that it modifies, tends in two different, even opposite, directions. On the one hand, insofar as it carries a certain taint of the "inglorious," of the guilty or dirty secret, it means something like "vulgar."[11] On the other hand, insofar as the secret is an almost inherently sexy will to power, *worldly* more glamorously means something like "sophisticated." Not infrequently used in this book as a convenient synonym for *sophistication*, *worldliness*, dirty in its glamour, glamorous in its dirt, indeed oscillates tellingly between "sophistication" and "vulgarity." But then so, I've been hinting, does *sophistication*. Glittering before us as the very antithesis of childhood humiliation and abjection, it turns out, for many who therefore rush to embrace it, to bring a humiliation and an abjection of its own. Sophistication, in the charming words of Jacques Lacan, is a veritable "gift of shit."[12]

But what if, instead of representing the cruel joke of a vicious circularity that only a multimillionaire can afford to bear, the dizzying, even nauseating, rapidity with which "high" turns into "low" served as an ingenious tactic for short-circuiting the middle? What, in other words, if the bizarre solidarity of the sophisticated and the vulgar, of the refined and the excremental, served to keep the everyday from settling into the mediocrity of the mundane? "Mundane," of course, is itself a third meaning of worldly. What I want to propose, however, is that it is this middle register of the worldly that the circularity of sophistication seeks to get around. In Proust, as we shall see, the mondain gets unmasked as the pseudosophisticated, but, if the "true" or metasophistication of the narrative itself consists in thus reducing high society to a dungheap — in uncovering its vanity, its stupidity, its mean-spiritedness — the hidden agenda of this engrossing demystification is to ensure that the one thing that the mondain does not end up as is the merely mundane.

It remains to be seen to what extent Proust, in developing his immense and intricate technology for the avoidance of boredom, steers clear of the extremes of depression and exaltation. Without conflating the ups and downs of sophistication with that psychic bipolarity, I would, however, underscore the tendency of sophistication's circularity to concern both its subject and its object. In the previous paragraph, for example, the vicissitudes of sophistication themselves slide almost imperceptibly between the sophisticate and the everyday life that his or her sophistication is busy wresting from banality. One advantage of worldliness over sophistication, we might note, is that it signals just such a mutually constitutive relation between its subject and the world. Worldliness, that is, reminds us that, if sophistication requires a kind of object-relations theory of its own, what that theory will have to account for is how sophistication maps out a certain fantasmatic way of circulating in and around the world — not, as may seem to be the case, of simply rising above it but, so to speak, of getting high off it by falling in love with it. With his vast wealth, which is also to say, with his vast cultural capital, Proust was of course well equipped to sustain a powerful — a powerfully ambivalent — worldly cathexis. But, if few people can marshal the same formidable resources against boredom, and if even fewer could keep up his level of interest in, say, the Faubourg Saint-Germain, I suspect that many gay people, at least, do have at their disposal, or in their usable pasts, typically in late childhood or early adolescence, the highly Proustian experience of falling, if not, at first, for some other person, then for some other place, some other world, magically different from the world of family and school, from a heterosexual everyday every day more banal and more oppressive.

Whatever that other world is called—Broadway, Hollywood, the opera, Green-wich Village, haute couture, high society, are some of its classic designations—it beckons not as a simple escape from the everyday but as a vision of the everyday transfigured: What would it be like to live there? But, whatever it is called, one probably got the message, without having to be told, that one had made a bad object choice—which is not to say, however, that the message had the power to scare one off. In many cases, perhaps, the effect was the reverse. A gift of shit almost from the start, but a gift none-theless, the fantasy world may have had, for many of us, the necessary, life-sustaining value of what Proust calls "interior food" (Time Regained, 910): at once filthy and sublime, this gift, in the very endless inversion of its fortunes, may have left its most precious trace in its recipients as an endlessly renewable (if latent) gift for inversion.[13]

Am I simply indulging in a potentially reactionary nostalgie de la boue? If my evocation of the secret treasure evokes as well the splendors and miseries of the closet, that, as Sedgwick has shown, is not only Proust's definitive gay theme but also his definitive gay subject position. Recall-ing Proust's closetedness may have the effect of dampening our Proust envy; it may also help us recognize at least one way—hardly an insig-nificant one, either—in which contemporary readers may in fact be less oppressed than their pampered hero. One need not glamorize the closet, however, to see in Proust's sophisticated naïveté a model for recapturing not so much a lost world as a lost libidinal intelligence, a capacity for having more than a blandly routinized relation to any world. The fantasy of being Proust keeps faith with a fantasmatic faculty itself: with, to amend Adorno, a childhood potential, not for unimpaired experience, but, less idealizingly, for making bad—that is to say, as Proust himself would say, good—object choices.

Strange Gourmet

The Guermantes Way, the third volume of Remembrance of Things Past, is pre-eminently the book of mondanité and therefore, as Gilles Deleuze suggests, preeminently the book of time wasted.[14] According to the recuperative logic of the Recherche, however, nothing ever really goes to waste: what looks like its slackest, least "composed," volume may in fact constitute the transitional center of the work as a whole; as for the activity described in this volume, what looks like so much aimless, profligate hanging out around so many vacuous aristocrats turns out, in the best tradition of the bildungsroman, to have been the decisive passage from adolescence to adulthood.[15]

Until now, I have been discussing the taste for waste as a regression to infantile perversity. Where adolescence has been mentioned as a site of buried excremental treasure, it has figured (as in "in late childhood or early adolescence") merely as childhood's annex. But perhaps, instead of assimilating adolescent to infantile perversity, we should consider its specificity, the uniqueness of the contribution it makes to the museum of bad taste. There is no need to assume that adolescence "deconstructs" the opposition between childhood and adulthood; one could argue, on the contrary, that it simply reinforces that opposition. But, if the structural intermediacy of adolescence accounts for its reputation as that awkward age, what is the content of this awkwardness? In our eagerness to reclaim the child, inner or otherwise, do we seek to evade (or, with greater cunning, indirectly to reach) her even more embarrassing, and even more exciting, older sibling?

As Maurice Bardèche has observed, The Guermantes Way is in some sense a "reprise" of Proust's earlier novel Jean Santeuil, with the difference that the former does not so much eliminate as dissimulate the "ridiculous" excesses of the latter.[16] In his biography of Proust, George Painter, sometimes as helpful in his schoolmasterly moralism as in his scholarly positivism, indicts those excesses—defects characterizing its immature author as well as its young hero—in terms stereotypically reserved for adolescence itself:

> Jean Santeuil is disfigured not only by technical lapses but by a moral fault which is inseparable from its main theme. It is a novel of revenges, of resentments felt and gratified, of self-adoration and self-pity. The hero is an ill-used young man, thwarted by unfeeling and philistine parents, insulted by wicked hostesses, self-satisfied snobs and pseudo-artists; a benevolent Providence ensures that he invariably scores off them all; and he is insufferably charming, handsome, intelligent and magnanimous.[17]

Jean Santeuil can be hard to take. But if a principle of dissimulation renders The Guermantes Way more palatable, the difference between the principle and what it dissimulates is not so obvious. Where Jean Santeuil wears his self-pity, his self-adoration, his vengefulness, on his sleeve, the narrator-protagonist of The Guermantes Way, only fleetingly visible, in the high beam of a certain unloving gaze, as "a hysterical little flatterer" (p. 367), owes his worldly success to his mastery of the art of playing it cool.[18] What disguise, however, more classically betrays the adolescent ardor of those who put it on than does this affectation of affectlessness? The very dead-pan ease with which the narrator moves through the Guermantes salon signifies that, in Bardèche's words, "Nous sommes en pleine fantaisie."[19] Nor can Proust (as opposed to "Marcel") be disimplicated from this fantasy. *Jean Santeuil*, it seems, leaves a bitter taste in the reader's mouth to the precise extent that it fulfills a wish for sweet revenge; skillfully softened, or rather, as Bardèche puts it, "habilement adoucie," by the "mature" style of *The Guermantes Way*, the *vanité* generating the wish finds a more lasting sweetness in that style itself.[20]

That *vanity* can describe both a self-adoring subject and an empty or worthless object should alert us to the possibility of an occult link between adolescent infatuation and the supposedly salutary demystification—the unflinching recognition of the world's nothingness, more particularly, of "the world," that is, high society, as what Marcel will call "le royaume du néant" (*La Prisonnière*, p. 780)—that passes for maturity. The empty object may be considered more accurately as an *emptied* one, the product of a "naively," perversely eroticized act of evacuation.[21] Demystification, in other words, does not necessarily mean decathexis. Although one of the great laws of the Proustian universe is the incompatibility of knowledge and desire, one of its less well-known, yet not, for all that, less powerful, counterlaws, best illustrated, as we shall see, by the case of snobbery, is the *interdependence* of knowledge and desire. Much as it may resemble a triumphant, conclusive renunciation of the object and of one's narcissistic investment in it, demystification may covertly be extending, *through* a fantasy of revenge, one's original guilty, ambivalent attachment. Far from signaling the death of desire, demystification may represent desire's most ingenious ruse.

It is not surprising, of course, when, in the horrible scene in the Champs-Elysées, where she suffers the stroke that portends her imminent death, the narrator's grandmother, emerging from the public toilet presided over by the snobbish "Marquise," ironically says to him (in her struggle to conceal her affliction), "I heard the whole of the 'Marquise's' conversation with the keeper. . . . Could anything have been more typical of the Guermantes, or the Verdurins and their little clan?" (p. 423). In her peculiarly delicate, metaphoric-metonymic way, Marcel's grandmother is simply telling him that she thinks that the Guermantes—in whose company, the badness of which she would appear to be admonishing him against, he will nonetheless, once she has died, spend most of the next four hundred pages—are full of shit.

Nor, perhaps, is surprise the exact effect when the egregious Legrandin shows up in the salon of Mme de Villeparisis shortly after treating Marcel to the following lecture:

> You know how I admire the quality of your soul; that is why I tell you how deeply I regret that you should go forth and betray it among the Gentiles. By being capable of remaining for a moment in the nauseating atmosphere of the salons—for me, unbreathable—you pronounce on your own future the condemnation, the damnation of the Prophet. . . . Good-bye; do not take amiss the old-time frankness of the peasant of the Vivonne, who has also remained a peasant of the Danube. To prove my sincere regard for you, I shall send you my latest novel. But you will not care for it; it is not deliquescent enough, not fin de siècle enough for you; it is too frank, too honest. What you want is Bergotte, you have confessed it, gamy stuff for the jaded palates of refined voluptuaries [du faisandé pour les palais blasés des jouisseurs raffinés]. I suppose I am looked upon, in your set, as an old stick-in-the-mud; I make the mistake of putting my heart into what I write: that is no longer done; besides, the life of the people is not distinguished enough to interest your little snobbicules. Go, get you gone, try to recall at times the words of Christ: "This do, and thou shalt live." Farewell, friend. (pp. 202–3; p. 452)

If, as I have said, surprise is not necessarily the effect of Legrandin's turning up—if not quite to eat shit, then conspicuously to kiss ass—in the very "nauseating atmosphere" he has just been execrating, this is because, almost from the beginning of Swann's Way, the masquerade of snobbery has been made so exquisitely, so vulnerably transparent to us. But, if (not without a little help from Thackeray as well) we have become proficient in seeing through a Legrandin, the very facility with which we do so may keep us from seeing what we do not already know: that Legrandin's "hypocrisy"—his pretending to hate what he really loves—is perhaps a little more complicated than we think; that his "hatred" is as sincere as his "love," insofar as loving "society" (le monde) while knowing it to be a bad object—the object you're not supposed to love—means cultivating an acute sensitivity to its badness, positively refining a taste for its gamy deliquescence (high society being "high" in more ways than one), a deliquescence like that, for example, of meat going bad.[22]

However knowing the reader may have become, Marcel's response to finding Legrandin in the Villeparisis salon is marked by an apparent ingenuousness:

Presently Mme de Villeparisis sat down again at her desk and went on with her painting. The rest of the party gathered round her, and I took the opportunity to go up to Legrandin and, seeing no harm myself in his presence in Mme de Villeparisis's drawing-room and never dreaming how much my words would at once hurt him and make him believe that I had deliberately intended to hurt him, say: "Well, Monsieur, I am almost excused for being in a salon when I find you here too." M. Legrandin concluded from these words (at least this was the opinion which he expressed of me a few days later) that I was a thoroughly spiteful young wretch [un petit être foncièrement méchant] and delighted only in doing mischief. (p. 272; p. 501)

Whether naïf or just faux-naïf, whether himself "sincere" or "hypocritical," Marcel here seems to read Legrandin less astutely than Legrandin reads Marcel. Not only, that is, does Legrandin recognize in Marcel a brother "snobbicule," a fellow "refined voluptuary" or connoisseur of the sumptuously fecal: he perceptively calls him on the malevolence (the méchanceté) that Marcel is so ingenuously — or perhaps so disingenuously — eager to disavow. More in touch, as some might say, with Marcel's anger than Marcel is, as well as more in touch with Marcel's hunger than Marcel is, more in touch, finally, with the close affinity between anger and hunger, Legrandin both identifies and embodies the obscenity of worldliness, an obscenity affecting not only the world as object but also the worldly subject:

"You might at least have the civility to begin by saying how d'ye do to me," he replied, without offering me his hand and in a coarse and angry voice which I had never suspected him of possessing, a voice which, having no rational connexion with what he ordinarily said, had another more immediate and striking connexion with something he was feeling. For the fact of the matter is that, since we are determined always to keep our feelings to ourselves, we have never given any thought to the manner in which we should express them. And suddenly there is within us a strange and obscene animal [une bête immonde et inconnue] making itself heard, whose tones may inspire as much alarm in the person who receives the involuntary, elliptical and almost irresistible communication of one's defect or vice as would the sudden avowal indirectly and outlandishly proffered by a criminal who can no longer refrain from confessing to a murder of which one had never imagined him to be guilty. I knew, of course, that idealism, even subjective idealism, did not prevent great philosophers from still having hearty appetites [de rester gourmands] or

from presenting themselves with untiring perseverance for election
to the Academy. But really Legrandin had no need to remind people
so often that he belonged to another planet when all his uncontrollable impulses of anger or affability [*tous ses mouvements convulsifs de colère
ou d'amabilité*] were governed by the desire to occupy a good position
on this one. (pp. 272–73; p. 501)

"Uncontrollable impulses of anger or affability": it is as though there
were such a thing as a beast of civility, a savage, monstrous, id-like creature driving us, against our better judgment, even without our knowledge, to perform the most depraved acts of *politesse*. But, while this passage
thus invokes the language of involuntarity and irrationality (to the same
degree, moreover, that Marcel continues playing the *ingénue*), it implies
at the same time a more "refined" insight into the deconstructive inti-
macy undermining the apparent binarism of the sophisticated and the
vulgar, of the *homme du monde* and the *bête immonde*: it interprets as cozily
systemic, rather than madly anarchic, the relation between, on the one
hand, worldly success and intellectual distinction and, on the other, the
bestiality, the stupidity, the garbage—as the French would say, the im-
mondices—on which that success and that distinction parasitically feed.
This feeding defines not only the dependence of the subject on the external object of his desire—the dependence, say, of a "jaded" worldling like
Marcel or Legrandin on the delectably putrid high society (the *monde immonde*) for which he hungers or of the great philosopher-gourmands on
the food they crave. Since the "obscene beast" is of course a beast within,
the feeding in question defines an *internal* dependence as well, suggesting
that, just as the great philosphers are great *because of* their gourmandise,
so, for example, might the narrator's "mature," "demystified" knowledge
of the world *consist in* a certain untranscended juvenile delinquency, one
that stops just this side of murder: more precisely, in the self-pitying, self-
adoring, and above all *vindictive* oral-sadistic fantasies about the world that,
long past the point at which he should have renounced it, keep him—
"un petit être foncièrement méchant" indeed, as Legrandin so incisively
recognizes—voraciously sinking his teeth into it.[23]

Marcel may not be playing it entirely straight, in other words, when,
after quoting what he takes to be a particularly silly remark by the Duchesse de Guermantes, he levels with us about the persistence of his crush
on her, a fixation whose intrinsic aggressivity he would thus take back:

"What a goose!" I thought to myself, irritated by her icy greeting.
I found a sort of bitter satisfaction [*une sorte d'âpre satisfaction*] in this

proof of her total incomprehension of Maeterlinck. "To think that's the woman I walk miles every morning to see. Really, I'm too kind. Well, it's my turn now to ignore her." Those were the words I said to myself, but they were the opposite of what I thought; they were purely conversational words such as we say to ourselves at those moments when, too excited to remain quietly alone with ourselves, we feel the need, for want of another listener, to talk to ourselves, without meaning what we say [sans sincérité] as we talk to a stranger. (pp. 308–9; pp. 526–27)

Less sincere, perhaps, in his avowal of insincerity than in the insincerity itself, Marcel may well mean the mean thing he says about the duchess — as much, in fact, as Legrandin means the méchanceté with which he bad-mouths the world of the salons. But, as we have seen, just as Legrandin's biting meaning, far from precluding the most lip-smackingly epicurean consumption of the food he reviles, evinces in fact the very finesse of his connoisseurship, so Marcel's bemused contempt for the duchess signifies not, as he would have us believe, a feigned disillusionment but rather the cruelty of Proustian love at its most perspicacious.

Although, in the original text, the duchess gets called not a "goose" but, less appetizingly, a buse — a buzzard — this renomination of an object figured elsewhere, as we shall see, as irresistibly succulent betokens less some failed or halfhearted attempt at aversion therapy than a perverse technique, like that still preferred by the subtlest (not to say the most jaded) of palates, for making the flavor of fowl more intoxicatingly "high" (that is to say, low) by rendering it even gamier.[24] The point, therefore, is not that Marcel does not "really love" the duchess: it is that he misrepresents what "really loving" her means. What is ultimately less — or more — than straight about the passage is not the first-order sophistication that consists in decathecting the duchess, or even the second-order sophistication that consists in decathecting the decathexis, but the third-order sophistication that consists in suggesting both that what gets the nasty little philosopher-critic "too excited" is his "bitter satisfaction" and that this "bitter satisfaction" is, in turn, the sweet taste of love.

As the sophisticated reader will have anticipated, however, we may not yet have reached the summit of the hierarchy of sophistications: what is necessary, that is, is an acknowledgment that the straightness of Marcel's "love" for the duchess must itself be taken with a grain of salt. Without, on the one hand, simply conflating "Marcel" (the narrator) with "Proust" (the author) or, on the other hand, not so simply rehearsing recent commentary on the dizzying play of hetero- and homosexualities in the *Recherche*,[25] we can settle for stating what should be fairly obvious: that, throughout Proust's novel, one discerns a whole range of closet effects. For instance, it is by now taken for granted that Albertine's gender may be as "ambiguous" as her sexuality. Because *The Guermantes Way* does not immediately announce itself as one of the gayer neighborhoods in *La Recherche*, however, it has been easy (even for those not easily taken in) to read the story of Marcel's "love" for the Duchesse de Guermantes relatively straight. Casting her as a mother surrogate, in the style of an older psychoanalytic criticism, does not exactly impede the always available heterosexualizing presumption, either, although it also tends to perform the cultural work of promoting Marcel's (and Proust's) image as a mama's boy.[26] That Marcel identifies with the duchess as much as—or to the extent that—he desires her can indeed be demonstrated, but then a question arises as to what that desirous identification itself means. What is at stake in Marcel's wanting (to be) her?

An answer awaits us, not surprisingly, in Legrandin's denunciation of Marcel for betraying his soul "among the Gentiles." For if, in keeping with the logic of "it takes one to know one," Legrandin thus unwittingly outs himself as a snob by outing Marcel, he also adumbrates a more oblique if no less pertinent connection between what will turn out explicitly to be his own homosexuality, on the one hand, and Marcel's more consistently camouflaged homosexual *positioning*, that is to say, his closetedness, on the other. If, in other words, Legrandin likens Marcel and himself to Jews, he also, in the same tirade, plays on the topos of snobbery and homosexuality as twin vices, hinting, for example, at more than one taste favored by the "jaded palates of refined voluptuaries" (*taste*, of course, being one of the privileged categories in terms of which homosexuality is constructed in Proust).

Working, then, by way of the novel's snob closet, Legrandin provocatively conjoins its Jewish closet with its gay closet; but, while the *Recherche* sets up a general analogy between the "race of Israel" and the *race maudite* of homosexuals, Legrandin's conjunction does not have the effect of making the Jewish and gay closets neatly interchangeable. Or rather, it does not have the effect of making *Gentile* and *heterosexual* neatly interchangeable. While the Guermantes and their circle, as the novel's insistent reference to the Dreyfus case makes clear, enjoy the arrogant self-satisfaction, not to mention the humiliating exclusionary power, of the tyrannical majority—the Guermantes are all anti-Dreyfusards, the dying Swann tells Marcel at the end of *The Guermantes Way*, because "at heart all these people are anti-semites" (p. 796)—their status as quasi-mythological divinities, as alluring racial others, as interdicted objects of desire *outside the family circle*—in short, as seductively *treyf*—aligns them symbolically with the very homosexuality that you don't have to be a nice Jewish boy to have been terrorized into knowing you'd better stay away from (and thus, needless to say, into finding all the more engrossing). As an overdetermined elite, minoritized and majoritized at once, the aristocratic Guermantes represent, in other words, the double fascination of a *homosexualized hetero sexuality*: the fascination of the forbidden object and the fascination of the oppressive agent. Indeed, a case could be made that, at the level of fantasy, the aristocratic salon figures generally in Proust as an "alternative family," one that, while exerting the captivating interpellative force of familialism itself, manages nevertheless, and at the same time, to be not only matriarchal but, so to speak, queeny as well, so that if, in Marcel's family romance, the duchess stands for the mother, the mother she stands for is simultaneously straight and gay. Without for a moment doubting the intensity of his "love" for her, we could compare it (by no means dismissively) to a certain gay male "love" for, say, Marlene Dietrich.

To draw that analogy, however, is to signal that Marcel is setting himself up for disappointment. The brightest star in the firmament of a homosexualized heterosexuality, the duchess, like so many of the compromise formations that define life in the closet, indeed proves an unreliable locus of erotic investment: even before Marcel crosses the threshhold of the hôtel de Guermantes, what he discovers is that the duchess, waspish queen bee of what, inspired by Paul Morrison's theorization of "ersatz heterosexuality," we might call a merely ersatz *homosexuality*, is in effect neither "gay" enough nor "straight" enough.[27] Her celebrated "wit" turning out to consist mostly of fat jokes, put-downs, and flat-footed, sophomoric puns, her powers of homophobic (or of anti-Semitic) abjection concomitantly lose much of their sex appeal as well. As a result, by the time Marcel, who, with typical fetishistic, masochistic obsessiveness, has not just worshipped the duchess but endured snubs from her that have only made him long the more to enter her charmed circle, finally gets embraced by the Guermantes with "parental affection" (p. 702), that affection no longer means much: if the duke and duchess have become as predictably familiar as real parents, they lack the authority of real parents to command, for instance, the fear that would induce a little "affection" in return.

Yet though we seem to be encountering here another great Proustian law, the law whereby you eventually get what you want, but only when you no longer want it, I would invoke again the less obvious counterlaw, whereby desire's apparent absence or negation serves as a cover for its

cunning, unregenerate persistence. (Finding out that high society is no
more glamorous than, say, high school is not necessarily a *complete* turn-
off—not, at least, to those for whom "high school" itself preserves a
certain erotic charge.) When Marcel says, "What a goose!" *and means* it, he
does run a certain risk of simply losing interest. But instead of handling
the situation either "heterosexually"—that is, by accepting boredom as
the structuring principle of his life and personality—or in the bolder,
braver, gay-affirmative way that some might wish for him—that is, by
coming out, by ceasing to look for love in the wrong places—he adopts
(although, to appropriate Jacques Derrida, "we are in a region . . . where
the category of choice seems particularly trivial")[28] the more ambivalent
and more ambiguous strategy, perhaps also the classically obsessional or
deconstructive one, of reliving, via the sadism of analysis, the first naïveté
(or first love) of ideological subjection as the second naïveté (or second
love) of ideological critique. If this technique for falling in love again suggests a certain libidinal conservatism—more censoriously, a certain adolescent refusal or inability (as self-hating as it is self-loving) to forgive and
let go—it also constitutes a distinctly Proustian solution to the perennial
grown-up problem of how love is to survive its (heterosexualizing) disap-
pointments, not to say a distinctly Proustian model for the revenge plots,
the angry, petulant, resentful plots *against* heterosexuality, animating some
of the most vital work in current gay, lesbian, and queer cultural critique.

Re-senting, re-tasting, re-finding the badness of the bad object, saving
that badness from falling into the mere banality of the merely deideal-
ized, may have the additional virtue, in other words, of helping one save
oneself. Perhaps it is this surreptitious economy that explains the oddly
exhilarating effect of Proustian "disappointment": "That Mme de Guermantes should be like other women had been for me at first a disappointment [*une déception*]; it was now, by a natural reaction, and with the
help of so many good wines, almost a miracle [*un émerveillement*]" (p. 719;
p. 815). The effect of the wines is indeed at best auxiliary: what is most
intoxicating is the discovery of one's own power not so much to turn
excrement into gold as to turn the merely *emmerdant* back into life-giving
merde: to transform a deglamorized *mondanité*—a fairy-tale world in danger
of becoming boring, annoying, oppressive—back into the precious nourishment that can be supplied only by *what's bad for you*, bad not just because,
having failed to deliver on what it seemed to promise, it has become con-
temptible but because, having been recontaminated by the bad subject's
bad taste, having regained an aura of the tantalizingly proscribed, it has
become newly *desirable* in its contemptibility.

All through *The Guermantes Way*, Proust practices (and gives us the recipe

for) such a gay alchemy, a gay science that we might also call a hom(e)op-
athy. "L'étrange gourmet" (p. 701): this is the term (rendered in English
as "the man of strange appetite" [p. 559]) that Marcel uses when, dining
with Robert de Saint-Loup in the restaurant in the fog, he overhears someone saying, "I should prefer glycerine. Yes, hot, excellent." It turns out to
be "simply a doctor whom I happened to know and of whom another
customer, taking advantage of the fog to button-hole him here in the
café, was asking his professional advice. Like stockbrokers, doctors employ the first person singular" (p. 559). Employing the same grammatical
form, Proust everywhere in his novel both prescribes for and administers
to himself—and thereby makes available for our own adaptation—a diet
designed in fact to prevent his palate from growing jaded, from becoming
"sophisticated" in the best (that is to say, in the worst) adult way.

Bad Tongue

No one in Proust is more jaded than Oriane, as her friends and relatives
call the Duchesse de Guermantes. What impels her to keep producing the
renowned delicacy that is the Guermantes wit—"The wit of the Guermantes . . . was a family reputation like that of the minced pork of Tours
or the biscuits of Rheims" (p. 627); "One of Oriane's puns? It's sure to be
delicious" (p. 636)—is nothing other than the boredom and restlessness
imposed on her, as a kind of life sentence, by the necessity (particularly
if she is to maintain her status as the most brilliant of brilliant femmes du
monde) to keep producing it:

> As though corrupted by the nullity of life in society, the intelligence
> and sensibility of Mme de Guermantes were too vacillating for dis-
> gust not to follow pretty swiftly in the wake of infatuation (leaving
> her still ready to be attracted afresh by the kind of cleverness which
> she had alternately sought and abandoned) and for the charm which
> she had found in some warm-hearted man not to change, if he came
> too often to see her, sought too freely from her a guidance which
> she was incapable of giving him, into an irritation which she be-
> lieved to be produced by her admirer but which was in fact due to
> the utter impossibility of finding pleasure when one spends all one's
> time seeking it. (p. 646)

The tribute that boredom pays to interest, Oriane's wit reminds Marcel,
in a passage whose méchanceté may or may not strike academic readers
as delightfully irreverent, of the purely mechanical, paradox-mongering
arbitrariness that allegedly constitutes the practice of criticism as a whole:

Mme de Guermantes was herself a great deal less advanced than she supposed. But she had only to be a little ahead of Mme de Parme to astound that lady, and, as the critics of each generation confine themselves to maintaining the direct opposite of the truths acknowledged by their predecessors, she had only to say that Flaubert, that arch-enemy of the bourgeoisie, had been bourgeois through and through, or that there was a great deal of Italian music in Wagner, to open before the Princess, at the cost of a nervous exhaustion that was constantly renewed, as before the eyes of a swimmer in a stormy sea, horizons that seemed to her unimaginable and remained for ever dim. (p. 643)

Like many of Proust's most "wicked" passages, this one affords a pleasure akin to that which one can sometimes get from reading, say, Bourdieu on philosophy: the pleasure of a certain extradisciplinary impertinence, whereby the massiveness and density of cultural production suddenly take on the wanton simplicity and clarity of a kind of child's play. This pleasure may, however, be diminished somewhat by the ease with which criticism gets accused of "sterility":

The Duchess, living this worldly life the idleness and sterility of which are to a true social activity what, in art, criticism is to creation, extended to the persons who surrounded her the instability of viewpoint, the unhealthy thirst [la soif malsaine], of the caviller who, to slake a mind that has grown too dry, goes in search of no matter what paradox is still fairly fresh, and will not hesitate to uphold the thirst-quenching opinion that the really great Iphigenia is Piccinni's and not Gluck's, and at a pinch that the true Phèdre is that of Pradon. (p. 644; p. 761)

We would not be the first to notice that even Proust's sophistication fails to preclude the occasional dip into doxa: in this case, into a familiar form of logocentrism, bordering on (and borrowing a certain pungency from) equally familiar forms of homophobia and misogyny.[29] At the same time, however, although Proust's account of Oriane's wit not surprisingly lacks an explicit feminist or gay-studies terminology, it manages to situate the delicious products of her distinctive oral aggression within the economy of what would nowadays be called compulsory heterosexuality. The narrative spends considerable time, for example, on the reasons for the "choice" by the ostensibly democratic, intellectual Oriane, "then of comparatively slender means" (p. 612), of "the wealthiest and the most nobly born" (p. 616) bachelor in the Faubourg Saint-Germain as her husband. It makes clear, moreover, that what counts as Oriane's intelligence by no means *ceases* to count once she thus appears to have devalued it. Sarcastically styling the duchess and the duke as "the sparkling lady and her impresario" (p. 637), Proust figures the "brilliant" heterosexual marriage as an interminable series of rigorously scripted public performances, in which the witty wife, having commodified her intelligence to become a star, had better keep on sparkling if she wishes to remain one.

In such an economy, the impresario's "pride" in his possession—a pride only superficially inconsistent, of course, with contempt for and abuse of it—can become so overmastering that, not content merely to run the show from behind the scenes, he cannot help getting into the act himself, assuming the classic role of the straight man. Indeed, the duke

> enjoyed bringing out his wife's wit. Now, whenever Mme de Guermantes had just thought up, with reference to the merits and defects, suddenly transposed, of one of their friends, a new and succulent paradox [un nouveau et friand paradoxe], she longed to try it out on people capable of appreciating it, to bring out the full savour of its psychological originality and the brilliance of its epigrammatic malice. Of course these new opinions contained as a rule no more truth than the old, often less; but this very element of arbitrariness and unexpectedness conferred on them an intellectual quality which made them exciting to communicate. However, the patient on whom the Duchess was exercising her psychological skill was generally an intimate friend as to whom the people to whom she longed to hand on her discovery were entirely unaware that he was not still at the apex of her favour; thus Mme de Guermantes' reputation for being an incomparable friend, sentimental, tender, and devoted, made it difficult for her to launch the attack herself; she could at the most intervene later on, as though under constraint, by taking up a cue in order to appease, to contradict in appearance but actually to support a partner who had taken it on himself to provoke her; this was precisely the role in which M. de Guermantes excelled. (p. 647; p. 763)

The married heterosexual couple as comedy team: many of Proust's own most succulent, psychologically original, and epigrammatically malicious morsels of prose owe their peculiar flavor to the unseemly insistence (like that of a grown man still intent on punishing his parents for crimes they committed twenty, even thirty years ago) with which, to use Painter's finger-wagging term, he "scores off" these icons of holy matrimony. But, if he does more than merely replicate the bitchiness that he has been exposing in Oriane, this is not just because he is in fact as "advanced" as she supposes herself to be. The reason why Oriane "isn't as smart as she thinks she is," one might argue, is precisely that she is forced to spend all her time trying to stay *ahead* of the game; Proust's (or Marcel's—at this point the difference seems negligible) advantage over her, one might argue further, is precisely that, determined to go slowly, to lose himself in naïveté, he has taken care to *arrive late*.

In *Proust and Signs*, Deleuze contrasts Proustian with Socratic intelligence: "In Socrates, intelligence still comes before the encounters; it provokes them, it instigates and organizes them. Proust's humor is of another nature: Jewish humor as opposed to Greek irony. One must be endowed for the signs, ready to encounter them, one must open oneself to their violence. The intelligence always comes after, it is good when it comes after, it is good only when it comes after."[30] If the enabling belatedness of Proust's intelligence recalls the unique temporality of Jewish humor, we might also, given the particular overdetermination of Jewishness in Proust, articulate that intelligence in relation not just to the *arrivisme* (i.e., the delayed arrival) of the snob—a character like Bloch would certainly help in the articulation—but to the perspective of a (non-Socratic) gay criticism "immaturely" persisting in its "spiteful" analytic fantasy of settling scores with the heterosexual regime to which the "well adjusted," in other words, heterosexuals, have learned not to give a second thought. Combined in the figure of Bloch, the Jew and the arriviste represent two of Proust's favorite kinds of humiliatable subjectivity: the third kind, never clearly separable from the others, even when he is neither a Jew nor an arriviste, is the gay man, of whom the Baron de Charlus serves as the novel's most salient instance. But if the most memorable scene of humiliation *and* of vindication in the entire *Recherche* revolves around Charlus, humiliated by the Verdurins and vindicated by the Queen of Naples, that scene, which occurs in *The Captive*, is in fact being played out throughout Proust's novel, thanks to the Jewish-snobbish-gay "humor" of a narrator, a veritable David against Goliaths, everywhere fantasmatically avenging his own humiliations.

To observe the obsessive vengefulness of *The Guermantes Way*, then, is to show what makes it one of the funniest volumes of the *Recherche*. As Deleuze suggests, its comedy is a comedy that comes only from coming after. Arriving in the Guermantes salon long after he conceived the desire to do so, after putting up with the duchess's humiliations, her evasions, her icy greetings, Marcel, as we have seen, finds his enchanted *mondanité* tottering on the edge of mundanity. His more-than-consolation, however, his heroically maladapted defense against the death-in-life threatened by this loss of his illusions, lies in the very resentment that has been accumulating as a result of the delay and its attendant indignities—a resentment no doubt redoubled by the failure of the fairy tale to live up to his expectations. Arriving late, that is (and already launching his retaliation by making the Guermantes keep dinner waiting for him while he looks at their Elstirs), Marcel is in a position to get even or, better, to get back, at once getting back at his worldly oppressors and getting back his interest in the world: *se venger, c'est se retrouver*.

As the obsessive, insistent character of re-sentment suggests, he accomplishes this rescue-revenge not only by coming after but by coming after and staying after, sticking around, *wasting time*, luxuriating in the waste that the haste of the "advanced" cannot help making: by sitting back and watching—watching critically, watching as a performance—the heterosexuality that his imperious hosts, their wits dulled by the very imperative to appear brilliant, are compelled merely to repeat.[31] Gay humor versus straight "wit": if he who laughs last laughs best, this is because, having been made to wait, he has learned how to take the time to get the joke that, in their hurry to arrive at the punchline, the distinguished jokers themselves cannot even know that they are making; where once the Guermantes wit might have caused him to crack up, might even, with all the proverbial force that makes the glamorous supercouple of "wit" and "sophistication" seem all but inseparable, have struck him dumb, now, a comedian in his own right, he not only absorbs its violence but, in thus taking it in, gives it back as well.

The aggressivity of comedy, or of comedians, is of course one of the commonplaces of our Freudianized culture; less familiar is a recognition of the extent to which this aggressivity takes as its object some prior aggressivity, someone else's attempt at murder by jest. If comic violence bespeaks the hipster's furious determination always to be in advance, never to be caught unawares, Proustian one-upmanship packs its greatest punch as a resentfully belated counterpunch, as a blow directed against those prepossessing arbiters of taste whose bullying "sophistication," especially when backed up by the apparently intractable weight of (Gentile) social and historical precedence or of a (heterosexual) prerogative to decide who gets put down and who does the putting, had until that point seemed, disspiritingly, to have not only the first but also the last word.

Proust's humor (too "warm," too benign sounding a term by far) makes it possible for us to see that the trouble with Oriane is not that she is too much like a critic: it is that she is not enough like one. There must, Proust maliciously speculates, be a Guermantes family genie who reminds this woman . . . , who cared only for reading and was no respecter of persons, to go out to dinner with her sister-in-law when eight o'clock struck, and to put on a low-necked dress for the occasion.

The same family genie [*le même génie de la famille*] represented to Mme de Guermantes the social duties of duchesses, at least of the foremost among them who like herself were also multimillionaires — the sacrifice to boring tea-parties, grand dinners, routs of every kind, of hours in which she might have read interesting books — as unpleasant necessities like rain, which Mme de Guermantes accepted while bringing her irreverent humour to bear on them [*en exerçant sur elles sa verve frondeuse*], though without going so far as to examine the reasons for her acceptance [*sans aller jusqu'à rechercher les raisons de son acceptation*]. (pp. 602–3; p. 732)

While the bite of the passage seems to depend on the ironic implication that no such mysterious genie is necessary to compel the duchess to do exactly what she wants, ardently pursuing the thing she professes to find boring while just as ardently neglecting the thing she professes to find interesting, we know that Oriane's boredom — the source of her "unhealthy thirst" for paradox — is to some extent authentic. Which is to say that she is under a compulsion, precisely that of the "family genie." A family genie, a genie presiding over the command performances of heterosexuality, this mean spirit mercilessly dictates that her genius, her wit, always frantically eager to shine, terrified of coming after, must never pause to reflect on the conditions (or the consequences) of its own production. If, as he tells us, Marcel never manages to follow the Guermantes way to its end, that way (like "bored" and "boring" theory itself, according to Paul de Man) is the path of its own self-resistance:[32] constitutively unable to go so far (back) as to figure out (*aller jusqu'à rechercher les raisons*) why she does what she does, or why she says she does what she does, the "irreverent" Oriane is never irreverent enough.

Certainly not irreverent enough to conduct the *recherche* that is the *Recherche*. We cannot all be Proust, of course, as we lamented at the beginning of this chapter. But what cheered us up even then was the glimpse of a possibility, if not of being Proust, then of living Proustianly, which is now beginning to look like the best revenge. Proust's great theme, as Deleuze suggests, is not time, or memory, but intelligence; and, although, as the case of Mme de Villeparisis, too free with her "sharp tongue" (or "mauvaise langue" [p. 245; p. 482]), too smart for her own good, so poignantly demonstrates, there does seem to be an inevitable connection between a certain intelligence and "l'insuccès mondain" (p. 483), the *Recherche*, whose almost miraculous life-saving efficacy may consist in its invention of that counterintuitive thing, a sophisticated optimism, stronger even than its more famous and more recognizably sophisticated pessimism, is finally about the inevitable connection between a certain intelligence and the *success* in the world, if not the worldly success, that we might simply call *happiness*. "Where life immures," the narrator writes near the end of the novel, "the intelligence cuts a way out [*Là où la vie emmure, l'intelligence perce une issue*]. . . . The intelligence knows nothing of those closed situations of life from which there is no escape" (*Time Regained*, 943; 484).

Proust's closet, then, whatever else we may say about it, however exempt we may feel from it, is not one of those situations. To be sure, he has not exactly escaped from it. But what is his intelligence if not the incessant activity of cutting holes in its walls? Boring in a rather different sense, the bored Oriane, imagining herself to "avenge[. . .]" (p. 632) her own childhood insults by compulsively applying her sharp tongue to the "witty" work of backbiting, never bites back, for all her *verve frondeuse*, at the keeper of her opulent prison:

> The Duchess's vagaries of judgment spared no one, except her husband. He alone had never loved her; in him she had always felt an iron character, indifferent to her whims, contemptuous of her beauty, violent, one of those unbreakable wills under whose rule alone highly-strung people can find tranquillity. (p. 646)

Some tranquillity. Demonically driven to stay on what passes for the cutting edge of the Faubourg Saint-Germain, the duchess, forbidden to bite back, must not *look* back either, lest she spy not just the short leash regulating her every "sortie" (p. 739) but the whip of the all-too-familiar family demon (if not the family genie) doing the driving.

A (gay revenge) fantasy of straight marriage as S&M, this scenario is no dirtier, really, than the one in which the duke and duchess figured as a kind of high-class vaudeville team. At once theatricalizing and humiliating—humiliating *because* theatricalizing, since to frame anything as a scene is to posit it as having a *behind*, an ob-scene—both these travesties, by making a spectacle of a sexuality that, when it does not simply pride itself on doing what comes naturally, fancies itself a class act, have the effect of *showing* the dirt, revealing the backstage or backside that no one, least of all the performers, is supposed to see.[33] Getting back means getting *at* the back, using one's bad tongue to get back, to get back at, the bad object tastefully hidden from view. In theatricalizing heterosexuality, Proust does not, however, simply homosexualize it again, restoring it to the borrowed splendor of a first naïveté. Not just a repetition, love at second bite, the more sophisticated, more cutting love that, having itself been cut, comes late, comes after, proceeds, like what Edelman has termed "(be)hindsight," from its own temporal posteriority toward the spatial posteriority that even straight men cannot always control.[34]

If the ass figures in the Recherche—and not just in the Recherche—as a privileged site of meaning-laden involuntarity, it is the gay ass in particular, of course, that seems most temptingly to arouse a hermeneutics of suspicion, which, pruriently stripping the gay man of the dubious distinction of whatever sophistication he might have seemed to enjoy, reassigns it to homophobic interpretation itself.[35] With his "derrière presque symbolique" (Sodome et Gomorrhe, 254), Charlus easily makes an irresistible target for such a hermeneutics; but again, Legrandin, although a relatively minor character, proves to be meatier than we might expect. On being introduced to the wife of a local aristocrat, Legrandin, as Gregory Woods has observed,[36] inadvertently reveals more than just his snobbery:

> This rapid straightening-up caused a sort of tense muscular wave to ripple over Legrandin's rump, which I had not supposed to be so fleshy; I cannot say why, but this undulation of pure matter, this wholly carnal fluency devoid of spiritual significance, this wave lashed into a tempest by an obsequious alacrity of the basest sort, awoke my mind suddenly to the possibility of a Legrandin altogether different from the one we knew. (Swann's Way, 135–36)

What if, every time the network news did a story on heterosexuals, we were treated to the aggressively desophisticating image of the "rumps" of a man and woman walking hand in hand? Training his razor-sharp gaze on the normative body's "bad" side, a place where straight women have reason to feel as vulnerable as straight men, Proust gets back at heterosexual culture by producing the verbal equivalent of that "carnivalesque" image, even though—or precisely because—he obligingly focuses on the obligatory gay derrière as well.

Sharply, smartly retardataire, Proust's sarcasm shows up as a refined taste for the waste precipitated (as though through the anus that, as D. A. Miller has pointed out, fantasmatically "reminds" of a cut) by the failure of the Guermantes's "success," a taste for the shit that their "wit," their esprit, reduced to a "wholly carnal fluency devoid of spiritual significance," leaves behind.[37] No mere nostalgia of mud, this second love re-searches for a bad object "different from the one we knew," for the way in which the object, going from bad to "worse," unwittingly—and unwittily—cuts into itself:

the way in which, necessarily cutting itself off from any knowledge of what is behind it, undercutting itself, boring (into) itself, it allows itself to be reglamorized, recathected, made interesting *again*. After his initial disenchantment, the narrator reports,

> Mme de Guermantes's mind [*l'esprit de Mme de Guermantes*] attracted me just because of what it excluded [*par ce qu'il excluait*] (which was precisely the substance [*la matière*] of my own thoughts) and everything which, by virtue of that exclusion, it had been able to preserve, that seductive vigour of supple bodies which no exhausting reflection, no moral anxiety or nervous disorder had deformed. . . . Mme de Guermantes offered me, domesticated and subdued by civility, by respect for intellectual values, all the energy and charm of a cruel little girl of one of the noble families round Combray who from her childhood had been brought up in the saddle, had tortured cats, gouged out the eyes of rabbits, and, instead of having remained a pillar of virtue, might equally well have been, a good few years ago now, so much did she have the same dashing style, the most brilliant mistress of the Prince de Sagan. But she was incapable of understanding what I had looked for in her—the charm of her historic name—and the tiny quantity of it that I had found in her, a rustic survival from Guermantes. Our relations were based on a misunderstanding which could not fail to become manifest as soon as my homage, instead of being addressed to the relatively superior woman she believed herself to be, was diverted to some other woman of equal mediocrity and exuding the same unconscious charm [*exhalant le même charme involontaire*]. (pp. 689–90; pp. 792–93)

How to distinguish between what the duchess charmingly, involuntarily "exhales" and what her mind—better, her wit, since *esprit* means both—"excludes"? Different names for the "substance" of Marcel's thought, the exhaled and the excluded mark the same difference between the "sterile" formalism of the duchess's pseudocritical performance and the fragrantly, flagrantly fertile material surplus that produces it and that it produces. The wealth that is not only its "cause" but also its "effect," this background suggests yet another variation on the term *an embarrassment of riches*. For what is "embarrassing" about the Guermantes is not just the proverbially filthy economic foundation on which their "brilliance" sits but the unconscious, uncontrollable semiotic proliferation, the caca-phony of a generalized body language, that, vulgarly exceeding that "brilliance," seems, as it were, to have been excreted by it. "But she was incapable of understanding what I had looked for in her"; "instead of being addressed to the relatively superior woman she believed herself to be": the only spirit even approximated by the brutally competitive duchess's *esprit* is the *team* spirit, the idiotic, almost flatulently unself-conscious exuberance, of the vigorous, supple-bodied Gentile jock goddess parodied most recently, with a queer-Jewish *méchanceté* worthy of Proust himself, by Sandra Bernhard in *Without You I'm Nothing*. "Deformed" by "no exhausting reflection," the charming Guermantes body involuntarily emits, for that very reason, plenty of fecund exhaust, a veritable feast for those who know how to make the most of it. Like the employers whose cook, as Françoise delights in telling Marcel's family, publicly referred to them as "dung" (fumier [p. 491; p. 654]) and thereby "wrung from them any number of privileges and concessions" (p. 491), the mediocre Guermantes, whose exhalations seem as much anal as oral, are most nourishing for Marcel when, going behind their backs and making asses of them, he finds ways to make their waste *matter*.

As befits the "cruel little girl" that she is, many of Oriane's *mots* are themselves about shit, which she archly euphemizes as "le mot de Cambronne" (p. 684), after the general who shouted "Merde!" when ordered to surrender at Waterloo: Zola, she quips, is "the Homer of the sewers. He hasn't enough capital letters to write the *mot de Cambronne*" (p. 684). Fond of playing scatologically on the surname of the odious Mme de Cambremer (which the lift boy at Balbec, by the way, mispronounces as "Camembert"), she typically jokes as well about food *as* shit:

> "All the same, one must admit that the fare you get there is of the very best," said the Duke, who fancied that in using this expression he was showing himself to be very old school. "I don't know any house where one eats better."
>
> "Or less," put in the Duchess.
>
> "It's quite wholesome and quite adequate for what you would call a vulgar yokel like myself," went on the Duke. "One doesn't outrun one's appetite."
>
> "Oh, if it's to be taken as a cure, that's another matter. It's certainly more healthy than sumptuous. Not that it's as good as all that," added Mme de Guermantes, who was not at all pleased that the title of 'best table in Paris' should be awarded to any but her own. "With my cousin it's just the same as with those costive authors [*les auteurs constipés*] who turn out a one-act play or a sonnet every fifteen years.

The sort of thing people call little masterpieces, trifles that are perfect gems, in fact what I loathe most in the world." (p. 667)

"I think it must be charming, a country where you can be quite
sure that your dairyman will supply you with really rotten eggs,
eggs of the year of the comet. I can just see myself dipping my bread
and butter in them. I may say that it sometimes happens at aunt
Madeleine's" (Mme de Villeparisis's) "that things are served in a state
of putrefaction, eggs included." (p. 691)

And so on. In thus thematizing waste, Oriane would stage her own
sophisticated relation to it, the relation not of the disgusted prude but
of the advanced intellectual and the audacious wit. Against this would-
be self-distinguishing, ironizing maneuver, as against similar would-
be tongue-in-cheek (metalinguistic) moves by the duke ("who fancied
that in using this expression he was showing himself to be very old
school"), Proust's tongue-teeth-mouth-pen — his composite organ for
kissing-biting-eating-writing[38] — goes to work in a cruel countermove
that we could describe as one of outwitting the Guermantes, were it not
the case that wit as a mode of rhetorical mastery, as a controlled and con-
trolling enactment of cultural authority, as a triumph of conscious design
over unconscious accident, in short, as not just sophistication's proverbial
consort but its ostensible apotheosis, is precisely what must be humiliated. It is through his superior naïveté that Proust may be said, rather,
to outsmart the Guermantes. If every one of Oriane's *mots* would, as we
have noted, impose itself as the *last* word, as the zinger that cuts off the
possibility of any riposte, Proust's comic revenge stems from the greater
audacity of one who, like an ill-mannered child, dares to talk back, de-
riding *le dernier* by reading it as "the worst."[39] He shows, in other words,
that the more the Guermantes wit tries sophisticatedly and brilliantly to
cover, the more it vulgarly and stupidly gives away; that, each time its
virtuosos make someone else the butt of their jokes, they blithely inflict a
more lasting violence on themselves, uncovering their own asses a little
bit more. Although neither the duchess nor the duke has his brother Charlus's "gros pétard" (*Sodome et Gomorrhe*, 12), the family wit (an oxymoron?),
far from proving itself the "superior form of intelligence" (p. 631) that
Oriane believes it to be, transcends its mediocrity only by unintentional
inversion, in the asinine sense of sinking below it.

Especially since, in accordance with the economy of vicariousness, the
mouth from which it issues, as we have suggested, sometimes resembles

the anus toward which other mouths seem irresistibly drawn. "For a Guermantes (however stupid), to be intelligent meant to have a sharp tongue, to be capable of saying scathing things, to give short shrift [*avoir la dent dure, être capable de dire des méchancetés, d'emporter le morceau*]" (pp. 604–5; p. 734). Yet this "intelligence" of even the stupid—that is to say, this stupidity—centers on the violence of a mouth that things not only go into but come out of as well, things like Oriane's *mots*, which in turn go into the mouths of her hungry public: " 'What do you think of Oriane's latest? I must say I do like "Teaser Augustus," ' and the quip would be served up again cold next day at lunch before a few intimate friends invited for the purpose, and would reappear under various sauces throughout the week" (p. 638).

Mots d'Oriane, mots de Cambronne. Words as turds. Oriane as oral anus. As we have seen, Thackeray's attitude toward such double vicariousness—where a fantasmatics of substitution and displacement organizes relations not just between bodies but between body *parts*—is one of ostentatious distance, even of "boredom." As we have also seen, that boredom itself works to conceal a certain excitement. One of the (numerous) ways in which Proust seems gayer than Thackeray is that, while appearing even more blasé, he indulges that much more lustily in a wasteful gastronomy itself bordering—as sensed by those who complain that Proust, no costive author, "needs an editor"—on logorrhea. Although Oriane functions for Proust much as Becky and Jos function for Thackeray—that is, as a foil, as the hapless, unknowing embodiment of a sophistication that *fails*—and although her functioning in this way is all the more gratifying in that she seems so much more brilliantly formidable than her Thackerayan counterparts, Proust scores off or outsophisticates her, not, like Thackeray, by contrasting her undisciplined overflow with his supreme authorial control, but by wallowing in, and thus by augmenting extravagantly, the overflow that only the most stringent (self-)discipline can create.

In one sense, Oriane's creative (if not her critical) practice seems to resemble Proust's. The members of the (even) dumber branch of her family, the Courvoisiers, are easily flustered by the annoyances and petty mortifications of everyday life:

> But Mme de Guermantes on the contrary drew from such incidents opportunities for stories [*récits*] which made the Guermantes laugh until the tears streamed down their cheeks, so that one was obliged to envy the lady for having run short of chairs, for having herself made or allowed her servant to make a gaffe, for having had at a

party someone whom nobody knew, as one is obliged to be thankful that great writers have been kept at a distance by men and betrayed by women when their humiliations and their sufferings have been if not the direct stimulus of their genius at any rate the subject matter [la matière] of their works. (pp. 640–41; p. 759)

Parodying Proust's art, Oriane's would represent an aesthetic recuperation of the quotidian. But, if the law that allows her récits to issue only in the narratively foreshortened, syntactically atomized form of mots does not quite cause the constipation that Oriane ridicules in her cousin's anorexic style of entertaining, it keeps her on a diet as unforgiving as her own sharp tongue. (Like many a funny lady, Oriane is her own worst enemy.) Parsimoniously pared down to antinarratives, to rigorously edited sound bites (brevity being the soul of wit), her witticisms, as witticisms, simply lack the diegetic, and thus the analytic, amplitude necessary for anything more than what might as well be a toothless charade, a dumb show, of avenging or redeeming the "humiliations" and "sufferings" of everyday life. Wit—not just Oriane's defective version of it, but wit tout court—is, well, tout court, which we might simply (mis)translate as "too short": the shortness of its cuts cuts against any critical edge that it might presume to enjoy. Proust may pretend to admire the terse symbolic eloquence of a Françoise, likening it to the "power of concentration" imposed on "writers . . . bound hand and foot by the tyranny of a monarch or of a school of poetry" (p. 491), but, as the sheer size of the Recherche attests, his aesthetic practice, as well as his aesthetic theory, has little affinity with the oppressive minimalism to which wit automatically binds itself. Constricted, for her part, by the tight little genre in which she works (that genre itself governed by the rigid conventions of marital display, of the couple who "entertain"), prevented by the short attention span of her audience from serving up anything more than the most easily digestible one-liners, captive, like "smart" women from Elizabeth Bennet on, of a tyrannical aesthetic of svelteness, Oriane, even (or especially) at her most mordant, is always in effect having to bite her tongue.

It would be nice if the feminist implications of Proust's gay ressentiment could be cordonned off from his tendency to punish heterosexuality mainly in the person of the heterosexual woman, whose privilege, if it keeps her from becoming a mere scapegoat, is itself inseparable from a certain self-mortification as well as from an abuse already, and all readily, visited on her by her impresario. One of the projects for Proustians of the current fin de siècle may be to find ways of doing Proust differently, not just outside the closet, but outside its dangerously substitutive logic of vindication. The least promising exit, however, is through a pious denial of aggression, whether Proust's or that which many gay men share with many women; better, I think, to recognize these aggressions, to figure out what they have done and what they can still do, before apologetically or apotropaically wishing all this badness away.

Carving out for himself, at any rate, a discursive space—a narrative space—as commodious as Oriane's is exiguous, Proust affords himself the opportunity vengefully to humiliate her more than she knows. For as the mock-honorific analogy in the passage above implies, the great writer is none other than the author of the *Recherche*, and any artistically enabling humiliations worth speaking of have had the Orianes of the world not, primarily, as their object—much as we feel the pain of one who has "allowed her servant to make a gaffe"—but as their source. If his humiliations at the hands of the "Gentiles" have served to stimulate his genius, the "subject matter" of his work consists in the counterhumiliations that, as we have seen, he performs by zeroing in on *waste* matter, by elaborating prodigally—indeed, with a vengeance—on what, at wit's end, the most "exclusive" exclude, on what, understandably eager to disavow it or, better, to refuse it, they would doubtless consider sub-ject, beneath themselves. In the case of the duchess, for example, this inferior substance, this refuse, is precisely the everyday life that sticks to her the more she tries wittily to spirit it away: "she furnished my mind with literature when she talked to me of the Faubourg Saint-Germain, and never seemed to me so stupidly Faubourg Saint-Germain as when she talked literature" (p. 679). However much the narrator likes to dignify the literature with which she furnishes his mind by representing it as the "poetic pleasure" (p. 734) of mythico-historical reverie, what is most enrichingly literary about the duchess is in fact the very Faubourg Saint-Germain stupidity that results from her Faubourg Saint-Germain attempts to sound smart: the trash, to put it crudely, behind her flash.

In other words, the vital stuff of *The Guermantes Way* is less the evocative *noms de personnes* on which it poetically ruminates than, to recall Adorno, the more "fundamental" material provided by all the little things people say without knowing that they are saying them, all the little ways in which their performance grotesquely subverts the benign social fiction of constative neutrality: "The overtones, the falseness, the artificiality, the urge to dominate, the flattery," in short, the innumerable *bêtises* that go to make up what an acutely inattentive listener—a novelist of *bad* manners—will learn to identify as the subtext of everyday conversation. If "talking literature" designates an attempted assertion of the aesthetic *over* the quotidian, Proust's most trenchant—that is, his most powerfully critical—masterstroke is his relocation of the aesthetic, his rediscovery of literature, *under* the surface that vainly keeps trying to hide it.

Here, *literature* means neither poeticizing abstraction nor the domineering *coups de théâtre* of a wit whose will to hermetic miniaturism only betrays the totalitarian character of its political aspirations. Rather, *literature* is the messy remainder of wit's would-be dazzling productions, what one finds when, in Henry James's suggestive phrase, one "goes behind"— behind the scenes that wit, precisely by self-consciously making them, involuntarily, embarrassingly *makes*, as certain children say of their excretory performances.[40] Going behind, going backstage, Proust gets back at the witty, not only by turning their theatricality against them, but, in the process, by subjecting them to a specifically *narrative* humiliation as well: he diachronically dilates on—that is, luxuriously analyzes—what wit itself, in its very bid for antinarrative self-enclosure, inadvertently starts to open up. Wit is sometimes valorized for its disruption of the narrative line; here it is narrative that turns out to disrupt wit. Telling the stories that should not be told, Proust revels, longer and more indefatigably than many readers can stomach, in the redundantly vast wasteland of stupidity, whose name in his novel is the Faubourg Saint-Germain, but which extends, for other readers, to include any world that, not despite but almost because of the fact that it turned out to be one more Vanity Fair—because, more specifically, to grow older is to learn that there is *no other world*—they can never stop loving.

To narrate at all, of course, can constitute a decidely unsmart career move. The hint of "naïveté" (or of "naivety") within "narrativity," the trace of *Narrheit* within "narrate": these are merely shorthand for a larger (almost postmodern) intuition that, in an age in which, as Oriane thinks, "to be easily bored [is] a mark of intellectual superiority" (*Time Regained*, 1041), the best way to get ahead is by refusing to get bogged down in story. To bring up the rear, as we know, is to risk looking like an ass oneself. To put it somewhat differently, the almost hysterically garrulous narrativity of Proustian analysis, for all its focus on the rear, is not particularly interested in achieving the ends of our culture's normalizing teleologies. Not only belated but regressive as well, Proust's tale of the tail, his narrativizing behindsight, insists preposterously on going back *and staying back*, dwelling on, and in, everything that a normal mind will have learned to disregard as beneath serious consideration. If even Proust at times promotes a sanitized and sanitizing association of literature with "poetry" over a franker recognition of his far greater investment in the psycho-bathology of everyday life, this public relations campaign only testifies to his keen perception of how infectious stupidity can be, how easily it seems to be spread, in a world where people will talk, from object to subject and back. No doubt Proust's tendency to clean up his act also fulfills a need to play down the obscene glee accompanying, for example, the parricidal phrase, all the more killing for its hit-and-run casualness, in which *Faubourg Saint-Germain*, venerated for so long as the local habitation of everything smart, suddenly finds itself modified by *stupidly*. But the reassuring oedipality of this speech act should not blind us to the fact that the parricide remains a parasite, dependent on his hosts for the surplus meanings that he vindictively turns against them and to his own profit.[41] Avenging humiliations, one courts the further humiliation of being seen as stuck in an adolescent *imaginaire*, unbecoming in more ways than one, in which all one can do is act out against increasingly shadowy authority figures.

This, of course, is not all that Proust does. Staying behind while others have gone ahead, or, like the duke and duchess, manically work to *stay* ahead, as though they were some anxious yuppie couple rather than the aristocratic luminaries that they manifestly are, Proust has the luxury of getting to the bottom of what most grown-ups cannot even afford to notice: "stupid" things like how people walk, how they shake hands, how they tell jokes, how they laugh, the clichés they use, the expressions that reveal their pretentiousness or their class backgrounds or their sexual tastes and histories, how they treat their servants, what they say behind their friends' backs, how they try to conceal (and thus betray) their snobbery, how they administer (and receive) snubs, how they give and get invited to dinners, how they dress or wear their hair, where they put their hats, how they advance their careers, how they cultivate their images, how they lie, how they bully (or placate) one another, how they make and try to recover from faux pas, how they affect simplicity, how they talk literature or politics, what and how they eat, how they show their boredom (or their interest), how they say good-bye.

If these examples seem remarkable only for their unremarkability, if they suggest nothing dirtier than the nitty-gritty of what Miller has called the novel as usual, this standard novelistic micropolitics, I would argue, is no longer quite so standard without the teleological alibi of a subsuming marriage plot. In Proust, what ought to have been subsumed, what ought to have remained merely the humble underside of novelistic discourse, rises to the surface and dominates that discourse. "If the narrator had had the will power of a Balzacian hero," complains Vincent Descombes, "he

would at least have attempted to marry a Guermantes."[42] It should be clear
by now, I hope, that the narrator's (and, a fortiori, the author's) lack of
willpower is precisely what this chapter has been celebrating as, to put it
naively, Proust's genius. What Descombes calls willpower, we would (re-
membering, e.g., Thackeray) call heterosexual melancholia: to attempt at
least to marry a Guermantes is to attempt narrative closure by enclosing
in a crypt— that is, by forgetting or disavowing—all the immature pleasures, including the pleasures of the mouth, that one can thereby imagine
as what one has maturely put behind or beneath oneself.

   Not surprisingly, given her boredom, Oriane herself suffers from melancholia. When he goes to take leave of her, Marcel finds himself detained
by her

> prodigality of charming words, of courteous gestures, a whole sys-
> tem of verbal elegance fed by a positive cornucopia within [alimentée
> par une véritable richesse intérieure] . . . : she would suddenly pluck a flower
> from her bodice, or a medallion, and present it to someone with
> whom she would have liked to prolong the evening, with a melan-
> choly feeling that such a prolongation [un tel prolongement] could have
> led to nothing but idle talk, into which nothing could have passed
> of the nervous pleasure, the fleeting emotion, reminiscent of the
> first warm days of spring in the impression they leave behind them
> of lassitude and regret. (p. 748; p. 834)

The source from which Oriane's prodigality flows is also the place to
which it must return since, unable either to renounce her pleasures or
to prolong them, she has no choice but the melancholic compromise of
internalizing them, consigning them to a cornucopia within. Practicing
sophistication as a panicky art of foreclosure and elision, she knows well
how dangerously longing informs prolonging. Where sophistication has
become an antinaive, antinarrative mystique of boredom, "intellectual superiority" may redound instead to one who reinvents sophistication as an
art of dawdling, of putting back in what those on the go have taken out. It
is the willpowerless narrator, last to arrive and last to depart, who enjoys
this sophistication of naïveté, who has the pleasure of releasing Oriane's
inner richness and prolonging it, with what we might call a general rather
than a restricted prodigality, into the banquet that, as internalized, it can
never afford to become on its own. The greatest philosopher-gourmand of
them all, Proust helps himself again and again to the rich food that, precisely by not marrying others, he succeeds in getting out of their bodies.

   Not that he himself entirely escapes the lesser sophistication of melancholia, a melancholia that, in his case identified neither with boredom nor with heterosexuality, takes instead the form of frequent idealizing references to, as we have seen, "poetic pleasure" or, more generally, to a somewhat disembodied "imagination." But, even when he seems to be exalting that imagination at the expense of the mere raw material on which it feeds, his heart, or his stomach—*coeur*, happily, can mean both— is really in the *post*melancholic gastronomy that seeks to recapture, with loving specificity, *what other people tasted like*. Indeed, at its richest, Proust's "imagination" is this gastronomy:

> We are bored at the dinner-table because our imagination is absent, and, because it is keeping us company, we are interested in a book. But the people in question are the same. We should like to have known Mme de Pompadour, who was so valuable a patron of the arts, and we should have been as bored in her company as among the modern Egerias at whose houses we cannot bring ourselves to pay a second call, so mediocre do we find them. The fact remains that these differences do exist. People are never completely alike; their behaviour with regard to ourselves, at, one might say, the same level of friendship, reveals differences which, in the end, counter-balance one another. . . . Types of mind are so varied, so conflicting, not only in literature but in society, that Baudelaire and Mérimée are not the only people who have the right to despise one another mutu-ally. These distinctive characteristics form in each person a system of looks, words and actions so coherent, so despotic, that when we are in his or her presence it seems to us superior to the rest. With Mme de Guermantes, her words, deduced like a theorem from her type of mind, seemed to me the only ones that could possibly be said. (pp. 780–81)

It is as though the whole of Proust's novel were an answer to the questions Bloch asks Marcel near that novel's end: "So the Prince de Guermantes can give me no idea either of Swann or of M. de Charlus? . . . But what was so different about them?" (*Time Regained*, 997). Marcel's immediate response: "To know that, you would have had to hear them talk yourself. But that is impossible. Swann is dead and M. de Charlus is as good as dead. But the differences were enormous" (*Time Regained*, 997–98). By now, of course, we have learned not to trust the short answer. What we, like Bloch, long for, what we cannot get enough of, is the long answer, the *prolonged* answer: the answer that we get from, and as, the enormous novel that is itself both the dinner table and the dinner at which we are almost never bored.

5

Expensive Tastes: Adorno, Barthes,

and Cultural Studies

Dating Adorno and Barthes

Is cultural studies potentially a Proustian discipline, a way of doing Proust in the late twentieth century? Consider, at least, that the naive sophistication that Proust practices to perfection might also serve as a formula for the composite perspective that links a wide range of cultural studies projects: the peculiar overlay of an interest in "low culture" with an optic of "high theory" (to echo the title of a representative volume).[1] That Adorno, dazzling critic of Proust, dazzlingly Proustian critic, from whom we have of course borrowed the notion of naive sophistication, also stands as one of the canonical precursors of contemporary cultural studies lends plausibility to the fantasy that the Proust *de nos jours* might find his Faubourg Saint-Germain in, say, Hollywood, her Duchesse de Guermantes on, say, CNN. That the equally if differently Proustian Roland Barthes functions as another, perhaps the other, non-British originary figure of cultural studies—the best-selling *Cultural Studies Reader* begins with selections from Adorno and Max Horkheimer's chapter on the "culture industry" in *Dialectic of Enlightenment* and from Barthes's *Mythologies*[2]—that these two critics are the A and B of cultural studies, further encourages the belief that the Proustian possibility, no more remote than one's remote-control channel changer, inheres in the very way we (the way some of us professors and graduate students, that is) live now.

But, while Adorno and Barthes might well be imagined to mediate between Proust and cultural studies today, it appears to be their fate, precisely *as* precursors, to be kept at a distance from the field they prefigure. Within a certain evolutionary narrative, their very earliness seems to entail another kind of naïveté, not that of treating "low" subjects, but rather a historically determined blindness, a theoretical immaturity resulting from the limitations of their particular time and place. In his introduction to the excerpt from "The Culture Industry," for instance, after cautiously reminding us of "the situation in which [the piece] was written"—contextualizing it with reference to the end of the Second World War, the authors' experience as refugees from the Nazis, their perspective as secularized high-bourgeois German Jews, the changes in the culture industry since the 1960s—Simon During, the editor of *The Cultural Studies Reader*, writes: "This helps explain how Adorno and Horkheimer neglect what was to become central to cultural studies: the ways in which the cultural industry, while in the service of organized capital, also provides the opportunities for all kinds of individual and collective creativity and decoding." And though, in introducing the excerpt from *Mythologies*, During allows as to how "the young Barthes" was hip enough to recognize "that mass-produced commodities can be beautiful," Barthes's analysis, During concludes, "is finally of a piece with Adorno and Horkheimer's line of thought."[3]

But even this naïveté gets entangled with its ostensible opposite. In Barthes and Adorno, a naive "neglect" of how the culture industry enables "all kinds of individual and collective creativity and decoding" coincides with an elitist ("mandarin," "patrician," "dandiacal") disdain for the masses and their culture that constitutes one readily available stereotype of sophistication itself. Instead of rushing to denounce or repudiate this stereotype, we would do better to acknowledge its truth content, to mark, at the outset, the sheer force of the distaste, if not the disgust, that Adorno and Barthes frankly manifest, not just vis-à-vis the products or the producers of mass culture, but also vis-à-vis its consumers.

Adorno's work fairly overflows with examples, most notoriously in his writing about jazz:

> The population is so accustomed to the drivel it gets that it cannot renounce it, even when it sees through it halfway. On the contrary, it feels impelled to intensify its enthusiasm in order to convince itself that its ignominy is its good fortune. Jazz sets up schemes of social behaviour to which people must in any case conform. Jazz enables them to practice those forms of behaviour, and they love it all the more for making the inescapable easier to bear.[4]

Piously though a latter-day Marxist like Fredric Jameson may labor to rehabilitate Adorno on mass culture ("Paul Whiteman [is] . . . the proper referent for what Adorno calls 'jazz,' which has little to do with the richness of a Black culture we have only long since then discovered"),[5] no amount of piety can white out, for instance, Adorno's assertion that "it is not as though scurrilous businessmen have corrupted the voice of nature by attacking it from without; jazz takes care of this all by itself. The abuse of jazz is not the external calamity in whose name the puristic defenders of 'real' unadulterated jazz furiously protest; such misuse originates in jazz itself" (Prisms, 122).

Barthes's offense against contemporary academic sensibilities is less egregious mainly because his frame of reference is European rather than American, his preferred target generally a French petit bourgeois culture racially marked as white. Still, it is hard to imagine that a critic practicing today could speak of the lower middle class as did the Barthes of Mythologies (1957): "What the petite bourgeoisie respects most in the world is immanence: every phenomenon which bears its own term within itself by a simple mechanism of return, i.e., to put it literally, every paid phenomenon, is agreeable to this class. Language is made to accredit, in its figures, in its very syntax, this morality of the retort." Or again:

> Billy Graham's "success" manifests the mental fragility of the French petite bourgeoisie, a class from which the public for these meetings, it appears, is chiefly recruited; the plasticity of this public to alogical and hypnotic forms of thought suggests that there exists in this social group what we might call a situation of risk: a portion of the French petite bourgeoisie is no longer even protected by its famous "good sense," which is the aggressive form of its class consciousness.[6]

Lucidly in touch with his own aggressivity, Barthes declares in his preface to Mythologies: "What I claim is to live to the full the contradiction of my time, which may well make sarcasm the condition of truth." And in "Myth Today," the theoretical essay that concludes the book, he writes, somewhat less grandiloquently, not only that his "connection with the world is of the order of sarcasm," but also, recognizing that sarcasm bites someone, that "the mythologist cuts himself off from all the myth-consumers, and this is no small matter. . . . To decipher the Tour de France or the 'good French Wine' is to cut oneself off from those who are entertained or warmed up by them."[7] While Barthes's sarcasm may cut both ways, its violence seems less self-inflicted than outer directed, less spectacularly cutting him off from than cutting into the community of myth consumers, who—somewhat suprisingly, given the book's aim of exposing bourgeois (as opposed to petit bourgeois) mystification—undergo a more consistent and more devastating laceration than do the "scurrilous businessmen" (and cynical publicists) on whom one might have expected the brunt of Barthes's trenchancy to fall.[8]

Whatever "Continental" prestige the names of Adorno and Barthes may lend to the enterprise of cultural studies, then, their texts nonetheless constitute something of an embarrassment for contemporary scholars in the field, where the relations between naïveté and sophistication normally take a more attractive form: where theoretically informed analysis coexists with an often populist enthusiasm for the noncanonical, the marginal, and the commercial. This current disciplinary protocol derives not just from a newer understanding of the openness or even transgressiveness of supposedly hegemonic cultural products, and not just from a post-1960s imperative to respect the pleasures of the nonelite other: it also reflects the fact that many members of the academy today *are* nonelite others. Or at least, *were*: perhaps the interplay between the naive and the sophisticated in contemporary academic writing about mass culture makes most sense as an attempt to invest one's cultural capital, whose acquisition is of course a function as much of class as of age, in objects one has had to renounce in order to acquire that capital in the first place.

In short, nothing dates Adorno and Barthes more definitively than their presupposition of a more or less rigidly socialized hierarchy of aesthetic values. Here again, for instance, is Adorno on jazz: "The organization of culture into 'levels' such as the first, second, and third programmes, patterned after low, middle, and highbrow, is reprehensible. But it cannot be overcome simply by the lowbrow sects declaring themselves to be highbrow" (*Prisms*, 127). Insistently, and indignantly, reading the degradation of mass or popular taste as the sign of an exploitative social system, both Adorno and Barthes remain confident nevertheless that that taste is in fact degraded. However obvious this assessment may have seemed to intellectuals of the 1940s and 1950s, it cannot help meeting with a cooler reception in a postmodern, post–baby boom Western cultural landscape, in which, wherever one turns, even in those few households still on intimate terms with European high culture, one will inevitably find *a television set*.

There is undoubtedly much to be grateful for in the democratic swerve, the inflection of cultural studies away from the arrogance and one-sidedness of an earlier intellectual and aesthetic regime. But, if neither Adorno's Biedermeier revulsion from the vulgar herd nor Barthes's high style of *mondanité marxisante* resonates very powerfully in academic discourse today, this is not quite to say that the bite of a pre-postmodern sarcasm has completely gone out of cultural studies. Consider, for example, Marjorie Garber's essay "Character Assassination: Shakespeare, Anita Hill, and JFK," which appears in the 1993 volume *Media Spectacles*, a showcase for some of the best work being done in the field. Commenting on the testimony of one J. C. Alvarez in the 1991 hearings on Clarence Thomas's nomination for the U.S. Supreme Court, Garber quotes Alvarez, a pro-Thomas, anti-Hill character witness, as "sneer[ing] self-righteously": "He [Thomas] must want to turn to her [Hill] and say 'Et tu, Brutus? You too, Anita?'" After pointing out Alvarez's mistake—which consists, needless to say, of substituting *Brutus* for *Brute*—Garber, as though sneering back, writes:

> That Ms. Alvarez has small Latin (and, I think it is fair to assume, perhaps even less Greek) makes her appropriation of Shakespeare, and Shakespeare's cultural power, even more striking. . . . Alvarez is speaking "Shakespeare," as "Shakespeare" has come to be spoken in the public sphere of American politics. Out of context, deprofessionalized, timeless, transcendent, and empty, the literary version of the American flag, to be waved at the public in an apparently apolitical gesture toward universal wisdom.[9]

Garber's animus, we should note, is not reserved for such small potatoes as J. C. Alvarez, as though she were concerned merely to reprofessionalize Shakespeare, reclaiming him, and his cultural power, for those who know their texts and contexts, those on whom canonical allusions ("small Latin and . . . even less Greek") are not lost. Much of her sarcasm, in fact, operates at the expense of the male senators ("the senator's eloquent peroration"; "the staffers of the indefatigably learned Senator Simpson"; "as Simpson noted to his learned colleagues"),[10] who, probably no less illiterate than Alvarez, command far more than her fifteen minutes in the spotlight and for whom *cultural* power is only one in a whole arsenal of weapons routinely available for brandishing at the American public.

Although seemingly indiscriminate, that is, Garber's biting wit may arise out of a quite specific political frustration, one experienced, I suspect, but rarely acknowledged, by a number of cultural studies practitioners: broadly functioning, I would suggest, as a *counteraggression*, that wit responds to the apparent impossibility of response in a "public sphere" dominated, and thus evacuated, by the likes of Senator Simpson and his learned colleagues, whose lack of learning, or whose frat-boy insouciance about what is at best an oafish semierudition, far from hindering their exercise of power, enables, enhances, and legitimates it, all by attesting their freedom from a feminizing, effeminating intellectuality. Barthes: "The professor is someone who finishes his sentences."[11] But the senator is someone who doesn't finish his, and who doesn't expect a reply either—

indeed, whose inarticulateness and indifference serve precisely to distinguish him from the professor. In America, anyway, the "public sphere" belongs to those who, while not petit bourgeois themselves, most convincingly simulate a petit bourgeois identification. Although J. C. Alvarez, ambitious Republican party functionary, fails laughably in her attempt to speak Shakespeare, her "failure" bears a remarkable resemblance to the "success" of the stars (and producers) of the show in which she can only play a bit part, the big boys who wear their not-so-gentle men's Cs as badges of honor.

This pessimistic reading of the political horizon not just of Garber's essay but perhaps of cultural studies as a whole goes against the grain of the official self-representation of *Media Spectacles*, which Garber coedited. We read in the introduction, at any rate, that "the essays in this collection perform, variously, the practice of academic scholarship not apart from or alongside cultural conflicts, but in the midst of them."[12] More than a mere spatial designation, "in the midst of them" commends these essays as salutary *interventions* in the rough-and-tumble world of political struggle. Coupled with a bold channel-surfing eclecticism — the volume boasts a heterogeneity of topics, from the Gulf War to the William Kennedy Smith rape trial to Hurricane Bob — this appealing notion of a newly engagé scholarship participates in the same upbeat conceptual repertoire as During's assurance that, while the culture industry serves the interests of organized capital, it "also provides the opportunities for all kinds of individual and collective creativity and decoding." By indicating in Garber's essay what I take to be residues of a more bitter wisdom — specimens of which I could have adduced from any number of other virtuoso performances in the field — I want to suggest that the *practice* of cultural studies in the 1990s is more naive, and therefore more sophisticated, than its *theory*. While the latter occupies an *imaginaire* defined by polyvalence and opportunities for all kinds of empowerment, the former knows its place in what for the most part remains an overbearingly, intractably nondialogical media culture, where "cultural conflicts" tend to be resolved by, and in favor of, those (like Senator Simpson waxing eloquent about "all this sexual harassment crap"[13]) with the biggest microphones. Cultural studies today, in other words, is closer to Barthes and Adorno than it thinks.

What would it mean for cultural studies to have a better knowledge of its proximity to these two "outmoded" forebears? To begin with, it might mean recognizing its own persistent *méchanceté* — the mark, if not of an inherent Proustianism, then of a specifically institutionalized literariness, a professorial deformation that, from the outset, significantly determines (or limits) the political efficacy of its "practice" and "performance." But it would also mean recognizing this méchanceté in the sense, precisely, of owning it, viewing it not, say, as a mannerism one might choose to abandon or tone down for the sake of better communication in the public arena but rather as the inevitable consequence of a certain refusal of communication, a certain foreclosure on the public arena—a refusal and a foreclosure constitutive of mass culture itself.

If Garber recalls Barthes and Adorno in her assassination of J. C. Alvarez's character, along with those of more powerful players in the Clarence Thomas–Anita Hill media spectacle, Barthes and Adorno provide considerable insight into why writing about the mass media can bring out the mass murderer in even the most cheerfully eclectic of critics. Insofar as Barthes's and Adorno's naïveté—their bad attitude toward mass culture—is also a sophistication, that is, it goes beyond (although it undeniably includes) a snobbish contempt for middle- and lowbrow tastes. Their legacy—which few contemporary critics seem eager to accept—consists not only in the violence of their naïveté but also in their extensive reflections on the larger situation of that violence. Should we think to replace the hackneyed theme of violence in mass culture with the somewhat fresher one of violence in academic essays on mass culture, Adorno and Barthes point instead, more helpfully, to the matrix of both these violences: to mass culture as violence, as organized, indeed industrialized, intimidation, about which it is all but impossible to write nicely.[14]

For Adorno to speak of a culture industry, after all, is for him to focus on just this systematization of brutality into business-as-usual. Perhaps the definitive feature of everyday life under late capitalism, the chillingly efficient deployment of mass culture as mass intimidation, moreover, does not simply result in a set of bad objects one can either censure from a distance or—if one prefers a more "politicized" model of criticism—intervene in strategically. Adorno never lets his reader forget the totalitarian character of mass culture's performativity, its fully corporal seizure of its subjects, which makes scenarios of intervention look at once redundant and quixotic. For instance: "The film has succeeded in transforming subjects so indistinguishably into social functions, that those wholly encompassed, no longer aware of any conflict, enjoy their own dehumanization as something human, as the joy of warmth. The total interconnectedness of the culture industry, omitting nothing, is one with total social delusion. Which is why it makes such light work of counter-arguments."[15] If Adorno naively (aggressively) exempts himself from the total social delusion, he sophisticatedly (aggressively) recognizes, at the same time, that

to be outside it is to be precisely nowhere, so effortlessly does the aggression of the culture industry itself preempt any position from which
to argue against it.[16]

And though, unlike Adorno, Barthes, especially the later Barthes, will
never be "political" enough for some critics, this dissatisfaction may say
more about their own ideological captivity than about the object of their
criticism.[17] For Barthes, both later and earlier in his career, in fact produces an exceptionally rich account of mass culture as a veritable intimidation machine.[18] Where Adorno obsessively speaks of the culture industry, Barthes throughout his oeuvre theorizes what he calls, variously,
myth, or the Doxa, or encratic language:

> Encratic language, supported by the state, is everywhere: it is a dif-
> fused, widespread, one might say osmotic discourse which impreg-
> nates exchanges, social rites, leisure, the socio-symbolic field (above
> all, of course, in societies of mass communication). Not only does
> encratic language never describe itself as systematic, but it always
> constitutes itself as an opposition to system: alibis of nature, of univer-
> sality, of good sense, of clarity—the anti-intellectualist resistances—
> become the tacit figures of the encratic system. . . . In short, it is
> a non-marked language, producer of a masked intimidation, so that it
> is difficult to assign it morphological features—unless we manage to
> reconstitute with rigor and precision what is something of a contra-
> diction in terms: the figures of the masked.[19]

Mass culture as mask culture: as though its all-encompassing violence
didn't make it hard enough to resist, we must also reckon with its policy—
in the language of an earlier media spectacle—of plausible deniability.
How do you deal with a bully who's got everyone convinced that he isn't
one? If, as Adorno argues, mass culture is already fascism, Barthes evokes
its peculiar horror (as well as its irresistible appeal) by doing everything
but calling it fascism with a baby face—not, as its apparent featureless-
ness might suggest, with no face. As Barthes (anticipating Althusser) puts
it, "This interpellant speech is at the same time a frozen speech: at the
moment of reaching me, it suspends itself, turns away and assumes the
look of a generality: it stiffens, it makes itself look neutral and innocent
[elle s'innocente]" (Mythologies, 125; 211).

Mass culture indeed innocents itself, we might risk the ineloquence of
saying—not because, since our eloquence gets us nowhere, we might as
well start talking like Alan Simpson, but because, in the face of a masked
intimidation, to which we should by no means resign ourselves, we need all the rhe-

torical resources we can get, barbarous jargon as well as belletristic irony. For even if we like mass culture—or, less globally and no doubt more accurately, even if we like certain genres or styles or moments or practitioners within it—our very liking of it may open us to (further) abuse by it. As almost any journalistic discussion of almost any cultural studies project shows (we are talking, to be sure, about a more or less "high" mass culture now), mass culture does not necessarily find itself honored by the attention—often respectful, sometimes even loving—that academic critics are suddenly paying it. Not that the point of doing cultural studies is to get a good review from Michiko Kakutani. But if the point is presumably to understand how mass culture works—and not merely to grade it in terms of its subversive goodness or its hegemonic badness—it makes sense to figure out what happens when one presumes to understand it, to engage the forces circulating in its field of intimidation. And, to assess those forces, one needs precisely to employ *figurative* arts: one needs, in Barthes's paradoxical phrase, to reconstitute the figures of the masked.

Physiognomic as well as rhetorical, these figures are also, of course, theatrical. But so is the attempt to reconstitute them: one cannot reveal the characteristic ruses of mass culture without staging them, without aggressively, parodically reenacting them, without making a spectacle of the media especially where—not wanting to scare us off with too many sneering figures à la Simpson and Alvarez—they wear their blandest or most unspectacular face. Much of the fascination, as well as much of the unseemliness, of Barthes's and Adorno's writing, I think, stems from their willingness to *make scenes*—to give a face to what would appear faceless and, in so doing, to show *themselves* in a less than flattering light. Grasping that mass culture's foremost intimidation consists in its endless, boundless production of an infuriating *innocence effect*, whereby, in Barthes's words, it "turns away" at the very moment of addressing you, so that any attempt you make to talk (back) to it can only seem excessive— nitpicking or imbecilic, perversely overingenious or crudely reductive, hysterical or paranoid, masturbatory or sterilely intellectualizing, sentimental or mean-spirited—Barthes and Adorno in fact go out of their way to *embrace* excess: renouncing both innocence and the pretense thereof, ruthlessly marking the unmarked, they exemplify practices of "creativity and decoding" that contemporary cultural studies itself, in its very pursuit of inclusivity, seems compelled to neglect.

These practices deviate from the norms of academic prose not in their creativity as such—indeed, creativity has *become* one of the norms of academic prose—but rather in the particular substance of that creativity.

What is Proustian about Barthes and Adorno, in other words, is not just their capacity for interweaving theoretical discourse with the kind of writing most typically encountered in the novelistic scene:[20] what is also Proustian about them—and what accounts better for their embarrassing "datedness"—is a certain compound of luxury and *sadism*, a volatile (or maybe just intolerable) mixture of intoxicating vengefulness, on the one hand, and something like the intellectual equivalent of conspicuous consumption, on the other.

Finding this mixture hard to take, cultural studies may have to neglect Barthes and Adorno; but, as I have suggested, they have not quite neglected it. My aim in the rest of this chapter will be to help cultural studies get in touch with these two inner children who remain disturbingly alive in it—disturbingly insofar as, however great one's admiration for them, anyone paying even minimal attention to their practices of creativity and decoding is liable to detect, in their distinguished ancestral voices, strains that recall not so much the plaintive cries of the inner child as the less endearing effusions of what our oddly censorious modern maturity might perceive as, simply, the *spoiled brat*. Mass culture itself, however, shows no signs of becoming nicer—more inclusive, more diverse, more amenable to "conversation": although it is now almost de rigueur to comment, whether ruefully or rhapsodically, on the Baudrillardean *hyperrealism* of our media-crazed society (everything is a soap opera, we're all potentially fifteen-minute celebrities, etc.), talking about mass culture's ontological delirium may have become a way of *not* talking about ways of talking (and thinking) that the very universality of the global masquerade—far less dizzy than it may want us to believe—has a distinctly nasty tendency to preempt, to discredit, to marginalize, or to exclude.

In this context, there may be some strategic value in risking theoretical unsubtlety by negotiating less abstract, less guarded relations with our enfants terribles, our naively sophisticated monsters within. Given that Adorno's and Barthes's own relations with the monster without, the immense, baby-faced monster that is mass culture (mouse culture?),[21] center on what Barthes calls the difficult, contradictory project of reconstituting the figures of masked intimidation, I will be focusing on a series of frankly scenic moments in their texts, not only texts that are more or less narrowly or consistently "analytic," but also those that are more or less openly or heterogeneously "autobiographical." In the process, I will be tracing a final, counterintuitive metafigure of sophistication itself—as what we could do worse than call *a naïveté without innocence*.

Toys

Thus far, I have been speaking of Adorno and Barthes almost as though they were a team, like, say, Adorno and Horkheimer. The differences between them are of course as important, and as salient, as the differences between the historical forces that shaped them and with which they variously reckoned throughout their lives and careers. One could schematize those differences, crudely, in terms of a certain stereotypical French/German binarism — or, only a little less crudely, in terms of a French/German-Jewish binarism. In other words, while Adorno's name evokes an ethic of philosophical "rigor" inseparable from an extraphilosophical experience of *pain* — the pain of Nazi anti-Semitism, the pain of exile, in short, what he famously called *damaged life* — the orbit of Barthes (whom I remember a graduate school classmate warning me away from as "lightweight") seems to define a space of glitteringly Parisian literariness unthinkable apart from a whole atmospherics of *pleasure*: "un peu de savoir, un peu de sagesse, et le plus de saveur possible." [22] This is to say that the differences could also be mapped onto a binarism of heterosexual versus homosexual, of melancholia versus gayness, such that, to signal the geography of our larger project, Adorno would figure as a twentieth-century Thackeray and Barthes as a latter-day Proust — which he in many ways already is.

But so, as we have suggested, is Adorno. To be under Proust's influence is not necessarily to relinquish one's heterosexual credentials; nor, as we shall see in looking at one of Adorno's more assaultive passages — or as we could tell from looking at some of Proust's, for that matter — does it in any way entail immunity from homophobia. Yet a first step toward nuancing too symmetrical a differentiation between our authors might consist of recognizing that, should we wish to find out not just how they represent naïveté but what they have to say about it, and should we, in the course of this inquiry, seek, for instance, an openly hospitable environment for a playful, erotic, *cathectable* naïveté — a naïveté affirmatively transvalued — we would do better to turn toward the toughly rigorous Adorno than to look for help from the deliciously hedonistic Barthes, in whose writings the term *naive* more or less consistently retains the negative charge that general usage assigns it. Extending far beyond his notion of Proust's "second naïveté," the itinerary of the naive in Adorno's texts is remarkable not only for its prominence but also for its relative prestige. That even as forbiddingly "German" and "philosophical" a text as his *Aesthetic Theory* features an entire section entitled "On the Changing Role of *Naïveté*" is perhaps less surprising than it may seem, given precisely the importance of naïveté in the German philosophical tradition. Nor does Adorno's preoccupation with the naive simply (or "naively") amount to a celebration of it. Still, where Barthes's explicit references to naïveté rather conventionally align it with a bad or pseudoinnocence ("what is inculpated here is any form of explicative, committed culture, and what is saved is an 'innocent' culture, the culture whose naïveté leaves the tyrant's hands free" [Eiffel Tower, 134]),[23] Adorno, thanks no doubt to his dialectical imagination, can write:

> Artistic production is truly naïve when it is unflinching in its opposition to petrified life. Measured by conventional standards, such art is said to lack naïveté. In actual fact it does contain naïveté, just as the artistic mode of behaviour contains an element of infantile insubordination and child-like rebellion against the reality principle and the values of society. This notion of naïveté is the opposite of the generally accepted one. . . . The naïve and reflexive elements of art have always been more interdependent than the nostalgic perspective during the advent of capitalism was willing to concede.[24]

It is not just the naive and reflexive elements of art, however, whose interdependence Adorno emphasizes. "The un-naïve thinker," he writes in Negative Dialectics, "knows how far he remains from the object of his thinking, and yet he must always talk as if he had it entirely. This brings him to the point of clowning. He must not deny his clownish traits, least of all since they alone can give him hope for what is denied him."[25] "Naïvety and sophistication are concepts so closely intertwined that no good can come of playing one off against the other" (Minima Moralia, 73), remarks Adorno, just before playing one off against the other; they are so closely intertwined in philosophical discourse itself that the latter can be articulated only in negatively dialectical relation to the former: in place of sophisticated—a word that travels even less well into German than into French—Adorno here and elsewhere writes unnaiv. Often likened to Derrida, Adorno, invoking the philosopher as clown, also resembles Bakhtin—whom, moreover, he in fact surpasses (which it is not too difficult to do) to the extent that he not only invokes but also plays the clown. For one of Adorno's strongest links with Barthes, despite their numerous and by no means negligible differences, is their shared predilection for critical genres that in themselves mimic "infantile insubordination and childlike rebellion against the reality principle and the values of society." Notwithstanding their regrettable insensitivity to hegemony's self-carnivalizing potential, that is, Adorno and Barthes, after all, are both masters (as one addresses a boy or young man) of the impertinently (un)naive forms prized by contemporary oppositional criticism: the essay, the aphorism, the fragment.

Both, too, obligingly discuss their Nietzschean fondness for short, semiautonomous forms, in ways that contemporary readers will find familiar. From Adorno's *Minima Moralia*: "If today the subject is vanishing, aphorisms take upon themselves the duty 'to consider the evanescent itself as essential.' They insist, in opposition to Hegel's practice and yet in accordance with his thought, on negativity" (p. 16). And from *Roland Barthes*, Barthes's own masterpiece-in-pieces: "I proceed by addition, not by sketch; I have the antecedent (initial) taste for the detail, the fragment, the *rush*, and the incapacity to lead it toward a 'composition': I cannot reproduce 'the masses' [*je ne sais pas reproduire 'les masses'*]" (p. 94; p. 97).

But what I want to emphasize is the less familiar disarmingness with which both Barthes and Adorno thematize their preferred stylistic miniaturism as a self-conscious redeployment of the forms, and forces, of childhood. In a stereotypically gloomy mood, Adorno asserts: "Whatever the intellectual does, is wrong. He experiences drastically and vitally the ignominious choice that late capitalism secretly presents to all its dependants: to become one more grown-up, or to remain a child" (*Minima Moralia*, 133). Even more secretly, however, Adorno reserves for himself a third, rather Proustian option: neither that of becoming one more grown-up, nor that of remaining a child, but, less depressingly, that of *becoming a child*. "The essay," he writes, "does not let its domain be prescribed for it. Instead of accomplishing something scientifically or creating something artistically, its efforts reflect the leisure of a childlike person who has no qualms about taking his inspiration from what others have done before him." [26] And, although, as we have said, Barthes's *énoncés* record a more or less commonplace aversion to the naive, his characteristically and avowedly fragmentary *énonciation* [27] constitutes a strategic refusal of "adulthood," of the oppressive bigness that, dubious privilege, comes with being *une grande personne*: "How can I manage to keep each of these fragments from never being anything but a *symptom*?—Easy: let yourself go, *regress*" (*Roland Barthes*, 172).

Even easier, perhaps, than Barthes thinks: for fragments are already regressive, or regressed, forms. To cite another Barthesian metafragment, fragmentary even in its syntax: "*Parodic affinity of the fragment and the dictation exercise: the latter will sometimes recur here, as an obligatory figure of social writing, a vestige of school composition*" (*Roland Barthes*, 45). Each fragment, in a sense, is itself a child: "Each one receives its image-system imprint [*sa marque d'imaginaire*] from that very horizon where it supposes itself loved, unpunished, exempt from the embarrassment of being read by a subject without indulgence, or simply: *who would observe* ['*qui regarderait*'] (*Roland Barthes*, 106; 110).

It may be objected at this point that, while a poetics of miniaturism and disjunction is supposed to signify "infantile insubordination and childlike rebellion," the aspect of childhood that seems most central to these formulations is not the naughtiness of the enfant terrible but, on the contrary, either the "good" child's eagerness to please or the simply lazy child's unconcern about "taking his inspiration from what others have done before him." Yet such an objection would forget (even as it would evince) both the frequency with which those eager to please arouse displeasure instead and how easily one can get away with theft if one calls it a taking of inspiration from others. It would also forget, for instance, that the affinity, according to Barthes, of the fragment and the dictation exercise is explicitly "*parodic*," just as the fragment parodies such other childhood forms as the riddle, the nursery rhyme, the fairy tale, and the cartoon. Indeed, what Barthes and Adorno effect, in their respective raids on the nursery, is not a nostalgic rehearsal of childhood but rather the more unsettling spectacle of an almost Pee-Wee Herman–like travesty—or tranvestism—of childhood on the part of "two grown men." By means of their regressions, in other words, they seek to mobilize a certain repertoire of infantility over and against not so much maturity per se as the normative appropriation of "childhood"—the systemic assumption of "childhood" as an alibi, as a mask of innocence—whereby encratic language, and mass culture in particular, simultaneously conduct and conceal their work of intimidation.

This is why, when Barthes confesses, "I cannot reproduce 'the masses,'" more is at stake than the not-so-secret self-congratulation that we might congratulate ourselves on recognizing. "Unable to" reproduce the masses, drawn instead toward the childlike littleness of the detail, the connoisseur of fragments confronts the *culture* of the masses—self-totalizing and self-infantilizing at once—with the image of an *alternative childhood*: of childhood as something other than bogus innocence, imperialistic pseudo-nature, monopolistic banality, mechanically reproduced adorability. No more "authentic" than childhood as universally abstracted, universally diffused mass-cultural alibi, this alternative childhood ultimately travesties, not childhood itself, but the mass-cultural *ventriloquization* of childhood that constitutes a travesty in its own right. Where mass culture, with what Adorno and Horkheimer call its "sly [i.e., spurious] naïveté,"[28] wears childhood as the face of anonymity, the sophisticatedly naive critic of mass culture insists on blowing (by reconstituting) that cover. Where mass culture infantilizes its products with a view toward masking or unmarking their intimidating performativity, the critic of mass culture stages a whole gaudy parade of fragment children, bringing out everything in "childhood" that *resists* neutralization, evacuation, and formalization. Where mass culture sublates "innocented" childhood, childhood *as* innocence, into a virtually invisible, if pervasive, technological effect, a generalized function of its worldwide operations, the critic of mass culture desublimates "child's play" with a vengeance, bringing it back as a rambunctious army teeming with the kinds of would-be child stars that audiences love to hate.

Cultivating the diminutive, in short, the critic of mass culture presides over a kindergarten of exhibitionists. Each fragment, for all its apparent timidity, is a little entertainer: "Each one . . . supposes itself loved, unpunished, exempt from the embarrassment of being read by a subject without indulgence, or simply: *who would observe.*" That is to say, each fragment wants, instead of simply being observed, placed under surveillance, to be read by a subject who would delight in it, savor it;[29] each one (whose status *as* fragment, whose brokenness, affiliates it, perhaps, with the *abused* child) vulnerably, pathetically demands indulgence—unlike mass culture, which, relentless in its efforts to keep us entertained, seems to have perfected the technique of giving the cold shoulder to anyone warm enough to appreciate not just its entertainment value but its performativity as well. "This interpellant speech," to re-cite Barthes, "is at the same time a frozen speech: at the moment of reaching me, it suspends itself, turns away and assumes the look of a generality."

On one side, then, mass culture's glacial, monolithic impersonality; on the other, the fragment's impish hyperpersonality. On one side, the monster of totality (to borrow the title of the last fragment in *Roland Barthes*); on the other, lots of tiny monsters, most impressive, not for their "innocence," or even for their perhaps equally nonexistent "charm," but rather for the sheer demonic intensity of their competition for readerly love. But it would be too easy to reduce the conflict to a question of big versus little, general versus particular. For if the art of the miniature collaborates with a politics of excess, then, conversely, the enormity of the culture industry signifies more than just the inexorable triumph of the enormous. Though much of the power of mass culture has to do precisely with its *massiveness*, that massiveness by no means prevents it from possessing its own massive art of the detail, its own monumental genius for the miniature. As everyone knows, complaining about the tyranny of the sound bite, for instance, has become one of the clichés of contemporary commentary on the media, practically a sound bite in itself. But the sound bite is merely one of the newer models of what is perhaps the primal genre, the generative unit, of mass culture as a whole: the commercial or, rather, the commodity. Ostentatiously fragmentary books like Minima Moralia, Mythologies, and Barthes's autobiography thus equip themselves all the more effectively to parody a mass culture indistinguishable, as Adorno and Horkheimer argued long ago, from advertising. If their construction evokes a boisterous children's playhouse, the spectacle being presented suggests a dazzling constellation of seductive, shiny objects: the point where childhood and the commodity form intersect, each fragment perhaps dreams of turning into a toy—one absent, however, from every toystore.

One of Barthes's Mythologies, of course, is devoted to the subject of toys, about which he disapprovingly observes: "French toys are usually based on imitation, they are meant to produce children who are users, not creators" (p. 54). And yet, later in the same book (no need to wait for a post-1968, poststructuralist phase), Barthes will proceed to destabilize this moralistic opposition between using and creating, flaunting (as though going out of his way to annoy Terry Eagleton) a self-indulgent mastery of the bourgeois art of living, in which consumption stylishly revises itself as a mode of production. But the Marxist Adorno is at least equally committed to refiguring the experience of consumption. In the preface to Minima Moralia, avowing that its "starting-point is the narrowest private sphere" (p. 18), he writes:

> The change in the relations of production themselves depends largely on what takes place in the "sphere of consumption," the mere reflection of production and the caricature of true life: in the consciousness and unconsciousness of individuals. Only by virtue of opposition to production, as still not wholly encompassed by this order, can men bring about another more worthy of human beings. Should the appearance of life, which the sphere of consumption itself defends for such bad reasons, be once entirely effaced, then the monstrosity of absolute production will triumph. (p. 15)

Although a mere caricature of true life, the sphere of consumption affords at least a possibility of critical leverage against an ever-encroaching regime of production. Mimicking, in its discontinuous proliferation of brilliancies, the very form of consumer culture, making a veritable potlatch of its vast cultural capital, Minima Moralia, moreover, seems to conceive itself as the caricature of a caricature, the utopian (monstrous) fantasy of a consumption that, instead of mocking true life, might epitomize it.

In fact, Minima Moralia includes its own fragment on toys. In a section whose rubric the English translator renders as "Toy Shop" (more resonant than the original "Kaufmannsladen," or merchant's shop [p. 257]), Adorno observes: "In his purposeless activity the child, by a subterfuge, sides with use-value against exchange value. Just because he deprives the things with which he plays of their mediated usefulness, he seeks to rescue in them what is benign towards men and not what subserves the exchange relation that equally deforms men and things" (p. 228). All this talk of "men," all these masculine pronouns—Adorno, we should note, speaks, semineutrally, of Kind and Mensch—make one want to call the "Toy Shop" fragment an invaginated pocket within the larger text. It recommends itself, that is, as a microcosmic description of the book as a whole. Use-without-usefulness might well serve as the slogan, not just for the child's cunningly insubordinate relation to the commodity world, but for Adorno's own parodic (kidding?) approach to the spectacular marketplace that is mass culture and a culture of consumption at once. For all its (well-founded) bitterness, Minima Moralia, whose fragment titles alone constitute a lavish display, suggests a fantastic toy shop in its own right, in which Adorno, seeking "to rescue . . . what is benign" in his wares, what is good in his goods, himself plays the roles of both merchant and child.

Parody as rescue? To be sure, this account itself sounds a bit benign, a bit inconsistent with the monstrous Adorno we have been conjuring up. What exactly gets rescued by Adorno in Toyland? Barthes, whose procedure, as we have said, closely resembles Adorno's, helps us toward an answer when, in "Myth Today," he borrows another metaphor from the world of childhood to explain the relation between form and meaning in myth:

> But the essential point in all this is that the form does not suppress the meaning [le sens], it only impoverishes it, it puts it at a distance, it holds it at one's disposal. One believes that the meaning is going to die, but it is a death with reprieve; the meaning loses its value, but keeps its life, from which the form of the myth will draw its nourishment. The meaning will be for the form like an instantaneous reserve of history, a tamed richness [comme une richesse soumise], which it is possible to call and dismiss in a sort of rapid alternation: the form must constantly be able to be rooted again in the meaning and to get there what nature it needs for its nutriment; above all, it must be able to hide there. It is this constant game of hide-and-seek [ce jeu intéressant de cache-cache] between the meaning and the form which defines myth. (Mythologies, 118; 203)

"One believes that the meaning is going to die, but it is a death with reprieve": if form (denotation, exchange-value) needs to keep meaning (connotation, use value) alive, the mythologist himself plays an important part not merely in perpetuating the reprieve, but in untaming meaning's "richness," in making sure that it comes back more aggressively than mythic (or ideological) form, accustomed to keeping it at a distance and to calling and dismissing it at will, may find convenient. The rescue missions conducted by both Barthes and Adorno, in other words, themselves imply the aggression of *returning* meaning by deformalizing it; their good deeds on behalf of meaning operate, at the same time, to the detriment of form. Where form, for example, wants and needs meaning as a place in which to hide, the parodic critic *disrupts* the game of hide-and-seek, refusing to allow ideology to naturalize itself thereby. What is the hide-and-seek of ideology, after all, but the process by means of which mass culture "innocently" produces its masked intimidation? Nowhere are Adorno and Barthes more touchingly childlike than in the sadistic (sarcastic) glee with which they rip off the mask and drag the bully out from hiding.

Thanks to Barthes's happy mixing of the ludic metaphor with an alimentary one (meaning as richness, as nourishment), we can imagine these children at play, rescuing what is benign in things, as children whose orality—as their sadism already indicates—has itself yet to be fully domesticated. Baby gourmands, they *overconsume*, conspicuously failing to submit their appetite (for rich food, and for a lot of it) to the impoverishing strictures of dietary good sense. For mass culture and advertising, of course, work, not just by producing and stimulating appetites, but by disciplining them as well, at times seeming cruelly to withhold from the spectator-consumer the very content they ostensibly offer. "The culture industry," Adorno and Horkheimer observe, "perpetually cheats its consumers of what it perpetually promises. The promissory note which, with its plots and staging, it draws on pleasure is endlessly prolonged; the promise, which is actually all the spectacle consists of, is illusory: all it actually confirms is that the real point will never be reached, that the diner must be satisfied with the menu" (*Dialectic*, 139).

Here it is Barthes's turn to be the more dialectical one, for, as early as *Mythologies*, he recognizes that, just as ideology does not so much kill meaning as attenuate it, so mass culture, instead of simply *denying* us the gratifications for which it makes us hunger, works on the craftier model of what he calls "operation margarine": "'A mousse? Made with margarine? Unthinkable!' 'Margarine? Your uncle will be furious!' And then one's eyes are opened, one's conscience becomes more pliable, and margarine is a delicious food, tasty, digestible, economical, useful in all circumstances" (p. 42). Mass culture in fact has no interest in fooling the epicurean ogre of an uncle (deliciously "French" detail), getting him to mistake margarine for butter. Which is not to say that it has no use for him: by wielding him terroristically as the negative example of the bad consumer—the selfish, dictatorial, old-fashioned consumer, from whom we cannot but wish to differentiate ourselves—it compels us to accept a dose of moderate, modern, socially approved pleasure, the pleasure of the young and the up-to-date, in exchange for the excessive, anachronistic pleasure we only thought we desired.

Mass culture itself, then, is operation margarine generalized: supplanting the uncle's ancien régime, it increases its chances of being received as a more "digestible" (if not more palatable) authority by implicitly proposing to banish any unsatisfied customer into an avuncular wasteland, not unlike that to which, say, Jos Sedley gets consigned. (From "The Culture Industry": " 'No one must go hungry or thirsty; if anyone does, he's for the concentration camp!' This joke from Hitler's Germany might shine forth as a maxim from above all the portals of the culture industry" [p. 149].) "What does it matter, after all," Barthes asks sarcastically, "if margarine is just fat, when it goes further than butter, and costs less? What does it matter, after all, if Order is a little brutal or a little blind, when it allows us to live cheaply? Here we are, in our turn, rid of a prejudice which cost us dearly, too dearly, which cost us too much in scruples, in revolt, in fights and in solitude" (p. 42). By virtue of this very sarcasm, Barthes identifies himself with those who continue to pay such exorbitant prices: he casts himself as what we might call the child from uncle—as revoltingly "sophisticated" worshiper at the shrine of a superannuated haute cuisine, and thus as revoltingly "naive" reminder of tastes whose expensiveness a well-adjusted, grown-up economy cannot tolerate.

An extravagance as much at the level of discourse as of diet ("It would seem that we are condemned for some time yet always to speak excessively about reality" [Mythologies, 158]), this deviant orality is its own punishment: the unhappy customer automatically excommunicates himself from the happy sociality of those he attacks—those who make up the rigorously noninteractive "community" ruled by the radically anticonversational principle of "It goes without saying," the very watchword, as Barthes suggests in the preface to Mythologies, of "ideological abuse" (p. 11). Sentenced to solitary confinement, the gastronome in an age of margarine, however, may enjoy the consolation of uncovering "richness" where it is least suspected: in the impoverishing operation itself. Where mass culture attenuates meaning (le sens), its parodist takes wicked (unauthorized) pleasure in giving sensuousness, thickness, body, flavor—not just "buttery flavor" (as new and improved products in the ongoing campaign of operation margarine like to promise) but, as it were, the flavor of butter itself—to the very process of attenuation. In a footnote at the end of "Myth Today," Barthes "admits": "Even here, in these mythologies, I have used trickery [*j'ai rusé*]: finding it painful constantly to work on the evaporation of ideology, I have started to make it excessively dense [*je me suis mis à l'épaissir excessivement*], and to discover in it a surprising compactness which I savoured with delight [*une compacité surprenante, savoureuse à moi-même*]" (p. 158; p. 247).[30]

Disingenuous in the best Proustian way, Barthes is trickiest when he pretends to be surprised by the pleasure resulting from what he presents as a mere supplementary *divertissement*. His project, mordantly antiformalist from the start, has as its major goal the exposure, through the reversal, of the diluting and homogenizing of *content* whereby mass culture renders invisible both itself and its hold over us. And, if, as one might predict, the acerbic Adorno proves less fluent in the language of cuisine than the savory Barthes, he can still claim a (suitably "Germanic") culinary imagination of his own, which he is equally capable of turning against mass culture's distinctive sorcery: "the tone adopted by every film is that of the witch handing food to the child she wants to enchant or devour, while mumbling horribly: 'Lovely, lovely soup. How you're going to enjoy it!' " (*Minima Moralia*, 201). Luxuriously sinking their teeth not only into other consumers but into an all-consuming mass culture itself, both Adorno and Barthes insist on getting content precisely out of the evaporation of content. To make that process dense at all, they know well, is "to make it excessively dense": any consumption other than that prescribed by mass culture itself is by definition overconsumption. Or, in the idiom of the classroom, whose possibilities for intimidation anyone who has ever been a teacher, or a student, will recognize (one can forget that Barthes and Adorno both held academic positions): to read for content *where there seems to be none* is already to read too much into whatever is being read. Too clever and too dense at once, too old and too young, "creative" critics like Barthes and Adorno could give creativity—and what is more popular than creative writing?—a bad name.

Tough Baby

Their international *éclat* may efface Adorno's and Barthes's less glamorous pedagogical commitments, but both of them, in their writing, return to the classroom as a privileged scene of intimidation, a paradigm—or nursery—for the violence of an extramural order that depends heavily, if not exclusively, on mass culture to lay down its laws. "They who could not put together a correct sentence," Adorno poignantly recalls, "but found all of mine too long—did they not abolish German literature and replace it by their 'writ' [Schrifttum]? . . . In Fascism the nightmare of childhood has come true" (Minima Moralia, 193). Adorno is not too homophobic, or he is just homophobic enough, to be able to observe, moreover: "A child who prefers to listen to serious music or practise the piano will have to suffer as a 'sissy' in his class or in the other groups to which he belongs and which embody far more authority than parents or teacher" (Prisms, 131).

So, in addition to a general infantile histrionics of the fragment, Barthes and Adorno produce particular scenes from childhood, in which childhood itself emerges, anything but innocently, as the schoolroom where, with or without "parents or teacher," a whole aesthetic education, a whole pedagogy of the sophisticated, the naive, and (perhaps most important of all) the faux-naïf, gets enforced. At first glance, these scenes seem almost too readable: the stage appears to have been set, as in so many after-school specials, European-style, so as to pit a highly individualized high-cultural sensitivity against a crudely undifferentiated, indeed massified, anticulture that exists only to terrorize it. High culture for the sissy, mass culture for the gang, whose members, it goes without saying, can never be anything but regular guys. "Virile/non-virile: this famous pair," Barthes asserts, "which rules over the entire Doxa, sums up all the ploys of alternation [tous les jeux d'alternance]" (Roland Barthes, p. 133; p. 136).

But these ploys of alternation remain ploys of alternation, whose wiliness neither Barthes nor Adorno fails to grasp. The relations between a virile mass culture and an epicene high culture, they give us to understand, obey a logic not of simple hierarchical opposition but of complicity, subterfuge, and cross-identification. Following up on his claim that "there is an amor intellectualis for kitchen personnel" (Minima Moralia, 28), Adorno, for example, writes:

> Someone appalled by the good breeding of his parents will seek refuge in the kitchen, basking in the cook's vitality that secretly reflects the principle of the parental good breeding. The refined are drawn to the unrefined [Die feinen Leute zieht es zu den unfeinen], whose coarseness deceptively promises what their own culture denies. They do not know that the indelicacy that appears to them as anarchic nature, is nothing but a reflex-action produced by the compulsion they struggle to resist. . . . Bettelheim's observation on the identification of the victims of the Nazi camps with their executioners implies

a verdict on the higher nurseries of social horticulture, the English public school, the German military academy. Topsy-turviness perpetuates itself: domination is propagated by the dominated. (*Minima Moralia*, 183; 206)

Whatever the merit of "Bettelheim's observation," which has by now attained the status of an obscene commonplace, Adorno's uncovering of the hidden solidarities of "the refined" and "the unrefined" would, among other things, remind us not to take mass culture as a culture of, by, or for the masses. Perhaps we hardly need to be reminded, as by so heavy-handed a coinage as "the culture industry," of what is so obvious— though high-bourgeois fascination with a foul-mouthed lumpenproletariat (especially when nonwhite) has, if anything, gained intensity in the ongoing romance with the real sustained not just by the "cultural elite" of Hollywood but also by the academy. The endless psychic and economic transactions between "the dominated," construed as essentially virile, and "the dominant," construed as essentially nonvirile, define a slippery space of mass-cultural fantasy irreducible, at any rate, to the more familiar scenarios of schoolyard terror.

For its part, the French lycée proves no less productive of strange bedfellows than do the English public school and the German military academy. While not explicitly addressing the question of the links between high and mass cultures, one of the most delightful anecdotes in Barthes's autobiography hints at the intricately chiastic machinery governing the attraction between the exquisitely hystericized intellectual and the brutishly normal collectivity:

> Truckling to what has an advantage over you [*Complaisance à l'égard de ce qui a barre sur vous*]; for example, at the Lycée Louis-le-Grand, I had a history professor who, requiring to be jeered as though it were a daily drug, stubbornly offered the students a thousand opportunities for making a racket: howlers, naïvetés, double entendres, ambiguous gestures, and even the melancholy with which he accompanied all this secretly provocative behavior; the students, having quickly realized this, abstained, on certain days, quite sadistically, from jeering him. (*Roland Barthes*, 150; 153)[31]

Offering a provocation of its own (in which deliberate "naïveté" becomes indistinguishable from received "sophistication") by blandly serving up the old joke about how the sadist, refusing to gratify the masochist, thus gratifies him, this passage flirts, like the professor with his students, with self-parody. But the joke may finally be on the reader too quick to assume that assuming the position of the student, in this fable, means assuming the (classically male) position of superiority. If the anecdote illustrates "truckling to what has an advantage over you," that is, it is not clear that the advantage attaches unproblematically to the sadistically jeering (and even more sadistically nonjeering) students or that the complaisance is all on the side of the melancholy, masochistically self-abasing professor.

The high degree of instability that turns many a pedagogical power relation into a version of the master/slave dialectic becomes even more acute when the already-eroticized roles of professorial sophistication and student unsophistication are so assiduously reversed. Yet, though the professor's "naïvetés" (tricked out with "double entendres, ambiguous gestures," etc.) devirilize him as surely as would the sophistications that, in their perverse artfulness, they uncannily resemble, the students are no more masters of this scene than their occasional abstention from jeering him is performatively neutral. For they do not just clinically administer (if necessary, by withholding) the "daily drug" he requires: as good consumers of his spectacle—in fact, like the stereotypically docile, addicted consumers of mass culture itself—they participate with him in a relation of codependency, needing a daily fix of their own, which only his "abject" performances can provide. And, while their all-too-social sadism, the mob violence proper to those of their age and class, thus lacks the critical bite of the bad, excessive consumer's, their implication in the sadomasochistic exchange, insofar as it compromises the credibility with which they might play this scene as the butchly normal versus the campily deviant, puts them closer to the sarcastic gourmand than one might expect. (Elsewhere in the same book, Barthes captions a photograph of himself and two classmates, all three the picture of adolescent dandyism: "In those days, lycée students were little gentlemen" [*Roland Barthes*, n.p.].) Nowhere, perhaps, is the students' own virility more loudly called into question, their own complaisance more loudly affirmed, than when, toughing it out, they give their "victim" the silent treatment. Who, one might ask, is truckling to whom?

"Ambiguous gestures" indeed. That is to say, far from meaning any number of radically indeterminate things, they tend to mean *one other thing* in particular. Or, as Barthes puts it: "Contrary to what one might expect, it is not polysemy (multiplicity of meaning) which is praised and sought out; it is quite precisely amphibology, duplicity; the fantasy is not to hear everything (anything), it is to hear *something else*" (*Roland Barthes*, 73). More often than not, as D. A. Miller has taught us to recognize, the "something else" that Barthes wants to hear (if seldom to speak) is not just sexual but specifically homosexual, even more specifically male homosexual.[32] That he wants to hear it *instead of* what usually gets said registers, of course, our culture's policy (as yet unperturbed by the recent phenomenon of an out gay presence in the cultural mainstream) of treating male homosexuality as the content most likely to be evaporated. Yet Barthes's fantasy of "double entendre," or the relative ease with which it can be realized, also testifies to that policy's not necessarily unintended effect of making gay content—which, if most likely to be evaporated, is therefore most likely to suffuse the culture—*everywhere* audible, at least for those who have ears to hear it.[33]

Or, in the language of the classroom again (where jeering, after a certain age, generally gives way to more prudently masked forms of intimidation), everything "has to be" about homosexuality, to the precise extent that nothing can be about homosexuality. Far from being the result of a contingent omission, the exiguity of overt gay content in the Euro-American "public sphere" (i.e., in the mass media) is at once among that sphere's enabling conditions and perhaps its most abundantly signifying product. As I have been suggesting, as a careful reading of Barthes and Adorno would suggest, the relation between elite criticism and mass culture bears more than a merely fortuitous similarity to that between male homosexuality and the representational order that "ambiguously" contains it. Typically relegating gay content to the status of a "tamed richness," for instance, the violence of this order constitutively requires and interminably rehearses the *internal abjection* of two figures of excess so closely related, so capable of standing in for each other, as to seem at times like twins: the gay man, of course, along with his almost equally unpopular *semblable*, the cultural intellectual—the insufferably, implacably demanding consumer who, by refusing to take his, or her, "pleasure" (at least what is advertised as such) like a man, would prevent others from taking theirs, from enjoying the illusion, that is, that they are getting what they like and liking what they get.

A regular *spoilsport*, as Adorno titles one of the fragments in *Minima Moralia*, that intellectual, currently embodied by the cultural studies academic critic, no more offends by mere intellectuality than the more obviously sexual outlaw, the gay man, offends by mere physicality.[34] For just as homophobia hates not only what gay men do in bed but also the smug contempt for family values—the presumption to know more, to know better than, say, what Newt Gingrich calls "normal Americans"— that gay sexual practices go so far as to flaunt, so anti-intellectualism hates those spoiled children whose interference with the culture industry's delivery of the goods spoils the spectator sport of consumption itself, the aggression (however passive) whereby women as well as men compete for the virilizing prize of normality, the manly distinction of undistinction.

To introduce the intellectual here is not to propose a *second* "ambiguity": it is to account for the first (especially in a social order where "anti-intellectualism reveals itself as a protest of virility" [Roland Barthes, 103]). As I argued in relation to Thackeray, homophobia both models itself on and disguises itself as a less contestably democratic-seeming antisnobbery. But even "liberal" discourses have adopted this procedure, modifying it only by further confusing snobbery with intellectuality itself. The culture industry, for one—some of whose best friends are gay—preemptively dispenses with its professional critics by seeing to it not just that they get caricatured as snobbish elitists but that, whether their criticism explicitly addresses gay issues or not, and whatever their own sexual identification, their "snobbery," like that of the villains in the recent blockbuster feature-length Disney cartoons, implicitly homosexualizes them as well.

The culture industry can dispense with these critics—it can "make [. . .] such light work of counter-arguments," as Adorno says—because it so liberally *dispenses* them, distributing them homeopathically (like the "marge" whose place within operation margarine is by no means marginal) throughout its system. When we read in "The Culture Industry" that "the enemy who is already defeated, the thinking individual, is the enemy fought" (*Dialectic*, 149), it might well occur to us that the figure of the abjected intellectual serves the culture industry in much the same way, and for many of the same reasons, that, as various gay and queer theorists have argued, the figure of the abjected homosexual serves the heterosexuality industry—the two industries having merged, in the best capitalist tradition, some time ago.[35] No need, under this double regime, for a literal-minded parade of the abjected ones—the fewer identifiable scapegoats, in fact, the better. What gets distributed throughout the en-cratic system is not so much images of intellectuals and homosexuals as a pervasive intellectual-homosexual *effect*, a kind of stylistic obscenity around and against which that system in turn organizes itself, all the while blithely pretending to be otherwise engaged.

For the genius of the system, the efficacy of its intimidation, resides in the *unspokenness* of its threat against would-be troublemakers. Though mass culture hardly prohibits the more or less open representation of gay men and intellectuals—by now, the two figures, often conveniently conflated into one, can appear as "recurring characters," even as comically endearing ones, on prime-time television—still, where "it goes without saying" remains the name of the game, saying what is *normally* unsaid, speaking what is *normally* unspoken, inevitably counts as high-risk activity in its own right, a way of "catching" the homosexuality or intellectuality one sets out merely to discuss. "All anti-intellectualism ends," Barthes writes, "in the death of language, i.e., in the destruction of sociability" (*Eiffel Tower*, 134). As all sissies know, however, and as most "thinking individuals" eventually find out, talking "too much" is itself extensively discouraged as antisocial behavior, worthy of the punishment—cruel but not unusual— of social death: the mortifying experience of speaking *and being ignored.*

Risking the charge of "paranoia"—or, even worse, of "self-pity"—these sentences, I hope, evoke the cost of intellectualizing about (i.e., ruining) the innocent fun and funniness that mass culture has in store for us. To look for homophobia and anti-intellectualism even in their apparent absence, after all, is simply to ask for trouble. Up against such menacing encratic happy talk, one might suddenly find Adorno's "humorlessness" oddly cheering [36]—cheering in the grim glee with which he diagnoses the paranoiac's problem as that of not being paranoid *enough*:

> Violence, on which civilization is based, means the persecution of all by all, and the persecution-maniac puts himself at a disadvantage only by blaming on his neighbour what is perpetrated by the whole, in a helpless attempt to make the incommensurable commensurable. He is burnt because he seeks to grasp directly, as with his bare hands, the objective delusion which he resembles, whereas the absurd order consists precisely in its perfected indirectness. He is sacrificed to safeguard the tissue of beguilement. (*Minima Moralia*, 163)

In fascism the nightmare of childhood has come true. In the less palpably violent order administered by the contemporary culture industry, however, what is most nightmarish, if you happen to be gay and/or intellectual, is not that they really are out to get you: it is that, through the "perfected indirectness" of mass entertainment, they already have you, as *the one whose pleasure must be excluded* in order for the party to go on at all.[37]

The vignettes from childhood—more precisely, from childhood and adolescence—that we discussed above helped suggest such a "dialectical" view of the relations between high culture and mass culture. Adorno's reflection on the upper-class child in the kitchen situated mass culture (easy to misrecognize as popular) within high, or dominant, culture, destroying the scene's imaginary enchantments by going behind it, behind the delighted child and the earth mother of a cook ("die Köchin," Adorno writes [p. 206]), to reveal *the parents* running the show from the wings. Mass culture's *power* to intimidate, the parable would remind us, ultimately derives not—as our own masochistic fantasies might lead us to believe—from the muscles of the mythically virile masses but from the pocketbooks of a discreetly self-absenting "organized capital." Conversely, though not symmetrically, Barthes's little scene of pedagogical humiliation allegorized the place of a certain high culture—of a certain dominated dominance—within mass culture, pointing to the latter's almost chemical dependence on an always-possible spectacle of "professorial" perversity.

Yet the fullest staging of these themes occurs in a fragment from *Minima Moralia* entitled—in the German text as well as in the English— "Tough baby." Presenting not quite a scene from childhood but, as the title indicates, a scene in which infantility plays an emblematic role, this fragment delineates a sadomasochistic pedagogy of intimidation that, in totalitarian fashion, traverses the boundary between the academy and the culture industry, between elite and mass cultures. The kindred figures of the homosexual and the intellectual loom prominently here as well— although the particular choreography in which Adorno enlists them implicates him, more unpleasantly than his initial self-reflexive pirouette would allow, in the intimidation whose features he traces:

> *Tough baby.*—There is a certain gesture of virility, be it one's own or someone else's, that calls for suspicion. It expresses independence, sureness of the power to command, the tacit complicity of all males. Earlier, this was called with awed respect the whim of the master; today it has been democratized, and film heroes show the most insignificant bank clerk how it is done. Its archetype is the handsome dinner-jacketed figure returning late to his bachelor flat, switching on the indirect lighting and mixing himself a whisky and soda: the carefully recorded hissing of the mineral water says what the arrogant mouth keeps to itself: that he despises anything that does not smell of smoke, leather, and shaving cream, particularly women, which is why they, precisely, find him irresistible. (*Minima Moralia*, 45–46)

The fragment does not end here; we will consider the sequel in a moment. For now, let us note Adorno's parodic reenactment of the suspect gesture of virility: at the same time that his sardonic sentences mock the hard-boiled body language of film noir machismo, they also insist on giving profuse, sibilant utterance to everything that "the arrogant mouth keeps to itself." Mouthing what should stay behind tight lips, putting himself on the side of an excessive orality, Adorno—whose masquerade of manliness betrays a keen eye, not just for the gestures of virility, but for its whole décor—almost comes to occupy the homosexual-intellectual position mentioned above.

Almost: as though horrified to see himself becoming a kind of George Cukor of critical theory, he now performs the contemptuous (misogynistic, homophobic) gesture of which he began by gesturing toward suspecting himself:

> If all pleasure has, preserved within it, earlier pain, then here pain, as pride in bearing it, is raised directly, untransformed, as a stereotype, to pleasure: unlike wine, each glass of whisky, each inhalation of cigar smoke, still recalls the repugnance that it cost the organism to become attuned to such strong stimuli, and this alone is registered as pleasure. He-men are thus, in their own constitution, what film-plots usually present them to be, masochists. At the root of their sadism is a lie, and only as liars do they truly become sadists, agents of repression. This lie, however, is nothing other than repressed homosexuality presenting itself as the only approved form of heterosexuality. (Minima Moralia, 46)

Winding up a tour de force of theoretical detective work with a triumphant, vulgar-Freudian unmasking of "nothing other than repressed homosexuality," Adorno provides us with another reason why he must strike us as *dated*. Here again, as in relation to class, sophistication and naïveté seem to bring out the worst in each other: in this case, where both turn on the simpleminded equation of male homosexuality with masochism, sophistication ends up looking obtusely abstract, naïveté obtusely reductive.

In such painfully reduced circumstances, Adorno cannot, for example, follow through on what might have become a deconstructive or gay-theoretical analysis of "the only approved form of heterosexuality." Yet, here again, as with the earlier bad configuration of the naive and the sophisticated, he may present us with a blessing in disguise (not just with a *blessure*). Or rather, in his continuing, and increasingly voracious, enactment of what is perhaps meant to figure as at least an *authentic* (i.e., nonhomosexual) sadism but instead realigns him with the quasi-gay exorbitance of the biting overconsumer, whose sadism is neither simply a disguised masochism nor simply an agency of repression, he offers the mixed blessing, the painful pleasure, of a homophobic performance that *outsmarts itself*. Which hardly means that the hissy fit that ensues is any the less homophobic:

> In Oxford two sorts of student are distinguished, the tough guys and the intellectuals; the latter through this contrast alone, are almost automatically equated with the effeminate. There is much reason to believe that the ruling stratum, on its way to dictatorship, becomes polarized towards these two extremes. Such disintegration is the secret of its integration, the joy of being united in the lack of joy. In the end the tough guys are the truly effeminate ones, who need the weaklings as their victims in order not to admit that they are like them. Totalitarianism and homosexuality belong together. In its downfall the subject negates everything which is not of its own kind. The opposites of the strong man and the compliant youth merge in an order which asserts unalloyed the male principle of domination. In making all without exception, even supposed subjects, its objects, this principle becomes totally passive, virtually feminine. (Minima Moralia, 46)

It would not be difficult to make an example of Adorno himself, as he has somewhat perfunctorily invited us to do, continuing the game of dialectical reversal by exposing him as the truly effeminate tough guy, under whose totalitarian gaze all differences collapse into the vast sameness where homosexuality "almost automatically" equals masochism equals passivity equals femininity equals fascism. Yet, even as Adorno's insatiably negative dialectic, devouring every apparent contradiction, seems to imitate the homosexuality that he has been busy setting up as at once a whole and a hole, the same process no less mimetically raises the possibility of a homosexuality *not* totally defined by an imperial thematics of castration. Like the wine that Adorno expressly excludes from the pharmacy of masochism, this second homosexuality signifies, not the rule according to which any man wishing to pass for normal must acquire a taste for the repugnant (learning to take it as a "daily drug"), but, on the contrary, an exception to the rule.[38] Just as Adorno's *Wein* seems to echo the baby's cry (*das Weinen*), just as "all pleasure has, preserved within it, earlier pain," so might this exceptional homosexuality stand as the very superlative of pleasure — of a pleasure whose cry, sounding undeniably like a whine, constitutes a bitter refusal of the acrid self-discipline incumbent on every candidate for the men's club.

   Out of this refusal is born another tough baby rather than the normative "straight" man that this fragment takes pains to break down. In the
manner of the butter-loving sadist of *Mythologies*, who gets richness out
of the very operation of impoverishment and so mocks the law of less is
more whereby margarine rules, this other biting child parodies the male-
homosocial "joy of being united in the lack of joy" by making lack itself
joyfully excessive. Treating himself to an orgy of erotic pessimism, getting high off his very depressiveness, Adorno homophobically fantasizes
the *more* that Barthes, not all that fantastically, ascribes to a euphorically
oral homosexuality — a homosexuality without castration: "The pleasure
potential of a perversion [*Le pouvoir de jouissance d'une perversion*] (in this case,
that of the two H.'s: homosexuality and hashish) is always underesti-
mated. Law, Science, the *Doxa* refuse to understand that perversion, quite
simply, *makes happy*; or to be more specific, it produces a *more* [*un "plus"*]:
I am more sensitive, more perceptive, more loquacious, more amused,
etc." (*Roland Barthes*, 63–64; 68).
   This *more*, moreover, resists being reduced to the more (*plus*) that is no
more (*plus*): to the more in more is less, the dreary corollary that governs
homosexual and intellectual alike under the endoxal reign of a moderation and common sense that, like the police at gay pride parades and gay
rights marches, can indeed be counted on to underestimate. As Adorno
has grotesquely shown, the composite figure of the homosexual intellectual, of the intellectual homosexual, lies embedded within a mass culture
and a high culture that themselves lie embedded within each other; thus
framed (not by Adorno alone), that figure serves ideally to reveal the dirty
secret of the masculinity that both cultures, themselves secretly united,
pretend to hold sacred, even while appearing to enjoy seeing it profaned:
the secret of the narcissistically totalizing domination that is "really" passivity, of the strength that is "really" weakness. It fails, however, to go
without saying that the more of intellectual-homosexual perversion — of
"good drugs" like wine and hashish — does not necessarily come down
to the anti-intellectually, homophobically prescribed more — linked with
"bad drugs" like whisky and tobacco — that is always less.[39] Since what
seems far more obvious, in fact, is the suspicion that being "more sensitive, more perceptive, more loquacious, more amused, etc." only reinforces one's internal abjection, perhaps we need "to be more specific"
yet about how perversion (to the dismay of many, it would please us to
say) *makes happy*.

Medusa

From *Roland Barthes*, another memory of youth and intimidation:

> The *Doxa* is current opinion, meaning repeated *as if nothing had hap-*
> *pened*. It is Medusa: who petrifies those who look at her [*ceux qui la*
> *regardent*] Which means that it is evident. Is it seen? Not even that:
> a gelatinous mass which sticks onto the retina. The remedy? As an
> adolescent I went swimming one day at Malo-les-Bains, in a cold sea
> infested with a kind of jellyfish we call medusas (what aberration
> led me to agree to swim there? I was one of a group, which justifies
> any cowardice); it was so ordinary to come out of the water covered
> with stings and blisters that the locker-room attendant phlegmati-
> cally handed you a bottle of potassium chloride as soon as you left
> the beach. In the same way, one might conceive of taking a (perverse)
> pleasure [*un plaisir (retors)*] in the endoxal products of mass culture,
> provided that when you left the immersion of that culture [*pourvu*
> *qu'au sortir d'un bain de cette culture*], someone handed you on each occa-
> sion, as if nothing had happened, a little detergent discourse. (p. 122;
> p. 126)

What is most perverse here—aside from the phlegmatic ease with which
the scene's atmosphere of teen eroticism *almost* gets allegorized away—is
the particular lesson that Barthes draws from this remembrance of stings
past. Proceeding, in this respect as well, "as if nothing had happened," he
seems to forget both that at least one of his major books (I am thinking
of *Mythologies*) is devoted precisely to "taking (perverse) pleasure in the
endoxal products of mass culture" and that, far from depending on the
obliteration effected by a "detergent discourse," this pleasure derives from
subjecting such a discourse (see, for a literal instance, "Soap Powders and
Detergents," in *Mythologies*), or any other cleansing agent, to the author's
own hypermaterializing sting—or countersting—operation. Repeatedly
assailed by a *Doxa* that, itself knowing no precept other than "as if nothing had happened," redoubles its insistent violence by blandly denying it,
Barthes, as we have seen, seeks not so much a "remedy" as revenge: more
sadist than masochist, this stung, blistered, *toughened* baby would turn pain
into pleasure by turning it back on its source.

But what compels Barthes to wash his mouth out with soap in the first
place? Why does he suppress his own oral history, preferring to dream
up a recipe for (perverse) pleasure that he has never bothered to put into

practice? Perhaps Barthes, anticipating the wariness of a cultural studies that will need to hold him at arm's length, contemplates recasting himself retroactively as, for example—to take up a hint dropped earlier—the sadly masochistic professor from the lycée, a safer stereotype of academic perversity, after all, than the more aggressively unvirile master of sarcasm responsible for writing *Mythologies*, among other texts. Or perhaps—more productively—Barthes's incorporative imitation of the *Doxa*'s detergent discourse signals a fantasized identification with mass culture inherent in his parodic aggression *against* it. To be more specific: insofar as the identification is fantasized, so is mass culture. That is, Barthes's perverse pleasure entails a fantasmatic exchange: if he assumes mass culture's "innocence" here, he reciprocally invests it with what (no longer assisting him in perversely cleaning up his act) we will call not his perversity but his perversion.

For though Barthes fails to include jellyfish—to be sure, hardly a staple of French cuisine—in the list of (conspicuously bourgeois) likes and dislikes that makes for one of the most appetizing moments in his autobiography, the fragment I have been discussing, entitled "Medusa," in fact goes on to imagine eating the *Doxa* thus figured, both confirming our sense of Barthes's identification with it and evincing that identification's homosexual-intellectual agenda:

> Queen and sister of the hideous Gorgons, Medusa was of a rare beauty with regard to the luster of her hair. Neptune having ravished and wed her in the temple of Minerva, the latter rendered her repulsive and transformed her hair into snakes.
>
> (It is true that in the *Doxa*'s discourse there are former beauties sleeping, the memory of a once-sumptuous and fresh wisdom [*le souvenir d'une sagesse somptueuse et fraîche autrefois*]; and it is indeed Athena, the wise deity, who takes her revenge by making the *Doxa* into a caricature of wisdom.)
>
> Medusa, or the Spider: castration. Which *stuns* me, an effect produced by a scene I hear but do not see: my hearing is frustrated of its vision: I remain *behind the door.*
>
> The *Doxa* speaks, I hear it, but I am not within its space. A man of paradox, like any writer, I am indeed *behind the door*; certainly I should like to pass through, certainly I should like to see what is being said, I too participate in the communal scene; I am constantly *listening to what I am excluded from*; I am in a stunned state, dazed, cut off from the popularity of language. (*Roland Barthes*, 122–23; 127).

Barthes's theme, it would seem *evident*, is not identification but exclusion—exclusion, moreover, that just as obviously advertises itself as "castration." Frozen impotently "*behind the door*," "cut off from the popularity of language," longing pathetically to "participate in the communal scene" from which he is barred, Barthes appears to have pulled out all the stops in taking on the mythic role not just of "any writer" but of the writer as homosexual as eunuch. So much gusto does he devote to framing and inhabiting this melodramatic tableau, in fact, that he might even be said to *chew the scenery*: in other words, to negate performatively the exclusion that he performs.

And what is this communal scene that the "man of paradox" can hear but not see? While its mythological décor heavily suggests the primal repetition of all-too-familiar heterosexual violence (rape, jealousy, revenge, castration), a paradoxical counterplot is busy cutting through this doxical caricature. As if rewriting it, at any rate, by reviving the communal scene of adolescence from the first part of the fragment, as if bringing back the group of swimmers from the lethe of abstraction to which allegory appeared to confine them, as if washing away only the blistering language of "aberration" and "cowardice," in short, as if "as if nothing had happened" hadn't happened, Barthes sets about not merely recalling but thereby projectively awakening and restoring the "former beauties sleeping" in the *Doxa*'s discourse. Refusing to view the *Doxa* simply as what is so obvious as to be invisible, Barthes, like a generous god, even like a fairy godfather, if only for a moment changes Medusa back from "a gelatinous mass which sticks onto the retina" to the embodiment of the "sumptuous and fresh wisdom" that she once was. "Queen and sister of the hideous Gorgons," "of a rare beauty with regard to the luster of her hair," she becomes, in this brief but extraordinary flashback, that gay archetype that even mass culture has not entirely forgotten: the ugly duckling who, finding the right swimming companions, finds herself to be a beautiful swan.

After this reverse metamorphosis, then, Barthes's enactment of "castration" indeed strikes one as *hysterical*—that is to say, unconvincing, dissembling, the displaced representation of some other scene. "Medusa, or the Spider: castration. Which *stuns* me. . . ." Stunned by castration? Though castration may well be stunning, this response, with its slight suggestion that the castration is happening to someone else, seems a bit estranged, a bit *beside the point* (if not *behind the door*). "I am in a stunned state, dazed, cut off from the popularity of language." Stunned? Or stoned? Medusa's petrifying effect, of course, precisely blurs the distinction between the two states; yet the sumptuousness and freshness of Barthes's language in the previous paragraphs, and even its hammy parataxis here (another manifestation of Barthes's "taste . . . for the rush"), evoke, say, *jouissance* far more than subjective destitution. Barthes insists on masquerading as a figure of lack so as to disguise the *more* of perversion as the *less* of castration.[40] By complaining, "My hearing is frustrated of its vision," "I hear but do not see," etc., by reducing himself to a blinded audition, he would render innocent his more consequential fantasmatic activity as a prodigious *mouth*, capable not only of releasing the *Doxa*'s hidden flavor but also — in the very "generosity" of this operation antimargarine — of taking the wise (if non-Minervan) revenge of making a sumptuous feast out of what stings him.

The scene from which Barthes purports to have been excluded, we might say, is all the while playing itself out, more richly, within his own oral theater. Unlike the false exteriority or internal abjection to which mass culture assigns homosexual-intellectual contestation, the false exteriority that Barthes claims to occupy here results from his own masking of the counteraggression with which he reconstitutes the figures of mass culture's masked intimidation. But, while he may thus foreshadow, after all, the current cultural studies compulsion to *make nice*, his guilty feelings attest, beyond what Bettelheim might call his identification with the oppressor, his far greater desire to get the oppressor to identify with him. Consider, from *Roland Barthes*, another fragment, titled "The Fear of Language," in which Barthes confesses, in a slightly coy third person, to "a guilty emotion of jargon":

> Writing a certain text, he experiences a guilty emotion of jargon, as if he could not escape from a mad discourse no matter how individual [*particulier*] he made his utterance: and what if all his life *he had chosen the wrong language?* He is all the more readily overcome by this panic here (in U.) where, staying home at night, he watches television a good deal; here is continually represented (remonstrated) a public language from which he is separated; this language interests him, but this interest is not reciprocal: to the television public, his own language would seem entirely unreal (and outside of aesthetic delight [*hors de la jouissance esthétique*], any unreal language is likely to be ridiculous). (pp. 114–15; pp. 118–19)

Barthes would seem guilty of nothing so much as overacting again — unless we recognize his "separation" from the language of mass culture as an alibi (one of his favorite words) for his ferocious ingestion and enriching perversion of that language, a crime that can be traced back at least as far

as *Mythologies*. The television public, Barthes claims, has failed to recipro-
cate his "interest" in it; but his interest has already led him to avenge that
failure by making mass culture over in his own naively sophisticated (i.e.,
perverted) image.

Fully understandable in light of this crime, Barthes's fear of his own
language is precisely a fear of jargon: in particular, the jargon that becomes all the more inescapable the more one tries to particularize one's
utterance; the jargon that, more choosing than "chosen," marks one as
belonging to the social group we might call the professionals of *jouissance esthétique*, the class of those who, instead of simply finding another
language "ridiculous," know how to infuse it with the more of (their)
perversion, as though appropriating it for their own theater of the ridiculous, in which, no longer pretending to ignore them, it finally, utopically
caters to their immoderate, unreasonable, expensive tastes. Ultimately,
then, Barthes's crime consists of his complicity in a discourse less "mad"
than privileged: what offends in the act of reading too much into other
people's language is that it implies *having too much* to read into it to begin
with. Nor is it quite the case, in late-twentieth-century U.S. culture anyway, that the *Doxa* takes no interest in the jargon of the privileged and the
perverted, a discourse it indeed represents (remonstrates) as "mad," so as
not to be driven mad itself by an invidious, unbearable suspicion: that
"excessive" cultural capital affords "excessive" happiness.

Not that the critic of mass culture feels no pain or that, falling short
of madness, he rises above anger: as I have been emphasizing, the delight
that impels Barthes and Adorno as critics comes from their vindictive re-
staging (reversing) of scenes of intimidation that they cannot help taking
personally.[41] But who believes that what most disturbs the *Doxa* of contemporary cultural studies is the display of an anger (as distinguished from
a sadism) for which politically respectable reasons can almost always be
adduced? More scandalous than any such "healthy" rage is visible possession of the means to make good on it. Biting back at mass culture
by desublimating its tamed richness, that is, presupposes the inheritance
of a richness less alimentary than socioeconomic (which is not to say
that these two richnesses can ever be isolated from each other). Eager, of
course, to play the scandal down, if not to cover it up, the spokespeople,
or admissions officers, for cultural studies tend to promote it as a genially
capacious, radically heterogeneous *antischool*, where equal opportunities
for all kinds of individual and collective creativity and decoding minimize
the possibility that some people will appear to be enjoying themselves at
the expense of others.

Though undoubtedly as overdetermined as any phobia, fear of academic jargon, then, inevitably bespeaks a knowledge of something scandalously unshocking: that the unequal distribution of wealth translates itself into an unequal distribution of *pleasures*. As we have noted, journalism, especially journalism of a culturally ambitious (i.e., emphatically antiscandalous) stripe, furnishes abundant evidence of this knowledge in its resentful register; cultural studies itself expresses it in its guilty one. Theatrically avowing his susceptibility of this knowledge, which leaves him guilt ridden to the point of "panic," Barthes, throughout his career, no less theatrically repeats the crime (identical, we have seen, with its punishment: "We are condemned . . . always to speak *excessively* about reality") for which his panic attack doesn't exactly make amends. The remainder of *Roland Barthes* alone amply demonstrates that what the fear of jargon produces is more jargon, as though fear—like jargon itself, according to some who would prohibit it—were an ecstasy-inducing drug. Barthes keeps on fearing his language so much that, terror stricken, he keeps on reveling in it, positively flaunting his indulgence in the luxury of cultural criticism, in cultural criticism *as* luxury.[42]

As Lee Edelman has argued, luxury—"defiant luxury," not least the luxury of intellectual analysis—may be a necessity for gay politics in the face of pervasive hostility toward "the 'narcissism' and 'passivity' that figure the place of gay male sexuality in the Western cultural imaginary."[43] To be sure, not all practitioners of cultural studies are gay; nor can the media's resentful fascination with the "excessiveness" of gay sex be reduced simply to their resentful fascination with the "excessiveness" of the cultural critic's cultural capital. Yet, as we have remarked, anti-intellectual and antigay ideologies are often "naive" enough to collaborate, sensing between *jouissance esthétique* and *jouissance érotique* so close an affinity that sexual gayness and intellectual happiness can seem wonderfully to indict each other, even or especially once pathologized as the mores that are really less. Indeed, it is against this incessant work of underestimation, of detraction—this caricatural violence whereby Medusa herself, so far quite successfully, fends off insane jealousy—that cultural studies, like the gay politics to which it is more than analogically related, must assert not only the extravagance of its pleasures but their exceptionality as well.[44] If it imagines itself as intervening effectively in what *Media Spectacles* calls "cultural conflicts," at any rate, cultural studies should stop playing into the hands of the *Doxa* by disavowing its pursuit of a happiness exceeding the mass enjoyment ("Must-see TV!") that mass culture everywhere implicitly prescribes as the normal, normative experience of itself.

Sophisticated even to the extent of feeling guilty about their sophistication, Barthes and Adorno set a more encouraging example through their insistence on, and their insistence on dramatizing, its provocative potential. "Political slogans, designed for mass manipulation," writes Adorno, "unanimously stigmatize as 'luxury,' 'snobbism,' and 'highbrow,' everything cultural which displeases the commissars" (Prisms, 26). Prevented by his own homophobia from connecting this stigmatized luxury with gay sexuality, Adorno (with Horkheimer) embodies exceptional, unbearable happiness in the convergent figures, not of the intellectual and the homosexual, but of the intellectual and the Jew:

> The thought of happiness without power is unbearable because it would then be true happiness. The illusory conspiracy of corrupt Jewish bankers financing Bolshevism is a sign of innate impotence, just as the good life is a sign of happiness. The image of the intellectual is in the same category: he appears to think—a luxury which the others cannot afford—and he does not manifest the sweat of toil and physical effort. Bankers and intellectuals, money and mind, the exponents of circulation, form the impossible ideal of those who have been maimed by domination, an image used by domination to perpetuate itself. (Dialectic, 172)[45]

Not only does Adorno fail to invoke homosexuality as an image of happy luxury: as we might have feared, homosexuality's official role in the essay in which this passage appears ("Elements of Anti-Semitism") is that of castrato cum whipping boy. Never does gay bashing look more "theoretically sophisticated," more distingué, than in Adorno's hands. Yet, tempting though it may therefore be to get rid of him, let us think twice before throwing out the tough baby with the bathwater. Especially given the current interest in articulating Jewishness with queerness with cultural studies, and especially given his own commentary on Proust, Adorno's theorizing of luxury in terms of Jewish and intellectual happiness, while it cries out for gay-affirmative triangulation, might itself enrich any gay-affirmative rereading of "narcissism" and "passivity."

In the "Medusa" fragment, Barthes dreams of bathing in mass culture: "pourvu qu'au sortir d'un bain de cette culture. . . ." Sign and site of infancy, femininity, sensuality, orientality—of "happiness without power"—the bath may serve here to emblematize the luxurious experience of mass culture, an experience not of cleansing but of contamination: the contamination of mass culture by "everything cultural which displeases the commissars." In their Proustian sophistication or second naïveté, Barthes and Adorno refuse to be merely "images used by domination to perpetuate itself." For insofar as the thought of it is "unbearable," the "impossible ideal" of happiness without power enjoys a certain power of its own, not unlike le pouvoir de jouissance d'une perversion. But this narcissistic, passive power cannot be subsumed by, or reconciled with, the pluralistic consensus, the happy law of chacun à son goût, now operative in cultural studies. Adorno and Barthes rarely underestimate the power that would underestimate theirs: they take seriously mass culture's function as a commissariat— only somewhat less sarcastically and sinisterly, a ministry—of pleasure, where what gets administered is not "all kinds of" pleasure but just enough pleasure and no more. For Adorno and Barthes, indeed, it is as though, despite mass culture's frigid impersonality, we were required to please it as much as it is supposed to please us, as though our horror of displeasing it—say, by asking for other kinds of pleasure, or for more pleasure—were enough to make us keep our mouths shut.

Taking more, of course, Adorno and Barthes seem to take away: taking pleasure, they seem to deprive others of theirs. Happiness without power, some might say, has too much power.[46] Hence the discomfort with which cultural studies today regards Adorno and Barthes. As I suggested at the beginning of this chapter, however, that discomfort does not necessarily result in any abdication of the power, or the pleasure, that eloquence and erudition both signify and make possible. Nor should it: where cultural conflicts revolve around the power of pleasure, and where mass culture's "populism" means restricted pleasure for everyone, cultural studies is by no means alone in needing all the excess it can get.

Notes

Introduction

1   There is a book-length study of sophistication: Mark Backman's *Sophistication: Rhetoric and the Rise of Self-Consciousness* (Woodbridge, Conn.: Ox Bow, 1991). Backman's book usefully relates sophistication to the Greek sophists and to sophistry, from which it is etymologically derived. Unfortunately, the book is short on concrete analysis and compelling argumentation and long on emptily Olympian wisdom and universalizing "philosophical" grandiosity ("Paradoxically, our sophistication has led to a weakening of confidence in the order and meaning of life" [p. 168]). In the works from which I have learned most about sophistication, its treatment is sophisticated but not "sustained"; i.e., these works are either essays rather than books or studies in which sophistication is considered as an adjunct or subcategory of some more prominently featured topic. Aside from the work of Pierre Bourdieu, which I discuss below—explaining that, for all its importance to this project, his book on distinction is *not* a book on sophistication—my main sources of inspiration include Lee Edelman, "Imagining the Homosexual: *Laura* and the Other Face of Gender," in *Homographesis: Essays in Gay Literary and Cultural Theory* (New York: Routledge, 1994), 192–241; D. A. Miller, "Sontag's Urbanity," *October* 49 (Summer 1989): 91–101; John Kucich, *The Power of Lies: Transgression in Victorian Fiction* (Ithaca, N.Y.: Cornell University Press, 1994); and Eve Kosofsky Sedgwick, *Epistemology of the Closet* (Berkeley and Los Angeles: University of California Press, 1990).

2   Amy M. Spindler, "Gucci Reinvents Jet-Set Sophistication," *New York Times*, 7 March 1996, C13.

3   Tim Dean, "Sex and Syncope," *Raritan* 25 (Winter 1996): 86.

4   Pierre Bourdieu, *Distinction: A Social Critique of the Judgment of Taste*, trans. Richard Nice (Cambridge, Mass.: Harvard University Press, 1984), 1.

5   In *Cultural Capital: The Problem of Literary Canon Formation* (Chicago: University of Chicago Press, 1993), 325–40, John Guillory offers an incisive critique of Bourdieu's exposure of the "impurity" of aesthetic pleasure, arguing "that the *specificity* of aesthetic experience is not contingent upon its purity" (p. 336). I have found Guillory's critique helpful in my thinking about Bourdieu's tendency to conclude that it is enough simply to reveal (i.e., to discredit) a given aesthetic practice or attitude as socially motivated.

6   "Je retournai vivement la tête vers Saint-Loup pour ne pas être reconnu de l'étrange

gourmet" (Marcel Proust, Le Côté de Guermantes, in A la recherche du temps perdu, ed. Jean-Yves Tadié et al. [Paris: Gallimard, 1987], 2:701). I discuss this passage and this phrase in the Proust chapter.

7   Bourdieu, Distinction, 493.

8   Ibid., 492. The Kant text from which Bourdieu is quoting is "Conjectural Beginnings of Human History," in On History, ed. L. W. Beck (Indianapolis: Bobbs-Merrill, 1963), 55–56.

9   See Bourdieu, Distinction, 260–317.

10   Louis Marin, Food for Thought, trans. Mette Hjort (Baltimore: Johns Hopkins University Press, 1989), 125.

11   For a lucid account of the naturalizing of taste in aesthetic discourse, see Barbara Herrnstein Smith, Contingencies of Value: Alternative Perspective for Critical Theory (Cambridge, Mass.: Harvard University Press, 1988), 72–77.

12   David Hume, "Of the Delicacy of Taste and Passion," in Selected Essays, ed. Stephen Copley and Andrew Edgar (Oxford: Oxford University Press, 1993), 11.

13   Immanuel Kant, Critique of Judgment, trans. Werner S. Pluhar (Indianapolis: Hackett, 1987), 52.

14   Jean Anthelme Brillat-Savarin, The Physiology of Taste, or Meditations on Transcendental Gastronomy, trans. M. F. K. Fisher (San Francisco: North Point, 1986), 44.

15   On the dangers of conviviality, on the way the possibility of cannibalism remains a determining subtext of the most advanced customs of communal eating, see Margaret Visser, The Rituals of Dinner: The Origins, Evolution, Eccentricities, and Meaning of Table Manners (New York: Grove Weidenfeld, 1991).

16   Marcel Proust, Time Regained, in Remembrance of Things Past, trans. C. K. Scott Moncrieff, Terence Kilmartin, and Andreas Mayor (New York: Vintage, 1982), 3:1068.

17   J. Laplanche and J.-B. Pontalis, The Language of Psycho-Analysis, trans. Donald Nicholson-Smith (London: Hogarth, 1983), 212.

18   Roland Barthes, "Reading Brillat-Savarin," in The Rustle of Language, trans. Richard Howard (New York: Hill & Wang, 1986), 251.

19   The canonical work here is Judith Butler, Gender Trouble: Feminism and the Subversion of Identity (New York: Routledge, 1990). See also Diana Fuss, Identification Papers (New York: Routledge, 1995).

20   Butler, Gender Trouble, 71.

21   Jacques Derrida, "Foreword: Fors: The Anglish Words of Nicolas Abraham and Maria Torok," trans. Barbara Johnson, in The Wolf Man's Magic Word: A Cryptonymy, by Nicholas Abraham and Maria Torok, trans. Nicholas Rand (Minneapolis: University of Minnesota Press, 1986), xxxviii.

22   Kucich, The Power of Lies, 34.

23   For an analysis of nineteenth-century fiction that achieves remarkable results by placing Austen, not on its periphery, but at its vital center, see Mary Ann O'Farrell, Telling Complexions: The Nineteenth-Century English Novel and the Blush (Durham, N.C.: Duke University Press, 1997).

24   Edward Rothstein, "Jane Austen Meets Mr. Right," New York Times, 10 December 1995, sec. 4, 1.

1   Delicacy and Disgust, Mourning and Melancholia,
Privilege and Perversity: Pride and Prejudice

1   *Jane Austen's Letters to Her Sister Cassandra and Others* (hereafter cited as *Letters*), ed. R. W. Chapman, 2 vols. (Oxford: Clarendon, 1932), 2:299–300.

2   On this aesthetic (which, the author is at pains to show, is by no means merely an aesthetic), see Bourdieu, *Distinction*. One of Bourdieu's central theses is that "taste classifies, and it classifies the classifier. Social subjects, classified by their classifications, distinguish themselves by the distinctions they make, between the beautiful and the ugly, the distinguished and the vulgar, in which their position in the objective classifications is expressed or betrayed" (p. 6).

3   The phrase "rectitude and delicacy" describes Jane Bennet (*Pride and Prejudice*, ed. Tony Tanner [Harmondsworth: Penguin, 1980], 168). (Subsequent references to the novel are to Tanner's edition and will be included parenthetically in the text.) Austen thought Elizabeth Darcy "as delightful a creature as ever appeared in print" (*Letters*, 2:297), but one does not have to endorse the snobbery of a Miss Bingley to notice in Elizabeth some of that "want of propriety" (p. 228) that Darcy observes in almost everyone else in her family. As even a sympathetic critic like Claudia Johnson has to admit, "Elizabeth's wit is occasionally marked by an unabashed rusticity bordering on the vulgar"; Johnson also remarks that Elizabeth's "celebrated liveliness" "verg[es] sometimes on unladylike athleticism" (*Jane Austen: Women, Politics, and the Novel* [Chicago: University of Chicago Press, 1988], 76). As for Darcy, it is significant that, while he makes a favorable first impression, before long "his manners gave a disgust which turned the tide of his popularity" (p. 58).

4   D. A. Miller, "The Late Jane Austen," *Raritan* 10 (Summer 1990): 79. Miller's sumptuously suggestive reading of Austen's body politics has provided me with abundant food for thought. Other critiques of Austen's marriage plot include, e.g., Joseph Allen Boone, *Tradition Counter Tradition: Love and the Form of Fiction* (Chicago: University of Chicago Press, 1987), 89–96; Franco Moretti, *The Way of the World: The "Bildungsroman" in European Culture*, trans. Albert Sbragia (London: Verso, 1987), 15–73; and Mary Poovey, *The Proper Lady and the Woman Writer: Ideology as Style in the Works of Mary Wollstonecraft, Mary Shelley, and Jane Austen* (Chicago: University of Chicago Press, 1984), 194–207.

5   An example of the incoherences that occasionally beset this discourse of reduction appears in an article by Gina Kolata, entitled "Squeezing Fat, Calories, Guilt, and More Profits out of Junk Food," on the "Ideas and Trends" page of the *New York Times* "Week in Review" section (11 August 1991, E5). On the one hand, " 'It is very clear that the consumer wants low-fat and low-calorie foods—there is no question about that,' said Nomi Ghez, an analyst at Goldman Sachs who follows the food industry." On the other hand (several paragraphs later), " 'We have been telling people for decades to give up most meats and dairy products, to eat vegetables, grains and fruits,' said Dr. Adam Drewnowski, the director of the human nutrition program at the University of Michigan. 'But this is not happening. People seem to be not entirely thrilled about eating naturally low-calorie foods like broccoli and grains. They turn up their noses and say, How about some chocolate chip cookies?' "

6   Patricia Parker, *Literary Fat Ladies: Rhetoric, Gender, Property* (New York: Methuen, 1987).

7   See, e.g., Eve Kosofsky Sedgwick, "Jane Austen and the Masturbating Girl," *Critical Inquiry* 17 (Summer 1991): 818–37.

8   Jacques Derrida, "Foreword: Fors," xxxviii. This chapter's epigraph, which I have just incorporated partially into the text, is from Derrida, "Economimesis," trans. Richard Klein, Diacritics 11 (Summer 1981): 23. The text, an analysis of Kant's aesthetics, informs my reference below to the relation between disgust and vicariousness.

9   For a shrewd discussion of incorporation in terms of "the melancholia of gender," see Butler, Gender Trouble, 57–72. Butler's account is extremely helpful in its inflection of psychoanalytic theorizing toward a more searching analysis of the politics of gender and sexuality. My highly condensed remarks on incorporation owe much to her impressive synthesis and reorientation of a number of Freudian and post-Freudian texts.

10 See John Kucich, "Transgression in Trollope: Dishonesty and the Antibourgeois Elite," ELH 56 (Fall 1989): 593–618. In my thinking about the genealogy and the dynamics of middle-class sophistication, I am greatly indebted to Kucich's essay—which appears, in revised form, in his The Power of Lies. For an excellent account of the essentially defensive function of Elizabeth's "playfulness," see Poovey, The Proper Lady, 196–99.

11 The term middle-class aristocracy comes from Nancy Armstrong, Desire and Domestic Fiction: A Political History of the Novel (New York: Oxford University Press, 1987), 160. For an account of Austen's role in articulating that "paradoxical configuration" (p. 160), see pp. 134–60. In his reading of Pride and Prejudice, Moretti's The Way of the World also provides a helpful analysis of the symbolic marriage between the middle class and the aristocracy.

12 I allude here to Julia Kristeva, Powers of Horror: An Essay on Abjection, trans. Leon S. Roudiez (New York: Columbia University Press, 1982).

13 According to R. W. Chapman, stout in Austen "perhaps never = fat"; but he indicates one possible exception in her letters, and one could adduce others (see Letters, vol. 2, index VII ["Jane Austen's English"], n.p.). As D. A. Miller would remind us, however, the economy of scapegoating virtually requires that any fat-affirmative gesture we glimpse here be accompanied by a compensatory violence against the "slight, thin" body: on "the aggression that the diminutive woman suffers in Austen no less than the large," see Miller, "The Late Jane Austen," 62–64. On the fat (female) body as "an alternative body-identity fantasy" in recent gay male culture, see Michael Moon and Eve Kosofsky Sedgwick, "Divinity: A Dossier, a Performance Piece, a Little-Understood Emotion," Discourse 13 (Fall–Winter 1990–91): 13. The notion of "chunks of literality" (p. 36) elaborated in that essay has had a stimulating effect on my thinking about fatty residues in Austen. I am further indebted to Michael Moon for the felicitous term revolting criticism, which he used as the title for a session at the 1990 Modern Language Association convention and which I echo at the end of this chapter.

14 See Norbert Elias, The History of Manners: The Civilizing Process, vol. 1, trans. Edmund Jephcott (New York: Pantheon, 1978). On the function of the lower bodily stratum in middle-class culture, see Peter Stallybrass and Allon White, The Politics and Poetics of Transgression (Ithaca, N.Y.: Cornell University Press, 1986).

15 For an acid and deliberately reductive reading of Derrida's sophisticated vulgarity, see Bourdieu, Distinction, 494–500.

16 Stallybrass and White, The Politics and Poetics of Transgression, 202, 201.

17 On the activist/elitist binarism in gay studies, see Lee Edelman, "The Mirror and the Tank: 'AIDS,' Subjectivity, and the Rhetoric of Activism," in Homographesis, 93–117. For an example of how this binarism gets framed and circulated, see Jeffrey Escoffier, "Inside the Ivory Closet," Out/Look 10 (Fall 1990): 40–48.

18 For an extensive and richly nuanced analysis of how the homophobically constructed gay man can figure as the "other face" of the heterosexual woman, see Edelman's "Imagining the Homosexual," 192–241.

19 Readers of Bourdieu's *Distinction* will recognize that I allude here to his differentiation between dominant and dominated fractions of the dominant class and to his elaboration of the conflict between those class fractions.

2 Bon Chic, Bon Genre: Sophistication and History in Northanger Abbey

1 Armstrong, *Desire and Domestic Fiction*, 106.

2 Ibid.

3 Although the novel was published posthumously in 1817, Anne Ehrenpreis cites Austen's sister Cassandra as claiming that it was "written about the years 98 and 99." Ehrenpreis also notes that a version of the novel may have been "drafted as early as 1794" and that, according to the author's "Advertisement," the work was "finished in the year 1803." (See the introduction to Ehrenpreis's edition of *Northanger Abbey* [Harmondsworth: Penguin, 1972], 9–10; further references to this work will be included parenthetically in the text.)

4 Armstrong, *Desire and Domestic Fiction*, 160.

5 For an example of the framing of Austen as transitional, see Raymond Williams, *The English Novel: From Dickens to Lawrence* (New York: Oxford University Press, 1970), 61. For a critique of the opposition between Austenian "worldliness" and Brontëan interiority, see my *Caught in the Act: Theatricality in the Nineteenth-Century English Novel* (Berkeley and Los Angeles: University of California Press, 1992), chap. 2, esp. pp. 27–29. For an astute and suggestive account of the production of a certain middle-class sophistication in Trollope, see Kucich, "Transgression in Trollope." On the curious variability of views about Austen's class position, see Johnson, *Jane Austen*, xviii. An extensive discussion of class, gender, and ideology in Austen may be found in Poovey, *The Proper Lady*.

6 This reference to "professorial taste" is perhaps the first signal of the considerable influence, throughout the present chapter, of Bourdieu's *Distinction*. In some sense, my comments on "history" here represent an extension of certain themes broached in my "Back to the Future: A Review-Article on the New Historicism, Deconstruction, and Nineteenth-Century Fiction," *Texas Studies in Literature and Language* 30 (Spring 1988): 120–49. Since I wrote that article, my thinking about the politics of the new historicism has been affected importantly by Alan Liu, "The Power of Formalism: The New Historicism," *ELH* 56 (Winter 1989): 721–71; and by Stanley Fish, "Commentary: The Young and the Restless," in *The New Historicism*, ed. H. Aram Veeser (New York: Routledge, 1989), 303–16.

7 Avrom Fleishman, "The Socialization of Catherine Morland," *ELH* 41 (1974): 666. For other versions of this "dialectical" reading, see, e.g., Sandra M. Gilbert and Susan Gubar, *The Madwoman in the Attic: The Woman Writer and the Nineteenth-Century Literary Imagination* (New Haven, Conn.: Yale University Press, 1979), 128–45; Johnson, *Jane Austen*, 28–48; George Levine, *The Realistic Imagination: English Fiction from Frankenstein to Lady Chatterley* (Chicago: University of Chicago Press, 1981); and Judith Wilt, *Ghosts of the Gothic: Austen, Eliot, and Lawrence* (Princeton, N.J.: Princeton University Press, 1980), 121–72.

8   Wilt, *Ghosts of the Gothic*, 127.

9   On the link between realism and "the complexity of human character," see Fleishman, "Socialization," 664.

10   "Lover-mentor" comes from Wilt, *Ghosts of the Gothic*, 147.

11   I have in mind, e.g., the essays on *Bleak House* and *David Copperfield* in D. A. Miller, *The Novel and the Police* (Berkeley and Los Angeles: University of California Press, 1988). On the complex relations between the middling and the extreme in the constitution of middle-class identity, see Stallybrass and White, *The Politics and Poetics of Transgression*

12   I am drawing here on Kucich's demonstration of how in Trollope middle-class moral norms are "rotated slightly upwards in the social scale" as well as on his insights into the formation of a middle-class elite, which "depends on a conviction . . . of the transcendent fluidity of its social and moral identity" ("Transgression in Trollope," 598, 615). When General Tilney calculatingly "admires the elasticity of [Catherine's] walk, which corresponded exactly with the spirit of her dancing" (p. 118), what he miscalculates is the extent to which this "elasticity" prefigures the (upper-)middle-class "fluidity" that Kucich uncovers in Trollope.

13   My thinking about refinement, especially later in this chapter, takes inspiration from some dense, rich paragraphs in Jerome Christensen, *Practicing Enlightenment: Hume and the Formation of a Literary Career* (Madison: University of Wisconsin Press, 1987), 115–16. For example: "If refinement is what makes the economy go, vicious luxury is what erases the bounds between a restricted economy and one generalized beyond any reason. Refinement's globalism is theoretically unchecked, its processive aggrandizement potentially and radically diseconomic" (p. 116).

14   For example: "Taste classifies, and it classifies the classifier. Social subjects, classified by their classifications, distinguish themselves by the distinctions they make, between the beautiful and the ugly, the distinguished and the vulgar, in which their position in the objective classifications is expressed or betrayed" (Bourdieu, *Distinction*, 6).

15   There is an extensive critical literature about the relations between the novel and historiography before, during, and after the nineteenth century. For a classic deconstructive treatment of these relations, see J. Hillis Miller, "Narrative and History," *ELH* 41 (Fall 1974): 455–76.

16   On female paranoia, see, e.g., Mary Ann Doane, *The Desire to Desire: The Woman's Film of the 1940s* (Bloomington: Indiana University Press, 1987). See also note 21 below.

17   Much new-historicist writing is explicitly antitheoretical, but, if such theorists as Freud and Lacan are right about the affinity between theory and paranoia, the dissimulated paranoia of the new historicism may itself dissimulate certain stubborn theoretical residues. For a cannily Foucauldian reading of *Northanger Abbey*, see Paul Morrison, "Enclosed in Openness: *Northanger Abbey* and the Domestic Carceral," *Texas Studies in Literature and Language* 33 (Spring 1991): 1–23. Where Morrison tends to posit his reading over and against Henry Tilney's naïveté, I am suggesting that Henry is himself already a Foucauldian and that he is teaching Catherine how to become one.

18   I allude here to the slogan "Always historicize!" with which Fredric Jameson begins *The Political Unconscious: Narrative as a Socially Symbolic Act* (Ithaca, N.Y.: Cornell University Press, 1981), 9. Although current, this imperative is not exactly new. Almost twenty years ago, Paul de Man disdainfully remarked that behind the then resurgent pressure to historicize "stands a highly respectable moral imperative that strives to reconcile the internal, formal, private structures of literary language with their external, ref-

erential, and public effects" (*Allegories of Reading: Figural Language in Rousseau, Nietzsche, Rilke, and Proust* [New Haven, Conn.: Yale University Press, 1979], 3). That de Man evades the historical imperative in favor of an even more "rigorous" (if also, or therefore, more "unreliable") critical practice (p. 19) perhaps suggests one of the differences between his stance and the present chapter's vis-à-vis historicism.

19   I am not arguing, in a totalizing fashion, that feminist and gay critics who invest in historicism thereby inevitably become complicit in their own oppression. Nor would it be difficult to cite examples of the oppressiveness of various formalisms. My point is that the historicist imperative, *as an imperative*, can exercise a normalizing function that precludes many of the pleasures, aptitudes, and insights—call them "literary," for now—that a lot of feminist and gay critics might well be reluctant to renounce. Although a sophisticated (or "new") historicism significantly mitigates some of the more rebarbative features of history as a *discipline*—and although Foucault's sophisticated gayness, e.g., no doubt has much to do with the sex appeal of the new historicism or at least with the charm it exerted in the 1980s—sophistication has normalizing, disciplinary implications of its own. (On the problematic overdetermination of charm, see the third section of this chapter.)

20   On the similarities between history, as decribed by Catherine, and Gothic fiction, see Wilt, *Ghosts of the Gothic*, 130.

21   On the way in which "the whole set of socially constituted differences between the sexes tends to weaken as one moves up the social hierarchy," see Bourdieu, *Distinction*, 382–83. Although the literature on female paranoia necessarily works with, or within, psychoanalytic paradigms that do not explicitly address questions of class, I have found provocative Mary Ann Doane's comment on how, in certain Gothic-influenced "woman's films," "the mixture effected by a marriage between two different classes produces horror and paranoia" (*Desire to Desire*, 173). In the light of this comment, Doane's characterization of female paranoia as simultaneously a foreclosure of the paternal, a hyperbolization of the paternal, and a fear of the maternal (p. 145) could be opened up into an analysis of the cross-class dynamics of *Northanger Abbey*, where Catherine Morland's paranoid *social* desire gets played out in relation to the symbolic positions occupied not only by her own parents but by General Tilney as a father figure, by Henry Tilney as an "androgynous" compromise between the paternal and the maternal, by Eleanor Tilney as an idealized version of the self, and so on.

22   See Bourdieu, *Distinction*, 329: "But above all, the autodidact, a victim by default of the effects of educational entitlement, is ignorant of the right to be ignorant that is conferred by certificates of knowledge, and it would no doubt be futile to seek elsewhere than in the manner in which it is affirmed the difference between the forced eclecticism of this culture, picked up in the course of unguided reading and accidental encounters, and the elective eclecticism of aesthetes who use the mixing of genres and the subversion of hierarchies as an opportunity to manifest their all-powerful aesthetic disposition."

23   Wilt, *Ghosts of the Gothic*, 151.

24   This is not to say, of course, that male charm is unambiguously valorized in fiction before the nineteenth century; in a discussion of an earlier version of this chapter, one respondent cited the character of Lovelace in *Clarissa* as a notable counterinstance, and others could no doubt be adduced. Much as I value this kind of sophisticated historicist suspicion, I persist in the "naive" historicist belief that one of the ways

in which Austen's novels enjoy a peculiarly indicative relation to both eighteenth- and nineteenth-century fiction is in registering as acutely as they do the effects of a changing sex/gender/class system. A fuller consideration of this system would locate Austen's charming young men vis-à-vis such other increasingly problematic male figures as the rake, the fop, the dandy, and the gentleman. In this context, see, e.g., Regenia Gagnier, *Idylls of the Marketplace: Oscar Wilde and the Victorian Public* (Stanford, Calif.: Stanford University Press, 1986), and Ellen Moers, *The Dandy: Brummell to Beerbohm* (Lincoln: University of Nebraska Press, 1978).

25   Bourdieu, *Distinction*, 208.

26   Christensen, *Practicing Enlightenment*, 118n.

27   This fantasy of social identification anticipates the imaginary structure that D. A. Miller sees as typical of Victorian fiction in general: "An affective schema as adolescent as the protagonists who command our attention therein: those whom we love struggle with those whom we hate, against a background of those to whom we are largely indifferent" (Miller, *The Novel and the Police*, 132).

28   Derrida, "Economimesis."

29   On this mechanism, see Sigmund Freud, "Medusa's Head," in *The Standard Edition of the Complete Psychological Works of Sigmund Freud*, trans. James Strachey (London: Hogarth, 1991), 18:273–74; and Neil Hertz, "Medusa's Head: Male Hysteria under Political Pressure," in *The End of the Line: Essays on Psychoanalysis and the Sublime* (New York: Columbia University Press, 1985), 161–91.

30   Gilbert and Gubar, *Madwoman in the Attic*, 167.

31   See Bourdieu, *Distinction*, 207–8.

32   This perspective on Austen's "style" owes much to D. A. Miller, "Austen's Attitude," *Yale Journal of Criticism* 8 (1995): 1–5.

3   *Kiss Me, Stupid: Sophistication and Snobbery in* Vanity Fair

1   As explained by J. I. M. Steward in his notes to the Penguin edition of William Makepeace Thackeray's *Vanity Fair* (Harmondsworth: Penguin, 1985), 813–14. All quotations from the novel will be from this edition; page references will be included parenthetically in the text.

2   Sedgwick, *Epistemology of the Closet*.

3   René Girard, *Deceit, Desire, and the Novel: Self and Other in Literary Structure*, trans. Yvonne Freccero (Baltimore: Johns Hopkins University Press, 1965), 73.

4   William Makepeace Thackeray, *The Book of Snobs*, ed. John Sutherland (New York: St. Martin's, 1978), 14. Subsequent quotations from this work will be from this edition; page references will be included parenthetically in the text.

5   On the connection between "ambiguity" and homosexuality, see Edelman, *Homographesis*, 201–2.

6   I allude here to Sedgwick's discussion (*Epistemology of the Closet*, 82–86) of "minoritizing" and "universalizing" models of homo/heterosexual definition.

7   As Winifred Hughes observes in her "Silver Fork Writers and Readers: Social Contexts of a Best Seller," *Novel* 25 (1992): 331, this fork will figure again in *Vanity Fair*, where, in one of Thackeray's illustrations for chapter 47, it resembles the devil's pitchfork.

8   Sedgwick, *Epistemology of the Closet*, 192. For a more benign reading of Thackerayan irony in relation to snobbery, see Robert P. Fletcher, "The Dandy and the Fogy: Thackeray and the Aesthetics/Ethics of the Literary Pragmatist," *ELH* 58 (1991): 383–404.

9   Thackeray does not represent snobbery as an exclusively male affair: even in the chapter under discussion, he extends it to include women, and in *Vanity Fair*, as we will see, he does not hesitate to uncover Becky Sharp as, among other things, a snob. Insofar as Thackeray tends nonetheless to portray snobbery primarily as an obscene exercise in one-upmanship, it is as though he were taking us behind the scenes of the middle-class theater of conspicuous consumption, exposing the performativity of its male producer–director–stage managers, who usually stay backstage, delegating the work of representation to their wives. In keeping with his posture of self-implication, Thackeray—or his satirical persona—refers to his wife as "Mrs. SNOB" (p. 102), but the particular imbrication of homophobia with misogyny in this text is such that the author seems to worry less about female snobs than about the power of snobbery to feminize men.

10 For a cogent discussion of Hannibal Lecter in relation to psychoanalytic theories of incorporation, identification, and sexuality, see Diana Fuss, "Monsters of Perversion: Jeffrey Dahmer and *The Silence of the Lambs*," in *Media Spectacles*, ed. Marjorie Garber, Jann Matlock, and Rebecca Walkowitz (New York: Routledge, 1993), 181–205.

11 Bourdieu, *Distinction*, 56.

12 For the canonical account of this process, see Moers, *The Dandy: Brummell to Beerbohm*, 193–214. On the difficulty of maintaining the gentleman/snob binarism, see Alexander Welsh, introduction to *Thackeray: A Collection of Critical Essays* (Englewood Cliffs, N.J.: Prentice-Hall, 1968), 1–14.

13 For the definitive analysis of the Victorian middle-class investment in sophistication, see Kucich, *The Power of Lies*.

14 This claim is at odds with the more familiar narrative of the relation between regimes of production and of consumption outlined by Jean Baudrillard: "We don't realize how much the current indoctrination into systematic and organized consumption is the equivalent and the extension, in the twentieth century, of the great indoctrination of rural populations into industrial labor, which occurred throughout the nineteenth century. The same process of rationalization of productive forces, which took place in the nineteenth century in the sector of production is accomplished, in the twentieth century, in the sector of consumption" (Mark Poster, ed., *Jean Baudrillard: Selected Writings* [Stanford, Calif.: Stanford University Press, 1988], 50). Against this diachronic schema, the reading of Thackeray conducted here assumes an almost synchronic link between rule by production and rule by consumption.

15 See Butler, *Gender Trouble*, 57–72. In the more recent *Bodies That Matter: On the Discursive Limits of "Sex"* (New York: Routledge, 1993), esp. pp. 233–36, Butler expands on the relation between gender performance and disavowal in ways relevant to the present discussion. Gender is obviously an issue here, but I am also interested in the connection between disavowal and *class* performance.

16 On the difference between a distinguished "taste of reflection" and a popular (i.e., degraded) "taste of sense," see Bourdieu, *Distinction*, 488–91.

17 Prurience and knowingness may seem an unlikely pair. In conjoining them, however, I follow the novel itself in at least one of its more telling "inconsistencies." I have in

mind the prurience with which Thackeray teases the reader as to the nature of Becky's relations with Lord Steyne and that constitutes one of the pockets or cysts of naïveté that, as I suggest below, Thackerayan sophistication works to dissimulate.

18   Miller, *The Novel and the Police*, 145.

19   I am not the first reader in whom this passage has struck the same proverbial chord: "Thackeray creates in this passage a perspective that takes away as it gives a probationary sympathy to Becky's ambition, and to a possible reader's response to it" (Fletcher, "The Dandy and the Fogy," 383).

20   Theodor Adorno, "Short Commentaries on Proust," in *Notes to Literature*, vol. 1, trans. Shierry Weber Nicholsen (New York: Columbia University Press, 1991), 180. On snobbery as a fictive rewriting of class relations, see also Girard: "In a society where individuals are 'free and equal by law,' there *should* be no snobs. But there *can* be snobs only in this sort of society. . . . Snobbism begins with equality. This certainly does not mean that Proust lived in a classless society. But the actual concrete differences between these classes have nothing to do with the abstract distinctions of snobbism. In the eyes of sociologists the Verdurins belong to the same class as the Guermantes" (*Deceit, Desire, and the Novel*, 70).

21   On the reversibility of the substitutive relation between kisses and bites, see Adam Phillips, *On Kissing, Tickling, and Being Bored: Psychoanalytic Essays on the Unexamined Life* (Cambridge, Mass.: Harvard University Press, 1993), 97: "If in a crude psychoanalytic interpretation kissing could be described as aim-inhibited eating, we should also consider the more nonsensical option that eating can also be, as Freud will imply, aim-inhibited kissing."

22   Theodor Adorno, *Minima Moralia: Reflections from Damaged Life*, trans. E. F. N. Jephcott (London: Verso, 1974), 46.

23   Adorno, "Short Commentaries," 180–81. On snobbery and homosexuality in Proust, also see—but see cautiously—Girard, *Deceit, Desire, and the Novel*, 208–9. For a reading of *Vanity Fair* that, like this one, but also unlike it, draws on Adorno, see Andrew Miller, "Vanity Fair through Plate Glass," *PMLA* 105 (1990): 1042–54. Miller's analysis is impressive, but his Marxian emphasis on "impoverished intensities of consumption" (p. 1048) in the novel suggests an agoraphobia (I mean a hostility toward the marketplace) that at times borders on erotophobia. In trying to offer a gay-identified, and gay-affirmative, reading of consumption in Thackeray, this chapter would resist, with Adorno's help, a project to which Adorno also lends his support: a certain way of pathologizing the erotics of the marketplace.

24   Adorno, "Short Commentaries," 180.

25   Cited in Gordon N. Ray, *Thackeray: The Uses of Adversity, 1811–1846* (New York: McGraw-Hill, 1955), 280. In *The Buried Life: A Study of the Relation between Thackeray's Fiction and His Personal History* (Cambridge, Mass.: Harvard University Press, 1952), 42–47, Ray argues that the character of Jos is based on George Trant Shakespear, a cousin of Thackeray's—but what, after all, is a cousin?—who was known as "a confirmed bachelor" (p. 43) and who apparently ended by committing suicide.

26   In "Fattening Up on Pickwick," *Novel* 25 (1992): 235–44, James Kincaid has argued that the Fat Boy in *Pickwick Papers* seductively embodies a universal drive "to become one with the fat about us, to make the whole world into flesh—into our flesh" (p. 238). If Thackeray's Fat Boy, to his detriment, does a better job of making our flesh creep, this more authentically phobogenic effect may result from the fact that, for all its re-

gressive utopianism, the drive he embodies is not regressive *enough*, does not point back to a sufficiently undifferentiated, pregendered eroticism. The problem with Jos, in other words, is less that he desires too much, as his inability to shed his "super-abundant fat" might suggest, than that he desires in the wrong way. What makes this fat man egregious is his too-evident gregariousness: what puts him outside the flock of normative, "adult" masculinity, thus separating the sheep from the scapegoat, is his unseemly, immature eagerness to be *one* of the boys. But if the fat man is really a fat boy—"Be a man, Jos" (p. 795), the exemplary Dobbin vainly implores him, only two pages from the end of the novel—the fat boy is really no boy at all. Like the eighth-grade sissy, who, hatefully obtuse if not also hatefully obese, remains fixated on his jockish classmates at the moment when those good citizens are obediently beginning to conduct the traffic in women, Jos arouses disdain because, instead of acting his age, getting ready to become a family man, he insists on trying make up for lost time by living "like a gay young bachelor," idiotically dilating a phase that everyone else has had the good sense and the good taste to have gone through.

27   Sedgwick identifies this joke, attributed to Groucho Marx, as the "foundational prin-ciple" (p. 151) of snobbery.

28   Jürgen Habermas, *The Structural Transformation of the Public Sphere: An Inquiry into a Category of Bourgeois Society*, trans. Thomas Burger with the assistance of Frederick Lawrence (Cambridge, Mass.: MIT Press, 1991), 43.

4   Taste, Waste, Proust

1   Adorno, "Short Commentaries," 176.

2   Edelman, *Homographesis*; see esp. pp. 3–23. I am also indebted in this chapter to the theorization of "waste" in two recent essays by Edelman: "Plasticity, Paternity, Perver-sity: Freud's *Falcon*, Huston's *Freud*," *American Imago* 51 (Spring 1994): 69–104, and "Piss Elegant: Freud, Hitchcock, and the Micturating Penis," *GLQ* 2 (1995): 149–77.

On *Proust* as a signifier for sophistication itself, or on "those" who are most prone to try to capitalize on that signifier (Stephen Sondheim: "Some like to be profound / By reading Proust and Pound"), Gregory Woods has written: "Those who are most appreciative of this dimension of the book are, perhaps, also most likely to buy such books as Borrel, Senderens, and Naudin's *Dining with Proust*, which lavishly recreates the novel's most significant culinary experiences, and to attend such occasions as 'The Music of Marcel Proust,' held in St. John's, Smith Square, London, to mark the seven-tieth anniversary of the author's death. . . . Those who have read the *Recherche*—those who have *endured*—see themselves as an embattled elite, making up for what they lack in aristocratic credentials with a display of aesthetic appreciation" ("High Culture and High Camp: The Case of Marcel Proust," in *Camp Grounds: Style and Homosexuality* ed. David Bergman [Amherst: University of Massachusetts Press, 1993], 121–22). And what of those who write such knowing sentences? In place of (perhaps unnecessary) commentary on the game of self-distinction that is being played here, I merely offer an avowal that, perhaps equally needless to say, itself constitutes yet another move in the game: as an owner of the cookbook in question (Jean-Bernard Naudin, Anne Borrel, Alain Senderens, *Dining with Proust* [New York: Random House, 1992])—see especially the recipe for grilled crawfish in white sauce (p. 146)—I pay tribute to it by taking its title for that of the present section of this chapter.

3   Theodor Adorno, "On Proust," in *Notes to Literature*, vol. 2, trans. Shierry Weber Nicholsen (New York: Columbia University Press, 1992), 315–16.

4   There is a substantial body of critical literature on orality in Proust. See, e.g., Serge Doubrovsky, *Writing and Fantasy in Proust: La Place de la Madeleine*, trans. Carol Mastrangelo Bové and Paul A. Bové (Lincoln: University of Nebraska Press, 1986); Jean-Pierre Richard, *Proust et le monde sensible* (Paris: Seuil, 1974); Kaja Silverman, "A Woman's Soul Enclosed in a Man's Body: Femininity in Male Homosexuality," in *Male Subjectivity at the Margins* (New York: Routledge, 1992), esp. pp. 373–88.

5   The paradoxicality—and the current urgency or appeal—of the dream of eliminating waste is pointed out by Moon and Sedgwick in "Divinity."

6   "I hope that by the end of this paper I will not have bitten off more of the hand that feeds me than I can chew" (Barbara Johnson, "Gender Theory and the Yale School," in *A World of Difference* [Baltimore: Johns Hopkins University Press, 1987], 32).

7   Adorno, "On Proust," 316.

8   Jean-François Revel, *Sur Proust: Remarques sur "A la recherche du temps perdu"* (Paris: Julliard, 1960), 69 (my translation).

9   Marcel Proust, *Remembrance of Things Past*, vol. 3, trans. C. K. Scott Moncrieff, Terence Kilmartin, and Andreas Mayor (New York: Vintage, 1982), 931. Subsequent references, with the exception of those to *The Guermantes Way*, will be to this edition. The edition of *The Guermantes Way* that I am using is the third volume of *In Search of Lost Time*, trans. C. K. Scott Moncrieff and Terence Kilmartin, rev. D. J. Enright (New York: Modern Library, 1993). All subsequent references will be included parenthetically in the text. Most are to *The Guermantes Way*; when I quote from one of the other volumes, the title is also indicated parenthetically. Quotations from the French text, many of which are interpolated into the quotations from the English version, are from *A la recherche du temps perdu*, ed. Jean-Yves Tadié et al., 4 vols. (Paris: Gallimard, 1987). Where I quote from both the English translation and the French original, the first page reference is to the translation and the second to the original.

10   Sedgwick, *Epistemology of the Closet*, 240.

11   Sedgwick writes that Proust's novel "puts its sociological acuity humbly at the reader's service in the most inglorious, least customarily acknowledged of our projects" (ibid.).

12   Jacques Lacan, *The Four Fundamental Concepts of Psycho-Analysis*, ed. Jacques-Alain Miller, trans. Alan Sheridan (New York: Norton, 1981), 268.

13   The image of the simultaneously sublime and obscene object is drawn from the writings of Slavoj Žižek, esp. *The Sublime Object of Ideology* (London: Verso, 1989) and *Looking Awry: An Introduction to Jacques Lacan through Popular Culture* (Cambridge, Mass.: MIT Press, 1991). The use to which the image is being put here is not, I suspect, consistent with Žižek's theoretical and political agenda or with his Thackerayan pose as heterosexual man of the world. For a trenchant critique of his work in terms of its gender and sexual politics, see Judith Butler, "Arguing with the Real," in *Bodies That Matter*, 187–222.

14   Gilles Deleuze, *Proust et les signes* (Paris: Presses Universitaires de France, 1976), 34: "Les signes mondains impliquent surtout un temps qu'on perd."

15   "S'il est un 'volume de transition,' c'est parce qu'il décrit le passage de l'adolescence à l'âge adulte" (Thierry Laget, "Notice," in *A la recherche*, 2:1492).

16   Maurice Bardèche, *Marcel Proust romancier*, 2 vols. (Paris: Les Sept couleurs, 1971), 2:109–12.

17 George D. Painter, *Marcel Proust: A Biography*, 2 vols. in 1 (New York: Random House, 1987), 1:251.

18 Just after discovering that he is no longer in love with the Duchesse de Guermantes, and just before receiving what he once coveted, an invitation to dinner from her, the narrator observes: "But even in the details of an attachment, an absence, the declining of an invitation to dinner, an unintentional, unconscious harshness are of more service than all the cosmetics and fine clothes in the world. There would be plenty of social success if people were taught along these lines the art of succeeding" (p. 511). In the original, the last sentence is even better: "Il y aurait des parvenus, si on enseignait dans ce sens l'art de parvenir" (p. 669). For an interesting discussion of this Proustian secret of social—and erotic—success, see Leo Bersani, *Marcel Proust: The Fictions of Life and Art* (New York: Oxford University Press, 1965), 177–78.

19 Bardèche, *Marcel Proust romancier*, 109.

20 Ibid., 110.

21 Proust suggests as much in his remarks on "self-interest," which, in the original text, appears with a more telling ambiguity simply as *l'intérêt* (p. 557): "Often one has to come down to 'kept' persons, male or female, before one finds the hidden springs of actions or words, apparently of the most innocent nature, in self-interest, in the necessity to keep alive" (*The Guermantes Way*, 352). Contrary to popular opinion, vanity (self-interest), far from precluding interest in the world, just is that interest.

22 If we do not already know this, however, it may because we have forgotten it—or because, two volumes and over a thousand pages earlier, it was put somewhat differently. Recounting his family's discovery that, despite his grandiloquent denunciation of snobs, Legrandin is himself a snob, the narrator writes: "This is not to say that M. Legrandin was anything but sincere when he inveighed against snobs. He could not (from his own knowledge, at least) be aware that he himself was one, since it is only with the passions of others that we are ever really familiar, and what we come to discover about our own can only be learned from them" (*Swann's Way*, 140).

23 Offering an analogy for Proust's second naïveté, Adorno gives us to think about the less happy case of another spiteful young wretch: "Proust looks at even adult life with such alien and wondering eyes that under his immersed gaze the present is virtually transformed into prehistory, into childhood. This has an aspect that is not at all esoteric but rather democratic. For every somewhat sheltered child whose responsiveness has not been driven out of him in his earliest years has at his disposal infinite possibilities of experience. I remember a classmate of mine who did not turn out to be anything special in the eyes of the world. We were perhaps twelve years old when we read Molière's *The Miser* in French class. My classmate pointed out to me that the teacher pronounced the title, *L'avare*, in a manner reminiscent of provincial dialect, a manner that betrayed inadequate education, an inferior milieu, and that when one heard this hard "r" one would never believe this otherwise excellent teacher spoke French at all. One might find an observation like this in Proust" ("On Proust," 315).

24 In a letter to the duc de Guiche, Proust offers further unflattering ornithological metaphors for the duchess and her original, Madame de Chevigné (née Laure de Sade) (Marcel Proust, *Correspondance*, ed. Philip Kolb [Paris: Plon, 1992], 20:349): "Sauf qu'elle est vertueuse, elle [la Duchesse de Guermantes] ressemble un peu à la poule coriace que je pris jadis pour un oiseau de Paradis et qui ne savait comme un perroquet

que me répondre 'Fitz James m'attend' quand je voulais la capturer sous les arbres de l'Avenue Gabriel. En faisant d'elle un puissant Vautour, j'empêche au moins qu'on la prenne pour une vieille pie."

25   See, in addition to Sedgwick, *Epistemology of the Closet*, 231–40, the account by Silverman, "A Woman's Soul," 373–88; to the extent that Silverman's aim seems to be to produce a *heterosexual* male homosexuality, her reading needs to be approached with caution.

26   See, Doubrovsky, *Writing and Fantasy in Proust*

27   See Paul Morrison, "End Pleasure," *GLQ* 1 (1993): 53–78.

28   Jacques Derrida, "Structure, Sign, and Play in the Discourse of the Human Sciences," in *Writing and Difference*, trans. Alan Bass (Chicago: University of Chicago Press, 1978), 293.

29   On, e.g., the conventionality of Proust's overt "philosophy," see Vincent Descombes, *Proust: Philosophy of the Novel*, trans. Catherine Chance Macksey (Stanford, Calif.: Stanford University Press, 1992).

30   Gilles Deleuze, *Proust and Signs*, trans. Richard Howard (New York: George Braziller, 1972), 166–67.

31   An analysis of gay-Jewish excess in Proust could do worse than by beginning with the following passage: "Mme Cottard picked up only the words 'a member of the confraternity' and '*tapette*,' and as in the Doctor's vocabulary the former expression denoted the Jewish race and the latter a wagging tongue, Mme Cottard concluded that M. de Charlus must be a garrulous Jew. She could not understand why they should cold-shoulder the Baron for that reason, and felt it her duty as the senior lady of the clan to insist that he should not be left alone" (*Sodom and Gomorrah*, 594).

32   From Paul de Man, *The Resistance to Theory* (Minneapolis: University of Minnesota Press, 1986), 19: "Technically correct rhetorical readings may be boring, monotonous, predictable, and unpleasant, but they are irrefutable. . . . Nothing can overcome the resistance to theory since theory is itself this resistance."

33   In "Death and Literary Authority: Marcel Proust and Melanie Klein," in *The Culture of Redemption* (Cambridge, Mass.: Harvard University Press, 1990), 26, Leo Bersani distinguishes between the symbolic violence implicit in "going *behind*" objects and the more attractively metonymic or nonsymbolic practice (he speaks of "appetitive metonymies") of moving "*to the side* of objects." My project in this chapter might be characterized as an argument for symbolic violence—or at least as an attempt to trace that violence's own appetitive trajectories, which, if they oppose the "mobility of desire" (p. 22) that Bersani wants to bring out in Proust, continue to impel some of the most performatively interesting gay/lesbian/queer reading and writing.

34   See Edelman's "Seeing Things: Representation, the Scene of Surveillance, and the Spectacle of Gay Male Sex," in *Homographesis*, 173–91.

35   On the homophobic necessity of "knowing" the gay man—signally, Charlus—behind his back, see Sedgwick, *Epistemology of the Closet*, 223–30.

36   Woods, "High Culture and High Camp," 129: "In fact, of course, the semiotic charge of Legrandin's backside lays bare the fact that he is homosexual. More specifically, he takes it up the arse."

37   D. A. Miller, "Anal Rope," in *Inside/Out: Lesbian Theories, Gay Theories*, ed. Diana Fuss (Routledge: New York, 1991), 134. In the next sentence, I connect this "cut" with an image at the end of an earlier essay by Miller, "The Novel as Usual: Trollope's *Barchester Towers*," in *The Novel and the Police*, 145: "And should one recognize Trollope for the proper name

of a cultural strategy that is still 'boring' us, boring through us (though the Novel is no longer the primary site or instrument of the drill), the shock would only widen." Earlier in the same paragraph, Miller makes the point that I have adduced in relation to Thackeray: "Boredom, as the example of pornography perhaps best illustrates, overtakes not what is intrinsically dull, but what is 'interesting' to excess."

38 On Proust's fantasy of an "organ for kissing," see Silverman, "A Woman's Soul," 373–88.

39 I have in mind here Jacques Derrida, "Racism's Last Word," trans. Peggy Kamuf, in "Race," Writing, and Difference, ed. Henry Louis Gates (Chicago: University of Chicago Press, 1985), 329–38. Derrida points out that le dernier can mean not only the last but also the worst (p. 330).

40 On the Jamesian elaborations of "making a scene" and of "going behind," see my Caught in the Act, 195–269.

41 For another instance of Proust's fascination with parricide—other, I mean, than the narrative violence that I have been discussing throughout this chapter—see his essay "Sentiments filiaux d'un parricide," in "Contre Sainte-Beuve," précédé de "Pastiches et mélanges," et suivi de "Essais et articles," ed. Pierre Clarac with Yves Sandres (Paris: Gallimard, 1971), 15–59.

42 Descombes, Proust, 153. The absence of a marriage plot can register as the absence of plot, period: in Narrative Discourse, trans. Jane Lewin (Ithaca, N.Y.: Cornell University Press, 1980), 167, Gérard Genette observes that the Recherche is "sometimes so liberated from any concern with a story to tell that it could perhaps more fittingly be described simply as talking."

5   Expensive Tastes: Adorno, Barthes, and Cultural Studies

1 Colin MacCabe, ed., High Theory, Low Culture: Analysing Popular Television and Film (New York: St. Martin's Press, 1986).

2 Simon During, ed., The Cultural Studies Reader (New York: Routledge, 1993).

3 Ibid., 30, 44.

4 Theodor Adorno, "Perennial Fashion—Jazz," in Prisms, trans. Samuel Weber and Shierry Weber (Cambridge, Mass.: MIT Press, 1992), 126–27. Subsequent references to Prisms will be included parenthetically in the text.

5 Fredric Jameson, Late Marxism: Adorno, or The Persistence of the Dialectic (London: Verso, 1990), 141.

6 Roland Barthes, The Eiffel Tower and Other Mythologies, trans. Richard Howard (New York: Hill & Wang, 1990), 51, 65–66. Subsequent references to this work will be included parenthetically in the text.

7 Barthes, Mythologies, trans. Annette Lavers (New York: Hill & Wang, 1972), 12, 156–57. Subsequent references to this work will be included parenthetically in the text. In certain cases, I quote from the French text—Mythologies (Paris: Seuil, 1957)—as well. Where two page references are given, the first is to the English text, the second to the French.

8 On "petit bourgeois" as a "universal operator of value" ("no one is safe from this evil"), see Roland Barthes, Roland Barthes, trans. Richard Howard (Berkeley: University of California Press, 1977), 144. Subsequent references to this work will be included

parenthetically in the text. I also quote at times from the French text, *Roland Barthes* (Paris: Seuil, 1975); where two page references are given, the first is to the English text, the second to the French.

9   Marjorie Garber, "Character Assassination: Shakespeare, Anita Hill, and JFK," in Garber, Matlock, and Walkowitz, eds., *Media Spectacles*, 30.

10   Ibid., 24, 31, 24.

11   Barthes, *The Pleasure of the Text*, trans. Richard Miller (New York: Hill & Wang, 1975), 50.

12   Garber, Matlock, and Walkowitz, eds., *Media Spectacles*, 10.

13   Cited in Garber, in "Character Assassination," 29.

14   Barthes: "One can without fear defy anyone ever to practise an innocent criticism" (*Mythologies*, p. 82). I wonder, however, about "without fear."

15   Adorno, *Minima Moralia*, 206. Subsequent references to this work will be included parenthetically in the text. In a few instances, I interpolate a word or phrase from the German text: *Minima Moralia: Reflexionen aus dem beschädigten Leben*, ed. Rolf Tiedemann (Frankfurt: Suhrkamp, 1980). Where two page references are given, the first is to the English text, the second to the German.

16   Adorno sometimes overtly thematizes his nonexteriority to the culture industry: "Every visit to the cinema leaves me, against all my vigilance, stupider and worse" (ibid., 25).

17   I have in mind, e.g., Terry Eagleton, who complains, homophobically, of "a privileged, privatized hedonism" not only in "the later Roland Barthes" but, not too surprisingly, in "the later Michel Foucault" as well (*The Ideology of the Aesthetic* [Oxford: Basil Blackwell, 1990], 7).

18   In his autobiography, Barthes lists titles of projected books: along with such intriguing possibilities as *The Discourse of Homosexuality* and *An Encyclopedia of Food*, he includes *Linguistics of Intimidation* (*Roland Barthes*, 149–50). While Barthes never actually published a volume with that title, a large part of his oeuvre is nonetheless devoted precisely to elaborating such a linguistics.

19   Barthes, "The Division of Languages," in *The Rustle of Language*, 121.

20   For a discussion of Barthes's practice of "the novelesque without the novel," see D. A. Miller, *Bringing Out Roland Barthes* (Berkeley and Los Angeles: University of California Press, 1992), 43–51.

21   A friend tells me that, in Hollywood, the Disney studio is referred to as "Mauschwitz." To be worked out, although not here, is the relation between the "fascism" of the culture industry and its status as "still too closely bound up with easygoing liberalism and Jewish intellectuals" (Theodor Adorno and Max Horkheimer, "The Culture Industry: Enlightenment as Mass Deception," in *Dialectic of Enlightenment*, trans. John Cumming [New York: Continuum, 1982], 123). Subsequent references to this work will be included parenthetically in the text.

22   Roland Barthes, *Leçon: Leçon Inaugurale de la Chaire de Sémiologie Littéraire du Collège de France* (Paris: Seuil, 1978), 46.

23   Another example: "[Mythology] attempts to find again, under the assumed innocence of the most unsophisticated relationships [*sous les innocences de la vie relationelle la plus naïve*], the profound alienation which this innocence is meant to make one accept" (*Mythologies*, 156; 244).

24   Theodor Adorno, *Aesthetic Theory*, trans. C. Lenhardt, ed. Gretel Adorno and Rolf Tiedemann (London: Routledge & Kegan Paul, 1970), 462.

25   Theodor Adorno, *Negative Dialectics*, trans. E. B. Ashton (New York: Continuum, 1973), 14.

26   Theodor Adorno, "The Essay as Form," in *Notes to Literature*, 1:4.

27   An *énonciation* that, at least once, he does characterize and avow as naive: "I . . . naïvely connect detail to detail" (*Roland Barthes*, 93).

28   Adorno and Horkheimer, *Dialectic*, 149.

29   On his mother's kindness: "I could not define it better than by this feature (among others): that during the whole of our life together, she never made a single 'observation' " (Roland Barthes, *Camera Lucida: Reflections on Photography*, trans. Richard Howard [New York: Hill & Wang, 1981], 69).

30   More often, Barthes's antidoxological procedure entails not a valorizing of density but a vigilance against it. See, e.g., *Roland Barthes*: "Like a watchful cook, he makes sure that language does not thicken, that it doesn't stick" (p. 162). Easy enough to dismiss as a stereotypically fashion-conscious gesture, a "seventies" attempt to produce the literary-critical equivalent of nouvelle cuisine, this sentence in fact represents a distaste for viscosity that runs throughout Barthes's work. Whether as an oppressive thickness or as an equally oppressive transparency, however, the doxa, according to Barthes, always makes itself look *natural*.

31   In the text, this passage appears in parentheses, which I have taken the liberty of removing.

32   Miller, *Bringing Out Roland Barthes*, passim. Barthes may not speak of homosexuality much, but, as Miller points out: "Even when not spoken about in his writing, homosexuality does not fail to be spoken any the less. On the contrary, though seldom a topic, it comes to inflect every topic, no matter how remote, through the operation of a means comparable, even continuous, with that inexhaustible fountain of revelation popularly known (in fear, scorn, or love) as *a gay voice*" (p. 25).

33   Miller makes this point in "Anal Rope": "If connotation, as the dominant signifying practice of homophobia, has the advantage of constructing an essentially insubstantial homosexuality, it has the corresponding inconvenience of tending to raise this ghost all over the place" (p. 125).

34   "And yet (a frequent trick of any social accusation), what is an idea for him, if not *a flush of pleasure?* 'Abstraction is in no way contrary to sensuality' (*Mythologies*)" (*Roland Barthes*, 103).

35   On homosexual abjection, see, e.g., Butler's introduction to *Bodies That Matter*, 1–23; and Edelman, "The Mirror and the Tank."

36   "Indeed, the worst fears of those for whom a Germanic dialectic is virtually by definition humorless in its very essence will be confirmed by the obsessive diatribes against laughter that appear and reappear throughout [*Dialectic of Enlightenment*]" (Jameson, *Late Marxism*, 145).

37   From *Roland Barthes*: "To be excluded is not to be outside, it is to be *alone in the hole*, imprisoned under the open sky: precluded" (pp. 121–22).

38   Contrast this wine with the wine of *Mythologies*: "Through wine, the intellectual comes nearer to a natural virility, and believes he can thus escape the curse that a century and a half of romanticism still brings to bear on the purely cerebral" (pp. 58–59).

39   Though the distinction between "good" and "bad" might seem to correspond to one between a homosexuality outside power and a homosexuality inside power, the discussion of privilege and perversity below (as in the first chapter of this book) should challenge that distinction. Both "mores" are produced by the social machinery. To say

that, however, is to say relatively little. The question is not, Are they produced? but rather, Once they are produced, what do they produce in turn?

40   Standing behind the door, moreover, Barthes occupies a space less of exclusion than of protection. As Miller suggests in "Anal Rope" (esp. pp. 134–39), far from epitomizing the sad truth of "castration," gay male sexuality may signify a happy exemption from it.

41   Such personalization can reduce commentators to a grotesque "common sense": see, e.g., Eagleton on Adorno's "overreaction to fascism" (p. 358)

42   Cultural criticism, as I am characterizing it here, differs considerably from what Adorno, in "Cultural Criticism and Society" (Prisms, 28–29), means by the term: "To accept culture as a whole is to deprive it of the ferment which is its very truth—negation. The joyous appropriation of culture harmonizes with a climate of military music and paintings of battle-scenes. What distinguishes dialectical from cultural criticism is that it heightens cultural criticism until the notion of culture is negated, fulfilled, and surmounted in one."

43   Edelman, "The Mirror and the Tank," 113, 117. See also p. xvii, on the systematic interdependence of homophobia and fear (or hatred) of jargon in a culture by no means reluctant "to police the language of intellectual analysis by construing the ('left-leaning') academy, and ('left-leaning') academic theory, in terms of the nonproductive self-enclosure that a phobic regime has already attributed to the cultural category of the 'faggot.' "

44   Cultural studies, again like gay politics, is understandably wary of appearing to posit a hierarchy of pleasures: any such hierarchy can always be mobilized against groups whose "privilege" itself by no means guarantees their safety—from, say, resentful assault. The point, however, is not to insist that our pleasures are better than theirs: the point is to show that there already exists a large-scale, systematic administration of pleasures, whose function is to make sure that nobody has "too much" fun—or that those who do are seen to pay for it. Few will be surprised, of course, to learn that our culture is hierarchical; a certain novelty, however, may still attend the demonstration of the extent to which hierarchical organization structures the most "private" recesses of the sphere of consumption. Not that staging this demonstration will do anything to win friends for gay and/or cultural studies critics. But, like good teachers, we're not out to win popularity contests.

45   I am using pleasure and happiness as cognate terms, even though Jameson (Late Marxism, 146) warns that "Adorno and Horkheimer . . . sunder pleasure decisively from happiness." It is certainly true that "happiness" generally enjoys a dignity in Adorno's work that "pleasure" lacks. But sometimes the hierarchy is suspended, as in the following passage from Minima Moralia: "Few things separate more profoundly the mode of life befitting the intellectual from that of the bourgeois than the fact that the former acknowledges no alternative between work and recreation. Work that need not, to satisfy reality, first inflict on the subject all the evil that it is afterwards to inflict on others, is pleasure [Lust] even in its despairing effort. Its freedom is the same as that which bourgeois society reserves exclusively for relaxation and, by this regimentation, at once revokes. Conversely, anyone who knows freedom finds all the amusements tolerated by this society unbearable and, apart from his work, which admittedly includes what the bourgeois relegate to non-working hours as 'culture,' has no substitute pleasures. . . . Only a cunning intertwining of pleasure and work leaves real experience still open, under the pressure of society. Such experience is less and less tolerated" (p. 84; p. 145).

46 Too much power, of course, means too much money: not least of the outrages allegedly perpetrated by cultural intellectuals today is that of getting paid for "doing nothing" (not teaching enough classes, not spending enough time with undergraduates, not addressing a general readership, etc.). But this resentment isn't only about perceived economic injustice: behind the caricature of the academic critic as parasite, as a sort of yuppie counterpart of the welfare mother, lies the angry suspicion that the "nothing" for which that critic is getting (over)paid is in fact a too-enjoyable something: an unproductive pleasure or the pleasure of *bad* productivity (not unlike that of the welfare mother, for that matter).

Works Cited

Adorno, Theodor W. *Aesthetic Theory*. Translated by C. Lenhardt. Edited by Gretel Adorno and Rolf Tiedemann. London: Routledge & Kegan Paul, 1970.

———. *Negative Dialectics*. Translated by E. B. Ashton. New York: Continuum, 1973.

———. *Minima Moralia: Reflections from Damaged Life*. Translated by E. F. N. Jephcott. London: Verso, 1974.

———. *Notes to Literature*. Edited by Rolf Tiedemann. Translated by Shierry Weber Nicholson. 2 vols. New York: Columbia University Press, 1991–92.

———. *Prisms*. Translated by Samuel Weber and Shierry Weber. Cambridge, Mass.: MIT Press, 1992.

Adorno, Theodor W., and Max Horkheimer. *Dialectic of Enlightenment*. Translated by John Cumming. New York: Continuum, 1982.

Armstrong, Nancy. *Desire and Domestic Fiction: A Political History of the Novel*. New York: Oxford University Press, 1987.

Austen, Jane. *Northanger Abbey*. Edited by Anne Ehrenpreis. Harmondsworth: Penguin, 1972.

———. *Pride and Prejudice*. Edited by Tony Tanner. Harmondsworth: Penguin, 1980.

Backman, Mark. *Sophistication: Rhetoric and the Rise of Self-Consciousness*. Woodbridge, Conn.: Ox Bow, 1991.

Bardèche, Maurice. *Marcel Proust romancier*. 2 vols. Paris: Les Sept Couleurs, 1971.

Barthes, Roland. *Mythologies*. Paris: Seuil, 1957. Translated by Annette Lavers as *Mythologies* (New York: Hill & Wang, 1972).

———. *The Pleasure of the Text*. Translated by Richard Miller. New York: Hill & Wang, 1975.

———. *Roland Barthes*. Paris: Seuil 1975. Translated by Richard Howard as *Roland Barthes*. (Berkeley and Los Angeles: University of California Press, 1977).

———. *Leçon: Leçon inaugurale de la Chaire de Sémiologie Littéraire du Collège de France*. Paris: Seuil, 1978.

———. *Camera Lucida: Reflections on Photography*. Translated by Richard Howard. New York: Hill & Wang, 1981.

———. *The Eiffel Tower and Other Mythologies*. Translated by Richard Howard. New York: Hill & Wang, 1986.

———. *The Rustle of Language*. Translated by Richard Howard. New York: Hill & Wang, 1986.

Bersani, Leo. *The Culture of Redemption*. Cambridge, Mass.: Harvard University Press, 1990.

Boone, Joseph Allen. *Tradition Counter Tradition: Love and the Form of Fiction*. Chicago: University of Chicago Press, 1987.

Borrel, Anne, Jean-Bernard Naudin, and Alain Senderens. *Dining with Proust*. New York: Random House, 1992.

Bourdieu, Pierre. *Distinction: A Social Critique of the Judgment of Taste*. Translated by Richard Nice. Cambridge, Mass.: Harvard University Press, 1984.

Brillat-Savarin, Jean Anthelme. *The Physiology of Taste or Meditations on Transcendental Gastronomy*. Translated by M. F. K. Fisher. San Francisco: North Point, 1986.

Butler, Judith. *Gender Trouble: Feminism and the Subversion of Identity* New York: Routledge, 1990.

————. *Bodies That Matter: On the Discursive Limits of "Sex."* New York: Routledge, 1993.

Chapman, R. W., ed. *Jane Austen's Letters to Her Sister Cassandra and Others*. Oxford: Clarendon, 1932.

Christensen, Jerome. *Practicing Enlightenment: Hume and the Formation of a Literary Career*. Madison: University of Wisconsin Press, 1987.

Dean, Tim. "Sex and Syncope." *Raritan* 25 (Winter 1996): 64–86.

Deleuze, Gilles. *Proust et les signes*. Paris: Presses Universitaires de France, 1976. Translated by Richard Howard as *Proust and Signs*. (New York: George Braziller, 1972).

de Man, Paul. *Allegories of Reading: Figural Language in Rousseau, Nietzsche, Rilke, and Proust*. New Haven, Conn.: Yale University Press, 1979.

————. *The Resistance to Theory*. Minneapolis: University of Minnesota Press, 1986.

Derrida, Jacques. "Structure, Sign, and Play in the Discourse of the Human Sciences." In *Writing and Difference*, trans. by Alan Bass. Chicago: University of Chicago Press, 1978.

————. "Economimesis." Translated by Richard Klein. *Diacritics* 11 (Summer 1981): 3–25.

————. "Racism's Last Word." Translated by Peggy Kamuf. In *"Race," Writing, and Difference*, ed. Henry Louis Gates Jr. Chicago: University of Chicago Press, 1985.

————. "Foreword: Fors: The Anglish Words of Nicholas Abraham and Maria Torok." Translated by Barbara Johnson. In *The Wolf Man's Magic Word: A Cryptonymy*, by Nicolas Abraham and Maria Torok, trans. Nicholas Rand. Minneapolis: University of Minnesota Press, 1986.

Descombes, Vincent. *Proust: Philosophy of the Novel*. Translated by Catherine Chance Macksey. Stanford, Calif.: Stanford University Press, 1992.

Doane, Mary Ann. *The Desire to Desire: The Woman's Film of the 1940's*. Bloomington: Indiana University Press, 1987.

Doubrovsky, Serge. *Writing and Fantasy in Proust: La Place de la Madeleine*. Translated by Carol Mastrangelo Bové and Paul A. Bové. Lincoln: University of Nebraska Press, 1986.

Eagleton, Terry. *The Ideology of the Aesthetic*. Oxford: Basil Blackwell, 1990.

Edelman, Lee. *Homographesis: Essays in Gay Literary and Cultural Theory*. New York: Routledge, 1994.

————. "Plasticity, Paternity, Perversity: Freud's *Falcon*, Huston's *Freud*." *American Imago* 51 (Spring 1994): 69–104.

————. "Piss Elegant: Freud, Hitchcock, and the Micturating Penis." *GLQ* 2 (1995): 149–77.

Elias, Norbert. *The History of Manners: The Civilizing Process*. Vol. 1. Translated by Edmund Jephcott. New York: Pantheon, 1978.

Escoffier, Jeffrey. "Inside the Ivory Closet." *Out/Look* 10 (Fall 1990): 40–48.

Fish, Stanley. "Commentary: The Young and the Restless." In *The New Historicism*, ed. by H. Aram Veeser. New York: Routledge, 1989.

Fleishman, Avrom. "The Socialization of Catherine Moreland." *ELH* 41 (1974): 649–67.

Fletcher, Robert P. "The Dandy and the Fogy: Thackeray and the Aesthetics/Ethics of the Literary Pragmatist." *ELH* 58 (Summer 1991): 383–404.

Freud, Sigmund. "Medusa's Head." In *The Standard Edition of the Complete Psychological Works of Sigmund Freud*, vol. 18, translated by James Strachey. London: Hogarth, 1991.

Fuss, Diana. "Monsters of Perversion: Jeffrey Dahmer and *The Silence of the Lambs*." In *Media Spectacles*, ed. Marjorie Garber, Jann Matlock, and Rebecca L. Walkowitz. New York: Routledge, 1993.

————. *Identification Papers*. New York: Routledge, 1995.

Gagnier, Regenia. *Idylls of the Marketplace: Oscar Wilde and the Victorian Public*. Stanford, Calif.: Stanford University Press, 1986.

Garber, Marjorie. "Character Assassination: Shakespeare, Anita Hill, and JFK." In *Media Spectacles*, ed. Marjorie Garber, Jann Matlock, and Rebecca L. Walkowitz. New York: Routledge, 1993.

Genette, Gérard. *Narrative Discourse*. Translated by Jane Lewin. Ithaca, N.Y.: Cornell University Press, 1980.

Gilbert, Sandra M., and Susan Gubar. *The Madwoman in the Attic: The Woman Writer and the Nineteenth-Century Literary Imagination*. New Haven, Conn.: Yale University Press, 1979.

Girard, René. *Deceit, Desire, and the Novel: Self and Other in Literary Structure*. Translated by Yvonne Freccero. Baltimore: Johns Hopkins University Press, 1965.

Guillory, John. *Cultural Capital: The Problem of Literary Canon Formation*. Chicago: University of Chicago Press, 1993.

Habermas, Jürgen. *The Structural Transformation of the Public Sphere: An Inquiry into a Category of Bourgeois Society*. Translated by Thomas Burger. Cambridge, Mass.: MIT Press, 1991.

Hertz, Neil. "Medusa's Head: Male Hysteria under Political Pressure." In *The End of the Line: Essays on Psychoanalysis and the Sublime*. New York: Columbia University Press, 1985.

Hughes, Winifred. "Silver Fork Writers and Readers: Social Contexts of a Best Seller." *Novel* 25 (1992): 328–47.

Hume, David. "Of the Delicacy of Taste and Passion." In *Selected Essays*, ed. Stephen Copley and Andrew Edgar. Oxford: Oxford University Press, 1993.

Jameson, Fredric. *The Political Unconscious: Narrative as a Socially Symbolic Act*. Ithaca, N.Y.: Cornell University Press, 1981.

————. *Late Marxism: Adorno, or the Persistence of the Dialectic*. London: Verso, 1990.

Johnson, Barbara. "Gender Theory and the Yale School." In *A World of Difference*. Baltimore: Johns Hopkins University Press, 1987.

Johnson, Claudia J. *Jane Austen: Women, Politics, and the Novel*. Chicago: University of Chicago Press, 1988.

Kant, Immanuel. "Conjectural Beginnings of Human History." In *On History*, ed. L. W. Beck. Indianapolis: Bobbs-Merrill, 1963.

————. *Critique of Judgment*. Translated by Werner S. Pluhar. Indianapolis: Hackett, 1987.

Kincaid, James. "Fattening Up on Pickwick." *Novel* 25 (1992): 235–44.

Kolata, Gina. "Squeezing Fat, Calories, Guilt, and More Profits out of Junk Food." *New York Times*, 11 August 1991, E5.

Kristeva, Julia. *Powers of Horror: An Essay on Abjection*. Translated by Leon S. Roudiez. New York: Columbia University Press, 1982.

Kucich, John. *The Power of Lies: Transgression in Victorian Fiction*. Ithaca, N.Y.: Cornell University Press, 1994.

————. "Transgression in Trollope: Dishonesty and the Antibourgeois Elite." *ELH* 56 (Fall 1989): 593–618.

Lacan, Jacques. *The Four Fundamental Concepts of Psychoanalysis*. Translated by Alan Sheridan. Edited by Jacques Alain Miller. New York: Norton, 1981.

Laplanche, Jean, and J.-B. Pontalis. *The Language of Psychoanalysis.* Translated by Donald Nicholson-Smith. London: Hogarth, 1983.

Levine, George. *The Realistic Imagination: English Fiction from Frankenstein to Lady Chatterley.* Chicago: University of Chicago Press, 1981.

Litvak, Joseph. *Caught in the Act: Theatricality in the Nineteenth-Century English Novel.* Berkeley and Los Angeles: University of California Press, 1992.

Liu, Alan. "The Power of Formalism: The New Historicism." *ELH* 56 (Winter 1989): 721–71.

MacCabe, Colin, ed. *High Theory, Low Culture: Analyzing Popular Television and Film.* New York: St. Martin's, 1986.

Marin, Louis. *Food for Thought.* Translated by Mette Hjort. Baltimore: Johns Hopkins University Press, 1989.

Miller, Andrew. "*Vanity Fair* through Plate Glass." *PMLA* 105 (October 1990): 1042–54.

Miller, D. A. *The Novel and the Police.* Berkeley and Los Angeles: University of California Press, 1988.

———. "Sontag's Urbanity." *October* 49 (Summer 1989): 91–101.

———. "The Late Jane Austen." *Raritan* 10 (Summer 1990): 55–79.

———. "Anal Rope." In *Inside/Out: Lesbian Theories, Gay Theories,* ed. Diana Fuss. Routledge: New York, 1991.

———. *Bringing out Roland Barthes.* Berkeley and Los Angeles: University of California Press, 1992.

———. "Austen's Attitude." *Yale Journal of Criticism* 8 (1995): 1–5.

Miller, J. Hillis. "Narrative and History." *ELH* 41 (Fall 1974): 455–76.

Moers, Ellen. *The Dandy: Brummell to Beerbohm.* Lincoln: University of Nebraska Press, 1978.

Moon, Michael, and Eve Kosofsky Sedgwick. "Divinity: A Dossier, a Performance Piece, a Little-Understood Emotion." *Discourse* 13 (Fall–Winter 1990–91): 12–39.

Moretti, Franco. *The Way of the World: The "Bildungsroman" in European Culture.* Translated by Albert Sbragia. London: Verso, 1987.

Morrison, Paul. "Enclosed in Openness: *Northanger Abbey* and the Domestic Carceral." *Texas Studies in Literature and Language* 33 (Spring 1991): 1–23.

———. "End Pleasure." *GLQ* 1 (1993): 53–78.

O'Farrell, Mary Ann. *Telling Complexions: The Nineteenth-Century English Novel and the Blush.* Durham, N.C.: Duke University Press, 1997.

Painter, George D. *Marcel Proust: A Biography.* 2 vols. in 1. New York: Random House, 1987.

Parker, Patricia. *Literary Fat Ladies: Rhetoric, Gender, Property.* New York: Methuen, 1987.

Phillips, Adam. *On Kissing, Tickling, and Being Bored: Psychoanalytic Essays on the Unexamined Life.* Cambridge, Mass.: Harvard University Press, 1993.

Poovey, Mary. *The Proper Lady and the Woman Writer: Ideology as Style in the Works of Mary Wollstonecraft, Mary Shelley, and Jane Austen.* Chicago: University of Chicago Press, 1984.

Proust, Marcel. "Sentiments filiaux d'un parricide." In *"Contre Sainte-Beuve," précédé de "Pastiches et mélanges," et suivi de "Essais et articles,"* ed. Pierre Clairac with Yves Sandres. Paris: Gallimard, 1971.

———. *Remembrance of Things Past.* 3 vols. Translated by C. K. Scott Moncrieff, Terence Kilmartin, and Andreas Mayor. New York: Random House, 1982.

———. *A la recherche du temps perdu.* Edited by Jean-Yves Tadié et al. 4 vols. Paris: Gallimard, 1987–89.

———. *Correspondance.* Edited by Philip Kolb. Paris: Plon, 1992.

————. *In Search of Lost Time.* Translated by C. K. Scott Moncrieff and Terence Kilmartin. Revised by D. J. Enright. 6 vols. New York: Random House, 1992–93.

Ray, Gordon N. *The Buried Life: A Study of the Relation between Thackeray's Fiction and His Personal History.* Cambridge, Mass.: Harvard University Press, 1952.

————. *Thackeray: The Uses of Adversity, 1811–1846.* New York: McGraw-Hill, 1955.

Revel, Jean-François. *Sur Proust: Remarques sur "À la recherche du temps perdu."* Paris: Julliard, 1960.

Richard, Jean-Pierre. *Proust et le monde sensible.* Paris: Seuil, 1974.

Rothstein, Edward. "Jane Austen Meets Mr. Right." *New York Times,* 10 December 1995, sec. 4, 1.

Sedgwick, Eve Kosofsky. *Epistemology of the Closet.* Berkeley and Los Angeles: University of California Press, 1990.

————. "Jane Austen and the Masturbating Girl." *Critical Inquiry* 17 (Summer 1991): 818–37.

Silverman, Kaja. *Male Subjectivity at the Margins.* New York: Routledge, 1992.

Smith, Barbara Herrnstein. *Contingencies of Value: Alternative Perspectives for Critical Theory.* Cambridge, Mass.: Harvard University Press, 1988

Spindler, Amy M. "Gucci Reinvents Jet-Set Sophistication." *New York Times,* 7 March 1996, C13.

Stallybrass, Peter, and Allon White. *The Politics and Poetics of Transgression.* Ithaca, N.Y.: Cornell University Press, 1986.

Thackeray, William Makepeace. *The Book of Snobs.* Edited by John Sutherland. New York: St. Martin's, 1978.

————. *Vanity Fair.* Edited by J. I. M. Stewart. Harmondsworth: Penguin, 1985.

Time: The Weekly Newsmagazine. 8 August 1994.

Visser, Margaret. *The Rituals of Dinner: The Origins, Evolution, Eccentricities, and Meaning of Table Manners.* New York: Grove Weidenfeld, 1991.

Welsh, Alexander. "Introduction." In *Thackeray: A Collection of Critical Essays.* Englewood Cliffs, N.J.: Prentice-Hall, 1968.

Williams, Raymond. *The English Novel: From Dickens to Lawrence.* New York: Oxford University Press, 1970.

Wilt, Judith. *Ghosts of the Gothic: Austen, Eliot, and Lawrence.* Princeton, N.J.: Princeton University Press, 1980.

Woods, Gregory. "High Culture and High Camp: The Case of Marcel Proust." In *Camp Grounds: Style and Homosexuality,* ed. David Bergman. Amherst: University of Massachusetts Press, 1993.

Žižek, Slavoj. *The Sublime Object of Ideology.* London: Verso, 1989.

————. *Looking Awry: An Introduction to Jacques Lacan through Popular Culture.* Cambridge, Mass.: MIT Press, 1991.

Index

Abraham, Nicolas, 25
Academy, the, 80–81, 112–15, 176, 169 n. 43. *See also* Theory
Adolescence, 83, 89, 109. *See also* Childhood
Adorno, Theodor, 12–14, 17–19, 69–71, 73, 77–79, 81–82, 112–49; *Aesthetic Theory*, 123, 166 n. 24; *Dialectic of Enlightenment* (with Max Horkheimer), 112–13, 122, 125, 127, 129, 130, 136, 140, 166 n. 21; *Minima Moralia*, 123, 124, 127–28, 131, 132–33, 135, 137–40, 160 n. 22, 166 n. 15, 168 n. 45; *Negative Dialectics*, 123, 167 n. 25; *Notes to Literature*, 69–71, 73, 77–79, 81–82, 160 n. 20, 160 n. 23, 160 n. 24, 161 n. 1, 162 n. 3, 162 n. 7, 163 n. 23, 167 n. 26; *Prisms*, 113, 115, 132, 148, 165 n. 4, 168 n. 42
Althusser, Louis, 119
Alvarez, J. C., 116–18, 120
Anality, 60–61, 103; and behindsight, 108–109. *See also* Homophobia; Waste
Armstrong, Nancy, 33–34, 39, 154 n. 11, 155 n. 1, 155 n. 2, 155 n. 4
Austen, Jane, 13–16, 21–30, 33–54; *Emma*, 24, 47; *Letters*, 21, 153 n. 1, 153 n. 3, 154 n. 13; *Mansfield Park*, 24, 47; *Northanger Abbey*, 16, 27, 33–54, 155 n. 3; *Pride and Prejudice*, 15, 21–30, 47, 54, 80, 153 n. 3; *Sense and Sensibility*, 24, 47

Backman, Mark, 151 n. 1
Bakhtin, Mikhail, 123

Bardèche, Maurice, 85–86, 162 n. 16, 163 n. 19
Barthes, Roland, 11, 14, 18–19, 113–49, 165 n. 8, 166 n. 14, 166 n. 18, 166 n. 22, 167 n. 29, 167 n. 30; *Camera Lucida*, 167 n. 29; *The Eiffel Tower and Other Mythologies*, 114, 123, 137, 165 n. 6; *Mythologies*, 112–14, 119, 127–31, 141–43, 146, 165 n. 7, 166 n. 14, 166 n. 23, 167 n. 38; *Roland Barthes*, 124–26, 133–34, 136, 141–47, 165 n. 8, 166 n. 18, 167 n. 30, 167 n. 34, 167 n. 37; *The Rustle of Language*, 119, 152 n. 18, 166 n. 19
Baudrillard, Jean, 121, 159 n. 14
Bernhard, Sandra, 103
Bersani, Leo, 2, 163 n. 18, 164 n. 33
Boone, Joseph Allen, 153 n. 4
Boredom, 79, 82–84, 93–94, 99–100, 108, 164 n. 32, 165 n. 37, and excitement, 105; and the novel, 111. *See also* Melancholia; Taste; Theory
Borrel, Anne, 161 n. 2
Bourdieu, Pierre, 5–9, 16, 53–54, 61, 95, 153 n. 2, 154 n. 15, 155 n. 6, 155 n. 19, 156 n. 14, 157 n. 22, 159 n. 16
Brillat-Savarin, Jean Anthelme, 9–11, 152 n. 14
Butler, Judith, 12, 63, 152 n. 19, 154 n. 9, 159 n. 15, 162 n. 13, 167 n. 35

Castration, 143–45. *See also* Homosexuality
Chapman, R. W., 154 n. 12
Charm: of young men, 46–54, 157 n. 24

Joseph Litvak is Professor of English at Bowdoin College.
He is the author of *Caught in the Act: Theatricality in the
Nineteenth-Century English Novel*.

Library of Congress Cataloging-in-Publication Data
Litvak, Joseph.
Strange gourmets : sophistication, theory, and the novel /
Joseph Litvak.
p.   cm. — (Series Q)
Includes bibliographical references and index.
ISBN 0-8223-2007-X (cloth : alk. paper). —
ISBN 0-8223-2016-9 (pbk. : alk. paper)
I. Fiction—History and criticism—Theory, etc.   2. Rhetoric.
I. Title.   II. Series.
PN3331.L58   1997
808.3—dc21   96-54812 CIP